SETTING EUROPE ABLAZE

SETTING EUROPE ABLAZE

Some Account of Ungentlemanly Warfare

by

Douglas Dodds-Parker

SPRINGWOOD BOOKS

First printing 1983 Springwood Books

Second printing 1984 Springwood Books

Springwood Books Limited
22 Chewter Lane, Windlesham, Surrey

ISBN 0 86254 113 1

Typeset by Inforum Ltd, Portsmouth
Printed and bound in Great Britain at
The Camelot Press Ltd, Southampton

Dedicated
to those who did not live
to see V-Day

Contents

PART 1	Recoiling	
	Preface	3
Chapter 1	Aggression Grows	7
Chapter 2	Italian-Ethiopian War, 1935–38	12
Chapter 3	Prague, 1938	16
Chapter 4	Public Security, Khartum, 1939	20
Chapter 5	Interlude in Ethiopia	23
Chapter 6	Windsor, 1939	27
Chapter 7	War Office, Spring 1940	35
Chapter 8	Middle East and Cairo, 1940	47
Chapter 9	Ethiopia, the first Victory, 1940–41	55
Chapter 10	SOE London, 1941	74
PART 2	. . . . the better to spring forward	
Chapter 11	Clearing the path, Algiers, 1942	109
Chapter 12	Building the springboard: Massingham, 1943	118
Chapter 13	Monkey, the Italian Armistice	136
Chapter 14	Back into Europe: Maryland	142
Chapter 15	Corsica: the real Maquis	152
Chapter 16	Europe well ablaze: Speedwell, 1944	160

Chapter 17	To a hollow Victory	203
Chapter 18	All to what Purpose?	211
Appendix		220

Abbreviations used

Individuals are referred to by names under which they are usually known; the omission of prefixes denotes no lack of respect.

AFHQ	Allied Force Headquarters, Algiers
Avalanche	Assault on Salerno, Italy, September 1943
Brimstone	(Aborted) Assault on Sardinia and Corsica
Dragoon	Assault on South of France, August 1944
DSC	Distinguished Service Cross (British Naval decoration)
D Section	Action Branch of British Secret Service
DSO	Distinguished Service Order (higher British inter-service decoration)
FANY	First Aid Nursing Yeomanry; original women's service, reformed to support SOE
Force 133	SOE, Cairo
Force 139	SOE, Poland and Central Europe, at Brindisi, Italy
Gauleiter	Nazi Regional Commissioner
GR	Equivalent in Middle East to MIR
Halifax	4-engined bomber adapted for parachuting
Husky	Assault on Sicily, July 1943
Joe	Designation, used by RAF, of agents for air transport
LRDG	Long Range Desert Group, operating in desert behind the lines
Lysander	Single-engined aircraft used for pick-ups
MC	Military Cross
Maryland	SOE in Monopoli, Italy
Massingham	SOE in Algiers
MIR	Military Intelligence Research. Original Special Operations unit in War Office, 1938–40

MI 9	Special Service to organise escape techniques and routes
Monkey	Negotiations for Italian Armistice, August 1943
Muskateer	(Aborted) Assault on Istria through heel of Italy
OSS	The Office of Strategic Services, SOE's American counterpart
Overlord	The Allied assault on Normandy, June 1944
RAF	Royal Air Force
SD	Sicherheitdienst. German near-equivalent to SOE
SHAEF	Supreme Allied Headquarters Expeditionary Force to command Overlord
SIS	The British Secret Intelligence Service
SOE	The Special Operations Executive, formed in July 1940
SOM	Special Operations, Mediterranean at Bari, Italy
Speedwell	SOE link with AFHQ
Torch	Assault on Algiers and North Africa, November 1942
WAAF	Women's Auxiliary Air Force
Whitley	2-engined bomber first adapted to parachuting in 1940
ZNO	Non-occupied zone of France

PART ONE

Recoiling . . . .

Preface

A distinguished Grenadier once said to me 'How, as a Grenadier, did you get mixed up in All This?'

'You had better ask', I replied, 'how being mixed up in All This, did I ever become a Grenadier?'

This is an account, written from memory long after the events, of a dark decade from 1935 to 1945. In 1935 Britain was *the* world power, whose leaders lacked the foresight to avert what Mr. Churchill later described as 'the unnecessary war'. 1945 saw British power and position in decline despite achieving victory.

These years included the run-up to the disasters of 1938 to 1942 and saw the victories of 1943 to 1945. During them there grew up a spirit of resistance to tyranny, domestic and foreign, among the most diverse groups and individuals, of all classes and creeds, culminating in the organised Resistance movements which were after 1945 to dominate so much of political life. How far 'Resistance', in Europe and beyond, contributed to military victory is for the historians to judge. It was ideological and nationalist, even tribal, a spontaneous reaction to oppression, of the soul even more than of the body. For so many the blitzkrieg, unannounced and swift, had given little chance for normal military defence. So Resistance was to restore in full measure the feeling of participation in final victory. To support Resistance Britain formed the Special Operations Executive (SOE) to find the innumerable groups, to supply them and indicate targets and timing. Without those in the field there would have been little action beyond the conventional battles. Thus SOE was the link from outside with those real resisters who, with the air and boat crews, faced indescribable dangers, day and night, for those long years. Their continuing regard, more than forty years on, for SOE's relatively puny efforts shows the depth of their attachment to shared ideals.

SOE's responsibility varied from minute attention to numberless details to persuasion at the highest political and military levels, failure in which could lead to loss of life or worse, on a scale beyond reckoning.

Few records of SOE's organization have survived. Instinct and training required minimum records and early destruction when outside the UK. There was little opportunity, even had regulations allowed, to keep diaries. Only Field Marshals and senior officials seemed, from their post-war publications, to have been beyond the risk of courts martial.

Perhaps some signals to London remain. But to judge from recent enquiries the words Massingham, Maryland and Speedwell are meaningless; and the lists of symbols and code-names are gone. This account is written to record some events not elsewhere made clear, and to try to pay some tribute to a few of the many allies who came together in those years.

My upbringing and education were partly responsible for my 'getting mixed up in All This'. I was fortunate that my home was in a university city, Oxford; my father a surgeon, descended from a succession of younger sons which meant tradition without inherited wealth; and my mother from a family with generations of service overseas. The quality of life in Oxford in the inter-war years may never be surpassed for those able to enjoy it; such a diversity of local and university friends, with the annual inflow of students, especially Rhodes Scholars, from all over the English-speaking world. Among the many opportunities offered, at home, school and at college, I learnt to read widely and to walk; to fly and ski, the new sports, in Norway, Poland and Switzerland; to fish and to shoot; and to row (recalling throughout life the words of the great Australian coach, Steve Fairbairn, 'You can teach 'em to row; you can't teach them to race') and to travel throughout Europe and North America on the lines that 'the cheaper you travel, the more you learn'.

My family was concerned with Europe. An uncle, Fred Wise, MP for Ilford, had been sent by Mr. Lloyd George to Germany in January 1919. His report, urging the supply of food and raw materials to Germany rather than taking reparations out, was suppressed as premature; too soon after the 1918 Election won to 'hang the Kaiser'. To those who saw the effects of inflation and unemployment among Germans, especially after the refusal of aid to Dr. Bruning in 1929, the swing to Hitler was scarcely surprising.

All that I saw in my travels made me doubtful that peace would be prolonged, forebodings underlined by events in China, Ethiopia and Spain; and I came to believe that any new world war would involve clandestine and guerrilla action. My interests and experience thus predisposed me in favour of Special Employment when it was later to come my way.

Chapter 1

Aggression grows

At the depth of the Depression I left college and was fortunate to be selected for the Sudan Political Service. So, in the 1930s, there followed a decade of constructive effort, with the best colleagues, Sudanese and British, that could be found anywhere. I shall always regret that circumstances were not to let me complete the usual twenty-five years in a country with a diversity of peoples, the pleasantest I have ever known. The rigours of the climate were offset by three months annual leave, taken between April and October.

On a map of Europe and the Middle East I set out a different route to be followed each year. The first, in 1933, took me to Palestine, Syria and Iraq. There I met John Cadman, Chairman of the then Anglo-Persian Oil Company, who flew me with him to Teheran, and round the main cities of Iran, in breaks between negotiations for a new oil agreement. Thence the American Minister, Mr. Wadsworth, drove me to Resht on the Caspian, to eat caviar at source, washed down by whisky left behind by Dunsterforce, the British troops there in 1919. Passing through Transcaucasia, a four-day train journey took me through the Black Soil land of Russia. Stations were filled with peasants, emaciated if not clearly dying, driven from their collectivised land. Later the Soviets admitted that some six million had perished. I reached Moscow the day the verdict was given in the notorious Metrovic trial of British engineers convicted on a false spying charge. Britain broke off relations and I was told to leave. Protesting over-loudly, I was warned to have a care by Mr. Cumming, the British journalist. He undertook to intervene on my behalf with Mr. Vyshinski, the Public Prosecutor, who was in the Metropole Hotel with us. I was allowed to stay my week, as pre-paid. All the Russians I met were very friendly, so many of them being survivors of the middle class under the Tsar. They still wore their best when attending the former elegant splendour of the Bolshoi Ballet.

A German Reichswehr training centre existed fifty miles from Moscow. Russians were clearly fearful of the danger of a resurgent Germany. With Hitler now in power, the totalitarian philosophy was similar, the disagreement was about who was to run any joint activity, a Teuton or a Slav. In Berlin, in April 1933, I found the same apprehension among journalist friends. They said that Hitler would one day have to be stopped. The sooner, the less need for war. I was taken to hear Hitler speak at the Sportpalast. He strode onto the platform amid dead silence. A deafening roar of the triple *Sieg Heil* greated his Nazi salute – a frightening and menacing response. All agreed during those pregnant years that the best chance to stop Hitler, as is now confirmed by German records, was at the reoccupation of the Rhineland in 1936. This had been demilitarised by the Treaty of Versailles; German troops entered without ammunition, to test the determination rather than the military strength of the Allies. Preoccupied with unemployment and inflation, we were to 'miss the bus' – and nearly to lose the war when it came five years later.

My service in the Sudan began with three years in Kordofan in the west, in sedentary and semi-pastoral districts. I was then posted to Khartum, to be Assistant Private Secretary to the Governor-General, Sir Stewart Symes. My ill-concealed regret at leaving the district work was met with sympathy by Sir Stewart. Under him I saw 'government' as a whole. He was Head of State as well as head of government, dealing with varied and complex problems, domestic and external. The Anglo-Egyptian Condominium was unique, deeply involved in Egyptian politics and concerned with neighbouring French, Belgian and Italian colonies.

The Imperial Airways flying-boat services had just begun, a farsighted decision to send all first-class mail by air to Australia and South Africa, through the Middle East. This brought many distinguished visitors to stop-over in Khartum. These acquaintances were to prove invaluable in the next ten years as many of them were to hold top responsibilities, political and military. A favourite, especially with the ladies and the children, was General Smuts. Arriving one evening at the end of the annual children's party, he became the natural Father Christmas, telling them endless stories.

In October 1935, on Sir Stewart's instructions, I went to Geneva to attend a meeting of the League of Nations. The main item was the Italian occupation of the Wal Wal oasis on the Ethiopian side of the Somali frontier. Partly to find an outlet for the ever-growing population of Italy after the USA cut down immigration after the First War, Mussolini was on the march to occupy Ethiopia. There was a chance to rally international support to stop him, if necessary by force, by closing the Suez Canal. The British then had only one brigade in Egypt, and it was believed that British forces were inadequate to stop the huge armies of Italy. Five years later the victory at Sidi Barrani by the Western Desert Force was to prove the contrary.

At Geneva I was introduced to Anthony Eden by Roger Makins, his Private Secretary, whose fag I had been at school. 'Have you a tennis racket?' asked Roger, 'Anthony wants a fourth player'. I had to regret that I had not brought this important weapon with me. Among the few there was Henry Hopkinson from the Cairo Embassy. We listened to Italy, represented by Baron Aloisi, being declared an aggressor – without any practical proposals to follow. As another Foreign Secretary was to say, 'Not a man, not a ship, not a gun was moved by any except the British'. It was the peak of the delusion of collective security, 'of sheep against the wolf'. I recall how naively shocked I was to see Pierre Laval, the French Foreign Minister, lean over the embarrassed Italian and roar with laughter in his ear.

Tension was growing from 1934. In Rome I heard Mussolini's warlike address to the people from the window in the Palazzo Venezia. Next day came the news of the murder of the Austrian Chancellor, Dr. Dolfuss, who had resisted so bravely Hitler's pressure for union. I caught the train that night and was the only passenger to alight the next morning in Vienna. Fearing Nazi occupation, every one else was going the other way. After the murder, the world waited breathless to see whether Hitler would march into Austria. However, Mussolini's despatch of troops to the Brenner frontier postponed the occupation for another four years. By then Italy had joined the Axis Pact. So, amidst growing fears of doom, I went to listen to music in Salzburg.

While events were clearly moving towards an international explosion, I spent some weeks in 1936 in the Balkans, Poland, Leningrad and the Baltic States. I spent two days at the Partei Tag at Nuremburg, the Nazi Rally. I was present later at Bayreuth, at a performance of *Lohengrin*, when Hitler came in and sat in the main box. Ever since I have thought 'Had I brought my pistol . . .'.

On my return to London I met Richard Pilkington, a Member of Parliament, who had just made the same round trip. We agreed that war could not be long delayed, and that we should visit the USA before it broke out. I checked with Frank Roberts, head of the Central Department in the Foreign Office, asking about timing. Taking the marker out of Hitler's *Mein Kampf*, he replied, 'Yes. You should be all right. There should be two or three years to go'. His judgement was, as ever, right.

So, in August 1937, Richard and I met aboard the *Queen Mary*; and in the next ten weeks covered 14,000 miles, from coast to coast, in Canada and the USA. In Washington, Sol Bloom, the Representative from New York and an inveterate host to the British, arranged for me to accompany Richard to the White House. The President asked me about Ethiopia; and perhaps recalled this when, three years later, he sent 10,000 Springfield rifles for use by the Emperor's forces. Although perhaps not addicted to the Anglo-Saxons, he was obviously the strongest supporter of freedom. I shall always believe that, thanks to Mr. Churchill and the President above all, I can write this as a free man.

I have mentioned these travels to give an idea of the experience gained in the 1920s and 1930s, of the countries and their political backgrounds, in which the British were later to be involved. Also, in the Sudan I had more time to read than usual. History showed that many political groupings in Europe were accustomed to taking direct action not always based on the decisions of governments to 'go to war', but on the atavistic urge of peoples to resist the tyranny of foreign occupiers. Especially when Britain stood alone, from 1940 to late 1941, it became her sole responsibility to judge how these legitimate political urges, often conflicting, could be harnessed to help evict the occupiers who were involved in a 'Geneva-Convention type' war with Britain, and to develop, indeed often create, the practical skills of clandestine survival, communications and operations in occupied territories. Only the Communists were so organised in 1939–1941 in all countries – and at that time they were helping Hitler. The Poles and Czechs, who had been operating thus for centuries, had formidable capabilities.

These experiences strengthened my growing realisation that urgent action was needed in Britain, as well as in the Sudan, to develop techniques beyond the normal military ones, both offensive and defensive.

CHAPTER 2

Italian-Ethiopian War, 1935–8

My direct involvement with subversion and irregular warfare came late in 1935 when I left the Palace for the Southern Fung part of the Blue Nile Province. This District stretches 300 miles along the Ethiopian frontier where the Blue Nile floods out of the highlands. The boundary was marked by cairns some six miles apart. This line had split the local tribes but as the Amhara rulers never came down from the escarpment 50 miles to the east, we ignored it, though careful never to cross it. All Ethiopians used Sudan markets and dispensaries with consequent goodwill.

Most of my three years there was spent on trek, by light truck in the six dry months and by mule in the rains. My District Commissioner was 250 miles to the north, and the Province Headquarters 200 miles beyond him. From both I was to receive unfailing support.

The Italian attack on Ethiopia had already begun. The British Parliament, recently elected on a 'no rearmament' programme, turned down the Hoare-Laval proposals which would have left a reduced area under the Emperor. They were universally condemned by all those who were unwilling to fight for, or even to supply arms to, Ethiopia, but some felt that they were better than the virtual abandonment of the Ethiopians. So the slaughter began, culminating in Marshal Badoglio's riding into Addis Ababa on a white horse, on 5 May 1936.

The Ethiopian regime disintegrated, the Emperor sought refuge in Britain. Later, his pilot, Carl von Rosen, Goering's nephew, crashed on landing at my base at Roseires. Three months after that the remnants of the Imperial Bodyguard, led by Mesfin, reached the frontier. They were a sorry sight, with many women and children. Years later Amaha Kassa, then Ambassador at the United Nations, said,

'I am still cross with you for taking away my rifle'.

'How old were you?', I asked.

'Eight, but you gave us bread, the first we had eaten for three months'.

A track was cleared along and a mile short of the 300 miles of frontier. All the thousands of refugees were told to build on the Sudan side of the track. This allowed our police better control when coming to collect firearms. In the next two years over 5,000 weapons were collected, some dating from the early 19th century; and most more dangerous to the aimer than to the target. Only two lives were lost, thanks to the courage and skill of the local police, under the Executive Officer, Mekkawi Suliman Akrat, later to become one of the highest Sudanese officials and always an outstanding personality.

The misdeeds of the Italians were to cause us serious concern. Great international issues meant nought to the local Ethiopian tribes to whom the Amhara were more remote than the British. Local administration, light though it was, meant much. So the activities of a Blackshirt officer were to make the word *tenente* a term of abuse. In late 1936 he arrived, setting up his post several yards on the Sudan side of the frontier at Gezzan. Despite my protests, relayed through Khartum, he refused to move. Indeed he made it clear in public that he scorned our remonstrances.

There followed a year of maladministration. He tried to stop the accepted freedom of movement by requiring written permits to cross the frontier. As most people were illiterate, and the more aimiable for it, this order was ignored. The 'culprit' would then be tied to a wooden frame, in the sun, and after a day or two taken to Battalion Headquarters tied to the tail of a mule. Many died. My protests, sometimes supported by photographs, of the atrocities, were again publicly treated with contempt. Trade, mainly in coffee and gold in exchange for clothing and food, dwindled away.

As the rainy season approached, with the Tenente still on Sudan soil, all pointed out that the rains were heavy and violent; that his shelters would not suffice; and he should build a good house with a strong roof. He accepted this advice. Many gave of their best, in materials and labour. All rejoiced at the magnificent result. I called to wish him a happy rainy season, avoiding the many horrible and dangerous diseases in Gezzan, while I was in the USA.

All waited. The first heavy rainstorm, of course, brought down the roof, built too flat and heavy by design, to the delight of all. The Tenente withdrew to Headquarters and was never seen again.

He had told me that he had entered the USA fifteen years earlier, but had not been naturalised. He must have been surprised when, returning later with an Italian decoration, he was refused re-admission.

There were many chances to maintain Ethiopian morale without contravening the instructions from London of 'no provocation of the Italians'. Our markets and dispensaries were kept open, often at night, to help all Ethiopians.

A more public occasion was when our police burnt down some huts built on the forbidden side of the frontier track. A protest through Rome was in such strong terms that I checked the line in secret, to find the protest unjustified. So I feigned apprehension, and suggested a full meeting to settle any damage. Hundreds from both sides of the frontier arrived, knowing the truth. More Italian feathered hats than had ever been seen, came along. Fires were lighted on the two marker cairns – and our rights fully vindicated as these showed the huts to have been a long way within the Sudan. And all the ranks of Ethiopia . . .

Throughout these three years I had been building up a considerable network of informants in north-west Ethiopia. This began in early 1936 when the death of King George V brought a number of noblemen from the Western Amhara-land, as well as local leaders, to express their sympathy. Despite all, they kept their high regard for the British Crown, remote though it was. I did what I could in return, as we watched their society beginning to collapse around them. Five years later many were to rally to the Emperor when he returned. HIM was, of course, a King of Kings and not always as popular as some of the lesser leaders. This was to be an important consideration in 1940–1. Meantime, with the increasing unpopularity of Italian rule, a spirit of greater respect for the Emperor spread to the outer Amhara lands. This was a factor to be added to the universal wish to evict the Italians. I was careful, following London's orders, to leave no trace of these contacts.

I took a greater risk when Mesfin, Commander of the Emperor's Bodyguard, came to say that he was returning to Ethiopia. He asked for help. As he publicly announced years later in Addis Ababa, I let him take some confiscated arms from my store, on the strict understanding that he would lie low until the Emperor returned. This seemed remote in 1938 – but within two years we were all at war together.

CHAPTER 3

Prague, 1938

Before leaving the Fung, I had volunteered for secondment to Palestine whose government had asked for two officers from my Service to help with the Arab revolt. I was told, however, that after the last three years I must do some normal administration. When going on transfer, I felt that I had done a little to make life more tolerable on the frontier. Some few preparations had also been made, keeping within the orders from London, for action if and when hostilities with Italy broke out.

I headed straight for Prague where, by mid-September 1938, German demands on the Czechs seemed certain to provoke war within weeks. I had introductions to the anti-Nazi Social Democrats, in particular to those of German origin who lived in the frontier (Sudeten) areas. Storch and Wenzel Jaksch were the leaders – the latter to survive and be a colleague at the Council of Europe. David Grenfell, a former Labour Cabinet Minister, was the only British Parliamentarian in Prague.

I spent ten days in the Ambassadors Hotel, moving round with some of the journalists there; John Whitaker, Knickerbocker, Reynolds and Phoebe Packard, and Maurice Hindus were the most cooperative. With them I was to witness the destruction of democracy in the most democratic country of Eastern Europe.

With every rumour forecasting war, I flew home. I called on friends in the forces, the Foreign Office and Parliament. Few offered signs of any coherent policy to confront Nazi determination. I was in a minority when I advocated playing for time; accepting some settlement to avoid immediate war on condition we went full ahead on rearmament.

I was in Whitehall, opposite Downing Street, when Mr. Chamberlain returned from Munich. He was wildly cheered by a large crowd.

'Give him a cheer', said a friend. After what I had seen in the

Sudan and Prague, I could not do so. I drove to Glasgow one night, to ask David Raikes for help. Our talks were interrupted by his going on the platform for the launching of the *Queen Elizabeth* by the Queen. As I had no top hat I could not accompany him. That night I drove back to Oxford. All the way the BBC kept replaying the Queen's speech . . . 'it will be all right . . .' That time, in some ways it was – just. I arrived home at 4.00 am to find my father and sister packing gasmasks in the Town Hall.

In Parliament bewilderment reigned. The overwhelming 'National' victory in 1935 had been tempered by the loss of a bye-election at Fulham to the Labour candidate on a strong 'no rearmament' pledge. Indeed, it was not until after the German occupation of Prague in March 1939 that the Labour Party would support conscription. Providentially in 1936 Philip Swinton, the Air Minister, had ordered the Hurricane/Spitfire fighters which were to win the RAF's Battle of Britain in 1940.

By chance, I was seated 'under the Gallery' in the Commons when, on 5 October, Mr. Churchill made his famous, many believe his greatest, speech – just after the Munich Settlement. He pointed out to the Government that

'. . . they neither prevented Germany from rearming, nor did they rearm ourselves in time. They quarrelled with Italy without saving Ethiopia . . . they neglected to make alliances and combinations which might have repaired previous errors, and thus they left us in the hour of trial without adequate national defence or effective international security . . . it must now be accepted that all the countries of Central and Eastern Europe will make the best terms they can with the triumphant Nazi Power'.

I felt that at last I had heard the words, and the voice, of reality. I could not believe my ears when I heard Mr. Churchill being howled down by all sides of the House. I had many friends there, several of whom were to die gallantly before long. I felt even further disheartened to find that reality, made stark by Mr. Churchill's inspiring oratory, could rally but a handful. Yet within two years he was being called 'The Greatest Englishman of all time'.

When I was introduced to the Tory Chief Whip as a witness from Prague, David Margesson asked me what I thought about British reactions; I spoke about Mr. Churchill's speech.

'Don't worry about him', he said, 'Winston has no judgement. And he is just sour as he is not in the Government'. I was to hear this standard riposte to Parliamentary critics many times in the future from Whips – and even had it applied to me by a Chief Whip.

I called on the Governor-General and Angus Gillan, head of my Service and a family friend. I told them, perhaps pompously, that I felt that I must do something active about the coming catastrophe. I realised that all who had not been in the Great War would want to do the same; but they had not shared my experiences on the Ethiopian frontier and in Prague. I would of course return to the Sudan if and when Italy attacked us. Both my greatly respected leaders agreed that if I felt so strongly I must leave.

In near despair, I flew back to Prague. All land routes were closed. I spent some time with Press and local friends. We saw the Czech troops leave the fortifications which they had earlier been trained never to abandon. Their morale in defeat was wholly admirable. There were few outbreaks of violence; though I spent an uncomfortable morning in Asch lying under a car while the police and Henleinists fought it out over our heads. In the Czechs and Slovaks we surely lost some fine fighting allies.

With other English speakers I was assaulted on occasion in the dark. The French, however, got more of the blame. They had formed and led The Little Entente to guard Central Europe. Soon their regular forces were to be defeated in the field with ours. Then in France, as in Central Europe, the spirit of individual resistance was to prove as indomitable as ever, and give help and glory to their countries.

Most of my time was spent trying to help refugees, in particular the anti-Nazi Sudeten Germans. A personal difficulty arose when at two in the morning a knock on my door heralded a request for me to go through a form of marriage with a lady, and so take her out safely on my passport. It was hard, sitting on my bed, to find reasons for not agreeing, since I was unmarried. Perhaps I could haved saved one life.

When ready to return to London, I found all land routes still closed, and all aircraft full. By chance, an offensive personal remark late one night to a lady suspected of being a Nazi agent – I still shudder at the memory – resulted in von Rheinbaben, a known Sicherheitdienst (SD) agent, being in the hotel lobby the next morning with an airline reservation for me to London. I took it gladly.

Back in Britain, my main efforts were directed at preventing the anti-Nazis being handed over to Hitler. A.L. Kennedy and Peter Fleming on *The Times* took details of a castle at Svetla where I had seen several hundred refugees, many of them women and girls who had been raped by the Nazis. A leader in *The Times* and talks at the Foreign Office produced a delay. Secondly, I called on Mr. Vincent Massey, the Canadian High Commissioner, who took up the cause and checked that this group, with many skilled glassworkers among them, could be accepted in Canada where the previous year I had heard of a deposit of silica needing glassmakers. Wenzel Jaksch later confirmed that they were rescued from Prague.

I felt that I had gained useful experience and personal contacts, though little had been accomplished. Above all Britain and her friends were not showing the determination to meet the fanaticism of their enemies. A night stop in Rome on my way back to Khartum found me outside the Italian Parliament during the notorious 'Corsica, Tunis, Nice' debate. There, too, flamed the spirit of fanaticism. Within two years Britain's spirit was to match and overcome their enemies. Within five years the spirit of resistance was to open a new era of freedom and bravery in Italy. It was to take a little longer in Germany.

CHAPTER 4

Public Security, Khartum, 1939

My last six months in the Sudan Service I worked in the Public Security Department. Jose Penney was a particularly talented Special Services Director. His twenty years work in Egypt and the Sudan had been a major factor in countering Egyptian and Italian subversion. Duncan Cumming, his Deputy, was later in charge of Italian Occupied territory in Libya as well as the Horn of Africa. The dozen years from 1941 of administration by a handful of officials, Sudanese as well as British, gave these areas the most progressive years of their troubled history. In particular, the four parts of Somalia were united until redivided later by the United Nations.

Another remarkable colleague was Edward Atiyah who, following his father, kept close touch with the increasing number of educated Sudanese. These were justifiably becoming ever more interested in taking greater responsibility for the direction of their country's affairs. The immediate issues were better understood in Khartum than in London. We had witnessed for several years the vicious attack on Ethiopia and the killing or driving out of all educated men and women. Many were refugees in the Sudan. This experience had shown the Sudanese what fate awaited them should the Italians overrun the Sudan. This fear, added to their natural comradeship, sustained their loyalty to our joint cause. More than one said to me, 'If you don't want to fight, get us the arms and let us fight'. After East Africa was cleared, more than 20,000 volunteered for service in North Africa.

Our second responsibility was the collection of intelligence on Italian forces in Eritrea and Ethiopia. I had made some continuing contribution to this. The Italian preponderance in manpower and material was overwhelming. Their Eritrean units, officered by Italians, were to fight well to the end. The Defence Committee in Khartum seemed to be trying harder than anyone in Britain, yet our efforts were delayed by slow arms production at home. Fifty Bren guns ordered in 1938 had not arrived by mid-1940. Despite all the handicaps, the fighting qualities of the Sudanese and Commonwealth troops were, from 1940 onwards, to prove more than a match against almost impregnable positions, such as Keren. But that was a nerveracking two years away.

As I had resigned and was thus 'in balk', I volunteered for any work on which there might be repercussions. Three episodes stand out. First, following the 'Corsica, Tunis, Nice' demands in Italy, a senior Italian official was sent to Addis Ababa to confer. Night stopping in Khartum, he was surprised to receive an invitation to dine in the Palace which he could not leave until 11 pm. Promptly at 8 his baggage was searched, a sealed bag found, opened, and photographed. The contents contained a proposal on the very highest level from Paris to Rome about 'Corsica . . .'. This was sent to Cairo and London who had not heard of the proposal from Paris. A warm letter of praise came from the Ambassador in Cairo, asking how it had been obtained. On being informed, he replied in most irate terms, 'no right to infringe diplomatic . . .'. Perhaps there was a tinge of conscience at past neglect?

The next problem proved constructive. Largely for the expatriate population, a few night clubs had been opened in Khartum in the 1930s. Cabaret turns came down from Cairo on short-term contracts. In December 1938 the Chief of Police told me that there were many in Khartum, from Germany and Austria, whose passports as from January 1939 were no longer valid for any of Jewish race. Unless they left before 31 December, before many of their contracts expired, they might be left in the Sudan. We decided that they must leave.

'But can we not help them?' I asked. 'You are the one who signs Sudan passports "For Governor-General". These are travel documents widely accepted in the Middle East . . . If you . . .?' We summoned representatives of the girls, and told them they must leave. Tears flooded the office. Then we asked, 'Would you care to try to reach Palestine with Sudan passports?'

Instantly the sun came out and we were offered all, but, with mixed regrets, excused ourselves. We saw them off at the station, which gesture alone cost us some misunderstanding. As suggested, they headed for Palestine where within the ten years validity of the passport, they could find a safer home.

The third problem was simpler. A charming young Italian Conte, working for the Italian airline, began to approach employees of Shell and other firms in the Sudan asking about fuel stocks. As usual these approaches were immediately reported to us. Telling the Sudanese to take any bribes offered and give them to charity, we waited until the Conte went on leave. Two days later a 'personal' letter reached his desk . . . 'before you leave, thank you for the maps . . .' We heard he had been sent to the political prison in the Lipari Islands. Perhaps this saved him from a worse fate.

CHAPTER 5

Interlude in Ethiopia

Just before I was due to leave Khartum, a sudden visit by the Viceroy of Ethiopia changed my plans. Amadeo Duca D'Aosta had suceeded Graziani whose cruelty had made Italian rule increasingly unpopular. He had felt it his patriotic and humanitarian duty to accept Mussolini's request. After service in the First War, ill health had kept him in the sun of Libya and Somalia until marriage had brought him to more formal duties. Both the Ducessa and he were of commanding presence, each standing six foot six inches tall, and of patently amiable disposition. Holding office at the Duimo near Trieste, he was present when Hitler met Mussolini for the first time. As the Italians stood waiting inside the castle, in strode Hitler in a dirty raincoat. Halting and raising his right hand, 'Heil Hitler', he cried.

From that moment, said Aosta, Mussolini hated Hitler. Aosta had also attended the Stresa Conference between Ramsay Macdonald and Mussolini. Trying to negotiate themselves without adequate trained diplomatic support, he said, the two parties left believing different things; the Italians, that they had been given a free hand for military occupation; the British, that they had agreed to an Italian economic sphere for trade only.

Aosta spent the night in Khartum. I was brought in to help with his numerous staff, and drove him round Omdurman. When he enquired, I told him that I had resigned because of the atrocities of his administrators; that I feared war would soon break out; and we would be fighting against each other. He agreed with all I said, adding that he had just returned from Rome where he had tried to persuade Mussolini not to attack Albania on Good Friday. He invited me to visit Ethiopia as his guest, to see what he was doing to try to check the maladministration. After getting the agreement of the Sudan military and civil authorities, I left the Sudan with the greatest regret. I was never again to find such 'job satisfaction' with so many good colleagues.

In the six weeks I spent in Ethiopia I found hospitality and facilities to which I would like to have become accustomed. Aosta was a Royal Duke, a Viceroy and a Commander-in-Chief, with staff and material support accordingly. His staff, personally selected by him, shared his outlook and approach to their difficulties. Despite the prohibition against mixing with the local population, they had the best relations with all races, colours and creeds. Aosta was clearly most popular with all except the extreme Fascists.

He took me with him when he roared round Addis in a small open car. Every few days, sending cars ahead, we would fly to some distant point. On landing he would take the nearest vehicle and drive round looking for any trouble. He would fly back while I returned by road later. Thus I covered 5,000 miles; to Gimma in the south-west, Dessie in the north and the Arussi in the south-east. These were approximately the three routes followed by our invading armies two years later.

Every evening in Addis there was a large formal dinner party, made cheerfully informal by my host and hostess. After dinner Aosta took me to the Great Ghibbi where he lived austerely, sleeping on a camp bed. There he would talk for hours about African administration and European politics. He was particularly interested in Britain's African administration, and in preparations for Sudan's independence when the threat of war and Egyptian intrigues were removed.

Before leaving he invited me to visit him in September at his house in Italy which he had inherited from the Emperor Maximilian. He wished to take me to see Mussolini, to show him that there were still British who would fight tyranny. When September came, we were at war.

I visited Jibuti, Aden, Suez and Malta on my way home. Within a year I was to visit all four in very different circumstances.

In London I was asked to join the SIS. Peter Fleming, one of the activists of those months, advised me to keep free of any definite job until war broke out; there was much to be done meantime on one's own. Peter was then helping to form MIR. I politely declined the SIS invitation, saying I wished to do something active, and not just collect intelligence. I was not told about the D section.

Of later value was a meeting in London. John Hamilton, then Sudan Agent in Cairo, asked me to meet Chaim Weizmann, the Zionist leader, and St John Philby, then working for the Saudi King. We discussed, hard though it is to imagine now, the possibility of transferring the British mandate for Palestine to the Saudis, and the difference between Zionists and Jews who, with Christians and Muslims, were all 'people of the Book'. When he heard I was setting out for Spain, Mr Philby told me to look out for his son, Kim, a journalist there.

He was to be one of the first we met when, late in June, John Wrightson and I travelled round the north of Spain on business. This first-hand experience of the moral and material devastation of that great country caused by the Civil War was to be useful when we reached North Africa three years later.

Passing through Paris, I called at a small hotel used by the Social Democrat International for refugees. They asked me to help in Poland as I could move round more freely than they. Many were Jewish who were under the greatest pressure. The immediate project was to organise the outflow of Czechs across the Carpathians to Gdynia and on to France to form the Czech Legion.

With French help, I flew to Cracow in southern Poland. There I found a group headed by the Mayor of Cracow, with the Czech General Pruheller, a Frenchman, a Russian and myself. Again the experience of 'green frontiers' was of value later – frontiers where there were ways, at a price, for crossing without authorisation.

On 22 August, however, the news of the Molotov/Ribbentrop Pact between Germany and Russia broke the relative calm. All had expected something to happen in September. A few had warned of such a Nazi/Soviet accord. None knew better than the Central Europeans of the age-long hatred and incompatibility of the Teutons and the Russian Slavs. For centuries their battles had been waged over the peoples of Central Europe. Here was war again.

'What will Russia do'? we asked our Russian colleague.

'We will lean against our fences' he replied, 'and if they are not kept strong enough, we will push them down'.

This was the exact method that Russia was to adopt. Eastern Poland, Finland, and the Baltic States, Ruthenia, Bessarabia were all occupied while others were busy elsewhere, and before the Nazi onslaught all but overwhelmed Russia herself.

There was little more we could do. We spent two days setting up 'lines' outside the former group, as we could clearly no longer trust the Russian, who from now on was an active enemy.

With some difficulty the aircraft on which we had arrived made a last trip. I arrived back in Paris to be invited by Litzi Auschnitt, wife of the Rumanian oil magnate, to the Paquin autumn show; and to stay at their house in Portugal 'for the duration'. Once again, I wondered if the scale of the coming catastrophe was realised.

Back again in Oxford, I visited President Benes and Jan Masaryk, who had sought refuge from Prague in England. After telling them of my visit to Cracow, they told me to keep in touch; which was valuable when later I was a junior officer concerned with Polish and Czech affairs.

CHAPTER 6

Windsor, 1939

I duly reported to the War Office. Having refused employment with SIS, I was, perhaps, saved from featuring in Mr. Kim Philby's biased account of the alleged haphazard recruiting for the Service. Guy Garrod, former Chief Instructor in the Oxford Air Squadron and now Air Member for Training, told me that I was on the list for employment on RAF Staff Duties in Cairo as I spoke Arabic, but he believed I wished to do something more active. Being over thirty years of age, it was unlikely that I would be taken for retraining for air duties. An interview with those who later formed MIR seemed more hopeful, but no offer came. In any event, I was told to get fully trained first before I could be employed.

Meanwhile among the Grenadiers who had served in Cairo in recent years were some old friends from Oxford days. They knew of my views on appeasement and of my resignation from the Sudan. They had suggested that I apply to join the Regiment. I had been told not to make formal application before hostilities began as I was still working abroad. I waited, therefore, until 1 September before, with great diffidence, writing in.

While waiting to hear the result, I had the good luck to be in the Gallery of the House of Commons to hear the Prime Minister announce at 11 am on 3 September that we were again at war with Germany. Paradoxically, the feeling of relief was immense. With others I had felt that continued withdrawal could finally put us in a position where any attempt to fight would be impossible.

On leaving the House, the Alert was sounded. All dived for shelter. The All Clear soon came. None knew the reason for the warning, but surmised that the Germans were quick on the draw. Only years later did I discover that the real cause was far different. The Marquis de Brantes, the French Military Attaché in London, trying to return from leave in France, had found the

Channel ports closed. So hiring a private plane, he flew across without giving due notice. He was the father of Mme Valery Giscard D'Estaing. Captured when involved in clandestine action in the Allied cause, he was killed at Mauthausen, a hero of the Resistance.

It was, therefore, with a sense of immense pride and relief that I received my calling-up papers. All other ideas of clandestine action I put behind me. Clearly my friends and I must be wrong. We were back in the concept of the 1914–18 type of warfare, only with tanks rather than horses. I only prayed that I might live up to the honour of joining a Regiment of such distinction. Being physically fit, I looked forward to serving with it throughout the war.

I had applied to join with all other Guardsmen, beginning to train at the Depot. I was told, however, that as I was over thirty, I was to be commissioned at once and sent to Windsor to join the Training Battalion. There I arrived, full of social and military apprehension. The next few months were, in fact, to be among the most enjoyable and instructive in my life. Having endured a modicum of responsibility and experience, I found surprisingly little difficulty in being a very minor cog in a large and admirable machine. 'Do what you are told', especially by the Non-Commissioned Officers, 'and you will be in order'. 'Learn not only to obey at once and without question, but to anticipate orders'. Politeness at all times – 'I thank you', 'Please' – not 'Yes' but 'Sir' – 'Sir, Sir'. 'On parade' and 'off parade'. On parade all were 'Sir' and all were saluted. Off parade only the Commanding Officer was saluted, and called, like all Senior Officers in the Brigade of Guards, by his Christian name rather than his surname. 'Colonel John', 'General Boy', such rules made life much easier. 'In civilian dress (would we ever put that on again?) lower your bowler hat below the shoulder'. 'In uniform, do not carry a parcel, get a lady friend to carry it for you'. Thus were polished, rather than ground, into shape a number of individuals of considerable poise and initiative outside the military machine.

Lieutenant Colonel John Pilcher was the Commanding Officer, with Arthur Hanning as Adjutant. Pat Robertson, his Assistant, showed us how to return a salute with a gesture inherited from removing a tricorne hat from a peruke wig. The

Company Commanders were mostly First War veterans recalled, like tame elephants, to get us into shape. They typified the classic reply to the question in their war, 'What was it like?' by saying, 'Oh, the war wasn't so bad. But the noise, and the people'.

We were quartered in Victoria Barracks where the Messes had to accommodate more than one hundred officers and three thousand Guardsmen. Our pay was, as Ensigns, 11/6 (57p) a day, with a ration allowance of 1/1½ (6p) – the same for all ranks. As few of us, contrary to popular belief, had much in the way of private means, we were glad to get that. After breakfast at 7 we were on parade for Adjutant's memoranda at 8. With a short break for lunch, training continued until 4 pm. An important part was to learn to look after each other. Thus an officer attended and waited until the end of the Guardsmen's meals to see if there were any complaints, before eating himself.

There were thirty of us 'elderly' officers, reservists and others, untrained but eager to join such a regiment. They came from varied occupations, adding to each others experiences. There were also many young officers just out of school. They brimmed even fuller with self-confidence, and were already trained in the fairly simple infantry tactics of 1939. Rodney Moore, recalled from staff duties, later commanded the Grenadier Group in the Guards Armoured Division and went to the top in his Military career; Peter Carrington, who, with Sergt. Robinson captured the key bridge at Niemegen and later, but for having been born into the Better House of Parliament, might have become Prime Minister; Rowley Cromer, to become a most effective Governor of the Bank of England – the list is long, and selection invidious. The distinction in later public life of those who survived showed the quality of our loss in the death of so many young of all classes, as significant in quality in World War II as in numbers in the First War. Particular friends who were lost included Dicky de Rougement, the Eton fast bowler, who could throw a grenade further and more accurately than any other, 'Stumps' Boyd and Christopher Ford. In addition to our company training, there was an officers Platoon, to give us the required skills in fieldwork and on 'the Square', which is such a basic requirement of the Brigade of Guards. All these small-scale skills were to prove invaluable in the years ahead. The winter of 1939–40 was very cold. This made the square very slippery for slow marching and turning, especially for any who had celebrated too well the previous evening. Since by some oversight, there was a shortage of gloves for the Guardsmen, none of them, and certainly no officer, was allowed to wear gloves until supplies for all were found. No coat collar was ever allowed to be turned up. Indeed Louis XIV's dictum was proved – 'No man of quality must display the effect of heat and cold, of hunger and thirst, of comfort or discomfort'. Such stoic acceptance, physical and mental, found in rowing and service in the Sudan as well, has stood me in good stead ever since. Again, time on the square gave the same feeling as in a good crew, when all moved in unison. Trusting the stroke, or officer, to lead, and to suffer most if he got it wrong.

A very good Sergeant, Chatterton, was in charge of the Officers Platoon. He was inevitably known, but not to his face by officers, as 'Ruth'. He spoke wisely when he told us of the need to return a salute, even if given from far away. If not returned, our names would be taken and we would be given extra duties. The good reason given was that our attention must always be sharp, so that when an enemy appeared we would see him. He also urged us to become fit.

'You gentlemen', he said (did we hear a faint doubt in his tone?) 'are to command the finest trained reservists in the world. And you are not even fit.' (Those in the front rank thought they detected, sotto voce, 'the consolation is that, if any of you by any chance were tempted to run away, you would not be able to run very far'.)

Thus encouraged, we tried to get fit. Every Wednesday morning the whole Battalion had to run round the Copper Horse in Windsor Park and back. I shared the periods of nausea behind the magnificent trees lining the Long Walk, which after the war had to be cut down – I hope not through our fault. On one night exercise, wet through and frozen, we were about to assault the Copper Horse when out of the dark came the voice of John Bailey, who had just missed the First War and had much enjoyed life since; 'God, what wouldn't I give for a week in the South of France now?' Whenever in later years I have felt specially dispirited, John's voice has echoed these sentiments to cheer me.

On occasions we did not feel altogether inadequate. After

being shown the working of the Service rifle in the indoor range, a random four were picked to try to hit the targets. All of us scored the maximum possible.

Outside military training, our first and enjoyable duty was to guard Windsor Castle. There were rumours of possible parachute attacks on the royal family who were in residence. Sentries were issued with live ammunition and told to fire if any did not obey a challenge first time. So well trained were the Guardsmen that when going on rounds, the officer had to give the order to halt exactly as one foot passed the other – like changing gear without using the clutch – or confusion might be caused. Punctually at 11.00 pm, I was dressed with steel helmet and gasmask strapped to chest. Outside in the blackout stood ready a drummer in front with a lantern, with a Sergeant and two guardsmen to follow. Apprehensively we set out. At the slightest sound I would give the order 'Halt', saying the word under my breath every time one foot passed the other. We arrived safely back, an hour and a half later.

On that occasion it was snowing. There was a crowd to watch as we marched up the slippery slope into The Castle, with the Battalion 'drums', the band, in front. I felt some slight qualm that perhaps it would have been better had I stayed in the Sudan after all. All went well on 'mounting'. The next day was even colder. The New Guard overshot their mark by a few feet, and then turned to face the Old Guard. At that moment my drummer, the bugler, raised his frozen bugle to his lips and blew a series of the rudest noises. His opposite number should have replied, but wisely remained rigidly at attention. So I stepped forward and offered the Keys, the token of our custodianship, to the Officer of the New Guard.

'Not now, old boy', he whispered. I stepped back. 'Oh God, it should have been now, shouldn't it . . .' but we carried on with regimental panache. I doubt if any but the NCOs noticed. All were so well trained that as long as the officers made a long sound followed by a short one, the Guardsmen knew exactly what to do.

Her Majesty Queen Mary took a gracious interest in our welfare, and expressed an intention to visit the Guard Room to see if the elderly officers were duly cared for. This called for immediate action as murals decorating the room were thought to be out of order for Her Majesty. After public duties, some of us went to tea in Royal Lodge where the royal family lived most of the time. This was a great encouragement to us all. On occasion, too, Sir Owen Morshead who was Librarian at the Castle, would show some of us round the royal collections. All were safely stored and protected against possible air attack, but we could see many interesting items in what must be the most comprehensive art collection in the world.

St. George's Chapel was another source of great pleasure. Many of the quiristers from the several Chapels Royal had been evacuated to Windsor. The quality of singing, always outstanding, reached even greater heights. The Grenadiers, being the Garter Regiment, and St. George's Chapel being the Garter Chapel, we had the right to occupy the Knights' stalls if free. This privilege was immensely enjoyed whenever possible.

HRH The Duke of Connaught was Colonel of the Regiment. On occasion he would visit Victoria Barracks. Once I heard HRH say, 'Of course, you young men have never seen life. You were never at the Courts in St. Petersburg and Vienna'. We all agreed that we had clearly missed much. He then went on, 'Of course, my godfather used to say to me that I had never seen life as I had not been to the Court of Louis XVI'. His godfather had been the Duke of Wellington who had petitioned the King to grant The First Guards the right to style themselves 'The First or Grenadier Regiment of Foot Guards' after their defeat of Napoleon's Imperial Guard at Waterloo. The Iron Duke had, in fact, died when the Duke of Connaught was but one year old, so the conversation could not have been a prolonged one. It was remarkable that two lives had spanned so many years.

When going to or from barracks, each company marched with one file on one side of the road and two files on the other, with a gas sentry marching fifty yards ahead. We were told that if Royalty were seen – and we had all the relevant car numbers – the company must be closed up and a Royal Salute given. One cold evening our company was returning to Victoria Barracks. Crossing the Long Walk, we observed two young ladies walking back to Royal Lodge. Oliver Bevan said to George Northumberland, 'Let's give them a song instead' . . . and broke into

Wish me luck as you wave me goodbye

Cheerio here I go on my way
Wish me luck as you wave me goodbye
With a cheer, not a tear, make it gay.

The two girls stood waving and smiling as we marched past,

Give me a smile I can keep all the while
In my heart while I'm away

George and Oliver were both killed a few months later at Dunkirk, as were so many of the Guardsmen, then or later. They too must have cherished that moment.

Till we meet once again, you and I,
Wish me luck as you wave me goodbye.

Strange, as Noel Coward once wrote, how potent cheap music can be, or is it so strange? I have never heard that tune again without reliving the moment.

Early in 1940 the authorities found too large a number of officers and Guardsmen overcrowding Windsor. A Holding Battalion was formed and marched to Kempton Park race course for quarters. George Northumberland kindly opened a wing of his house at Sion nearby. There we were to live, in the greatest elegance, in 'blue' uniforms with congenial company and conversation after dinner – but in great discomfort from the intense cold. After further training in the area, the authorities decided that our military duties should extend beyond guarding Windsor Castle, Staines Railway Bridge and the night club, The Bag of Nails. So individual officers, especially the 'elderlies', were sent off on various courses. I was sent to Cambridge for an eight-week course, being assured that at its conclusion I would return to Windsor.

It did not occur to me that I was not to see the Regiment again as a regimental officer. It was to be one of my greatest regrets that I never had the satisfaction of serving in a battalion on active service. As younger men became available, the 'elderlies' were sent off to other duties. Only one, I believe, ever went into battle with a Grenadier Battalion. The rest went to all kinds of different action. Peter (Milton) Fitzwilliam, for instance, was Specially Employed with George Binney manning the converted motor gunboats which made such a contribution to victory ferrying ball-bearings across the Skagerak from Sweden to Britain. As membership of the Regiment and the privilege of wearing its uniform required active service, I was always careful to obtain the leave of Regimental Headquarters to take up and continue in Special Employment. The Lieutenant-Colonel, Colonel John Prescott, and above all the Adjutant, Major Arthur Penn, were always most considerate. They were good enough to accept that there were physical hazards on occasions off as well as on the battlefield.

I can never repay what I owe to the Regiment for the training and friendship given me, and for the standards they inspired. My efforts in pursuit of my duties in the war years were immensely facilitated by the right to wear the uniform. Since 1945, in private and public life I have constantly come across members of the Regiment quietly and efficiently doing more than their share, in charitable work, in the police and public services, and in Old Comrades Associations – the kinds of voluntary work which sustain our type of democracy.

CHAPTER 7

War Office, Spring 1940

The weeks spent in Cambridge were another strange interlude. The Course, later known as 'The Gauleiters', had aims far different from those of the Nazi leaders. MIR had organised it to bring together and classify a number of officers who had specialist knowledge of foreign countries, and who might be available and suitable for action rather than intelligence in the (by MIR) expected holocaust. The instruction was comprehensive, from international law and economics to varieties of sabotage, physical and commercial. Much of the teaching proved valuable in the many complex problems of the years ahead. I am happy to record that I learnt proportionately more in those weeks at Cambridge, enjoying too the great hospitality of the cellar of Trinity College, than during my years at Oxford. But then I had the greater incentive to learn, to save my skin.

It is not for me to try to write the story of the various British Special Services and their interaction. I can only tell, briefly and I trust responsibly, of those parts of which I had direct knowledge. Until the mid-thirties the only British Special Service with authority to carry out clandestine activities overseas was the SIS. Their task was to collect intelligence, not to take action. Indeed, very few other countries had any capability for taking action.

Only a few men had seen the likelihood of some non-military action, and had begun, despite financial restrictions, to prepare for it. The D Section of SIS was set up under Colonel Laurence Grand. At about the same time a small group of farsighted and experienced Army officers, Joe Holland, Gerald Templer and Colin Gubbins, had come together in MIR, in Room 365 in the War Office. They shared many ideas, stemming from personal service in the First War, and afterwards in Russia, in the Troubles in Ireland, and later in India and Palestine. Indeed, overseas Public Security departments were more practised than Whitehall, as was demonstrated in the Sudan.

Sometimes the placing of these activities under the umbrella of Intelligence led to confusion. Since so much of the work concerned 'foreigners', Intelligence, rather than Operations, seemed to senior officers to be their best home. In truth, some brilliant Intelligence Officers were to find great difficulty with 'Action', especially of an 'ungentlemanly' nature. Their training and skill lay in evaluating the strength and likely reaction of the enemy. The need in Action services, as in Operations, was the vision: how to turn the evaluations into counter-action, in unorthodox ways.

Ethiopia was soon to provide a study ground for the five phases of liberation of an enemy-occupied country. In terms of modern conflict, there was, first, the collection of intelligence by various means, usually secret; second came the organisation of action, normally clandestine, the so-called Special Operations. In these individuals worked in civilian dress, using 'unacknowledgeable' methods. This was, in Mr. Churchill's phrase, the 'ungentlemanly warfare' in which the Geneva Convention rules do not apply and the price of failure was often a slow and terrible death. *Insaisisable sabotage*, that in which it was impossible to track down the saboteurs, had been for long developed by the Communists. During the years from 1939 to 1941 when the Soviets were in alliance with the Nazis, some British Communists were patriotic and far-sighted enough to share their skills with us.

In the third phase, that of guerrilla warfare, much the same methods were used but the individuals wore uniform. Often this made little difference; in the later years of our advance into the Continent, all found behind the lines, in uniform or not, were shot out of hand, by Hitler's personal orders.

Fourthly came the warfare of the regular forces; and, finally, a period of Military Government until the back areas were quiet and could be handed back to their own authorities. Some individuals participated in all five phases. My duties in the next five years were to lie in the second and third phases. My experience on the Ethiopian frontier, in Public Security in Khartum, and in extensive travels and study round Europe were little enough, but more than many had been able to acquire. My experience had been with action and counter-action, as gamekeeper as well as poacher.

Summoned one day from Cambridge to the War Office, I went to Room 365, proud of my blue greatcoat and cap, and saluted as taught at Windsor. 'Ah, a real soldier at last?', said an officer with a quizzical but friendly glance. Luckily my coat collar held up my chin. This was my first meeting with Colin Gubbins, for and with whom I was to work for the next five years in perfect understanding and mutual loyalty. A born leader of men – and women – he was to become one of the outstanding personalities of World War II, still widely remembered with respect and affection long after most senior officers have been forgotten. His energy, physical and intellectual, was boundless. One of the first to study the possibility of Special Operations in practice, he had given endless time to the study of tactics, guerrilla and clandestine; and to the signals, codes and cyphers, weapons, explosives, disguise, false papers and lightweight equipment so necessary to success; and to training in their proper use.

He had survived the rigours of the Blitzkrieg in Poland, finding his worst fears of the strength of Germany confirmed. He had been put in command of the Number 4 (Polish-Czech) Mission, the link with the Polish and Czech Forces located in France under French Command. He was applying all his efforts in trying to persuade the military authorities to take more urgent action for work in occupied territories; this needed understanding of their political background as well as their military potential. Meanwhile he was also charged with organising 'lines' of communication across still neutral countries to Poland and Czechoslovakia.

It was an immense privilege and honour to be for the next five years a junior member of the group which formed the nucleus of Special Operational Planning and Action – Peter Fleming, Peter Wilkinson, Tommy Davies, Douglas Roberts, George Taylor, Bickham Sweet-Escott, Dick Barry and Robin Brook; and in the field at first Gerry Holdsworth, Andrew Croft and Malcolm Munthe. Together under Colin Gubbins we worked on, despite some attempts from commercially successful late-comers to take charge. They were seldom aware of the original struggles to get recognition and make the necessary preparations.

It is always invidious to make such a selection of names. Many others were to make major contributions in the later war years. But without the early efforts of this small group those efforts could not have been so fruitful.

During these winter months I paid many visits seeking like-minded supporters. R.T. Clark, directing the BBC News Department, though deeply concerned in Marxism, watched closely events in Central Europe. I was invited by Parliamentary friends now in uniform to tell them about my visits to Prague, and the German tanks I had seen. 'We know the Germans use many mock tank bodies on car chassis to increase numbers' said one. I replied pompously, 'If you believe that the difference is not clear from six feet away, I'll not waste your time . . .' Their views were founded on loyal support for the Government. 'We believe the Prime Minister knows best. He has sources . . .' they claimed, not unkindly, implying that I was too junior to know. But from Khartum I knew how scanty those sources were.

Churchill, busied in the Admiralty, had little spare time. Eden and Duff Cooper, both of whom had resigned from the Government, were doing little openly for fear of causing public dismay. The Labour Party was still in opposition although I had the chance to talk to Herbert Morrison about the possibilities of Special Operations. Other friends in the Foreign Office who had served in the First War tried to advise. One event which had speeded recruitment was the murder of an Oxford contemporary in Germany. He had kept personal contact with von Reichenau and other German generals said to be anti-Nazi. This the Gestapo disliked, killing him and announcing his death as due to a car accident. When the truth became known it had the reverse effect to that intended, and others came forward to offer help.

Finally, from early 1940 efforts were made to have staff talks (through officers in civilian dress) with Belgium, Denmark and the Low Countries; these were rebuffed. When the assault came in May, the preparations were negligible.

Further north preparations could be partly cloaked by 'unacknowledgeable' support for the Finns, who had been attacked by Russia and had defended their freedom with magnificent courage and skill, and with worldwide acclaim but little help. Here my gamekeeping was to change to poaching. At the end of the Cambridge Course, I was summonded urgently to London, with a colleague who had spent the previous ten years in Japan. Told our destination was Scandinavia, we were fitted out with sheepskin clothing. Forbidden to tell anybody that I was leaving the country, I had not even time to call my family before catching a train to Edinburgh. We were told our destination was Finland, so we started to study phrasebooks – Finnish being particularly difficult, we had learnt little before being told that our journey had been cancelled. The advance party vanished without trace . . . Other colleagues in the Baltic in those months had great difficulty in getting out.

So I returned to London, to wait on call in my club. At this time, I heard later, General Wavell had visited London. Hearing about MIR, he had asked for a unit to be formed for his headquarters in Cairo. Its main purpose was to be ready to take action against any Russian incursion from Transcaucasia across Iran towards India. The officer put in charge, Colonel Adrian Simpson, had been ADC to the Grand Duke Nicholas in the 'Savage Division' from the Caucasus, in the Russian Army in the First War. Douglas Roberts, who had been born in the Caucasus, was to take me with him to join General Wavell in Cairo.

When summoned I reported to Room 365, five minutes ahead of time, as trained at Windsor. Roberts, from Russian-born habit, arrived five minutes late. While I was waiting, standing rigidly at attention, a young officer looked up and asked me if I knew anything about Poland. I replied that I knew a little, having got out of Poland seven months before. The officer said, 'I am Peter Wilkinson, you must be the one I'm looking for, let's go somewhere we can talk quietly'.

So we walked across to my club. Thus through the fog of special service recruitment and these errors was my future changed – and that of the next recruit to arrive who, as I had apparently not arrived, must have joined Roberts's group. Peter Wilkinson briefed me to take his place in Room 365 as the representative of Number 4 (Polish-Czech) Military Mission. Its headquarters were at 88 rue de Varennes in Paris. Wilkinson had taken over from Gubbins who had been appointed to form and command the Independent Companies, the forerunners of the Commandos. These were to take part in operations in Norway, to cut the German iron ore supplies from Narvik – but were anticipated by the Germans who invaded Norway first.

Room 365 was, in March 1940, a centre of repressed frustration.

In the small room next door was Colonel Joe Holland, the last of the three who had conceived the idea of establishing this nucleus of an organisation for plans and individuals, to prepare against the day when war would erupt, and when methods and equipment, offensive as well as defensive, would be needed. They had made some progress in the previous six months, but their reception was little more positive in the War Office than at Westminster. They were more concerned with the third, or paramilitary, phase of Special Operations, leaving to the D Section of SIS work on the second, or clandestine, phase. Colonel Laurence Grand, always impeccably dressed in civilian clothes with a flower in his buttonhole, would pay regular calls to coordinate plans over equipment and manpower and facilities. This example was to help me greatly before long. Personal willingness to cooperate, or not to, was to play a major role in all our efforts. In those early months I found nothing but the keenest wish to work together, in face of extraordinary national danger and the understanding of the ill effects on those in the field of any quarrels at base. None were looking for a career, but only for the survival of our country, in freedom – and, we hoped, of ourselves.

In Room 365 sat six officers I have mentioned already: Davies, concerned primarily with Western Europe; Fleming, with Scandinavia; Roberts with the southern flank of Russia, then in alliance with Germany; and myself, under Peter Wilkinson in Paris, with Central Europe. Ralph Gregg and John Kennedy looked after supply and personnel. Next door sat our 'Smart Girls': Joan Bright, Ann Jackson, Leslie Wauchope and Vera Long, all of whom were to contribute so much in the troubled years ahead.

My formal task was to represent Number 4 Mission in London. The Polish Army had reformed in Angers, in western France, where the Czech Legion was also quartered. The French were primarily responsible for equipping them, but the British kept in touch. General Carton de Wiart had led the Mission through the shortlived Blitzkrieg in 1939 in Poland. He had lived in Poland and was always at hand to help.

I was soon in trouble. The Poles had the best special services in Europe. They had needed these more than most during and between their centuries of occupation and partition. Judging from their experience in 1939, with the treacherous Russian stab in the back, and seeing the comparative lack of readiness or understanding in Western Europe, they had, while praying for a miracle, tried to prepare for the worst. They had written a Top Secret note, forecasting the date and place of the attack on the Low Countries in early May, suggesting the possibility of these countries and much of France being overrun; and asking for equipment and help in setting up a network of radio sets to work into Britain if the worst befell. I duly presented this request to a senior Intelligence Officer. On reading it, he said, 'Captain Dodds-Parker, were you not an officer in the Brigade of Guards I would send you back to regimental duty for spreading defeatism'.

'I thank you, Sir, for leave to speak.'

'Please.'

'I did not ask to come here. I was sent. I will return to Windsor this afternoon if you agree. I am only passing on the Polish appreciation, based on their experience and preparing against the worst . . .' We both calmed down.

Some days later I was again in a difficulty. Somehow the French had found out about this Polish initiative. The French Second Bureau, headed by Colonels Rivet and Villeneuve, had decided that Number 4 Mission was creating trouble between them and the Poles, over whom they wished to keep complete control. They therefore wished the Mission to leave Paris. Peter Wilkinson, as Head of Mission and a regular soldier, did all he could, but the British authorities were unsympathetic. Later, walking downcast to the War Office, I met Henry Hopkinson who told me that he was now on the Supreme War Council. I told him of my problem and asked his help. At once he said 'Let's go and see Gladwyn Jebb in the Foreign Office'. We found him standing in his office, a part of the Locarno Room. He listened patiently, then asked, 'What do you want?'.

'It's now late April', I replied, 'the Poles forecast the attack in early May. If the Mission can be kept in Paris until mid May and nothing has happened by then, I suppose we shall have to heave.'

'As I know you both, I will do all I can to keep you in Paris till mid May.' He did so; for this help the Poles and the Mission were most grateful.

When early May came, Peter told me to stand by in London

while he kept watch in Paris. As forewarned, just after midnight on 10 May, the Belgian and Dutch radios began to report attacks by Germans. The events of the next few days and weeks are now history. Earlier staff talks and preparations might have mitigated the coming disaster even if too late to prevent it. A year later I was concerned with putting into Europe, by air and sea, many brave men and women, sent to set up organisations and communications in circumstances rendered the harder and more dangerous by the lack of prevision. But by then, under Churchill's instruction and example, we were too busy to recriminate.

All in Room 365 had been fully occupied in the previous few weeks. Peter Fleming had gone to Norway with General Carton de Wiart. Gubbins was also there. Andrew Croft and Malcolm Munthe were already 'in the field' in Scandinavia. Supporting them took all our time.

Following the German invasion, unannounced and unprovoked, of Norway, British plans had been anticipated. Full accounts have been given of this short and disastrous campaign, dissipating British forces soon to be required in the Low countries. Among them a Guards Brigade took supplies and individuals to join Colin Gubbins. At Euston Station I saw off each unit, played away by the regimental bands of the Scots and Irish Guards. Everybody joined in giving each unit an enthusiastic send off – the only occasion I witnessed such a display throughout the war. Among those who left to join Gubbins was Kermit Roosevelt, son of President 'Teddy' Roosevelt, as a major in the Scots Guards.

When the evacuation from Norway was ordered, all our colleagues returned safely, if slowly. Croft, Munthe and Fleming survived for further duties.

Each of us in MIR had been charged with thinking ahead to meet the problems which could arise. Tommy Davies, among other plans, arranged for the evacuation from Holland of the large stocks of industrial diamonds there. A destroyer was made available one evening. Thirty-six hours later he was back, with many suitcases full of the precious stones. He had also, it appeared, been present when the Central Bank had destroyed their stock of sterling banknotes, and had signed a document stating 'I certify that . . . destroyed × million £s of sterling banknotes (signed) T. Davies, Capt., Grenadier Guards'. I understood that later the note brought due repayment.

My additional responsibility was to plan requirements if and when Italy entered the war against us. I had spent much time and thought in the previous years in the Sudan making outline plans. With this knowledge I sought further arms and money. President Roosevelt had promised to send 10,000 Springfield rifles, with two million rounds of ammunition. One difficulty was to get them to the Sudan before Italy entered the war as American ships, under the Neutrality Act, were forbidden to enter the war zone.

During the Italian Occupation, the Ethiopians had never trusted any substitute for the Maria Theresa dollar whose true silver content could always be tested by biting it. It was essential to obtain a supply of these. Enquiries were made at the Mint, which was ready to begin manufacture. Suddenly a letter arrived from the Foreign Office, saying that if this was discovered by the Italians, it could be most embarrassing, if not worse, so in the extremely delicate situation at that moment the manufacture must cease. Geoffrey Thompson, a senior Foreign Service Officer, whose servant had been killed a few feet from him by an Italian bomb in Madrid in the Civil War, offered to help, if necessary at the cost of his career. Luckily someone had a bright and better idea. There was a Mint in Bombay which made dollars for Aden where they were also in use. An order was placed for the supply of two million a month, beginning in August, which was the earliest they could manage.

So the days, and nights, went by from March until 10 May. Of necessity we were restrained by top security, but also by some degree of opposition, some examples of which I have given. We had sympathy with those charged with the highest decisions, but we also had our duty to prepare for unpleasant events. At the end of the 'phoney war', with the unknown factor of Italian intentions, the Cabinet had to play the hand, hoping for the best. MIR had to prepare for the worst. I can find no action taken by MIR before 10 May which proved embarrassing or was not useful.

Another initiative hived off from MIR was the beginning of the organisation of escape routes from Occupied Europe. I had had some experience in Ethiopia and Spain and Poland, where permanent frontier dodging over 'green frontiers' was a national sport. Norman Crockatt formed MI(9) which was to prove one of the real success activities of Special Operations.

There was almost a sense of relief when 10 May came. Overnight Room 365 came into its own. I do not believe that any orders came from above. Many who had doubted the para-military schemes of our middle-rank leaders became firm supporters. They seemed to welcome the presence of individuals who had ideas, had made some preparations, and were ready to carry out these projects themselves; the basic feature of Special Service.

Thus, this original small group in MIR, and the D Section, were to remain the mainspring for planning and action. The number of those in the field, who ran the greatest risks and achieved the real results, increased steadily. Others, usually in uniform, were to run transport in and out of occupied territory – in themselves military operations. In between was built up a unique administrative organisation to undertake the essential support services: radio links, codes, weapons and explosives, parachute and sea containers, night landing techniques, 'toys' for 'fun and games'; clothing and documentation, training, in all a large scale effort, within five years to be worldwide. There were many, too many, failures but, in all the circumstances, considerable success.

It took a year to get all these ideas sorted out. Meanwhile British resistance continued. The victory of the RAF in the Battle of Britain gave pause to those abroad who believed all was lost. After all, Britain had always said that had the Germans reached the Channel ports in March 1918, the First War would have been lost. In 1940 virtually all Western Europe was lost. Only the benighted British under Churchill's leadership, and the Commonwealth, and the Poles and Czechs, and the first Resisters, did not see it that way. Their numbers might not have been great, but their quality and determination were unsurpassed.

The next two weeks in late May 1940 saw decisions being taken at last. Wilkinson summoned me to Paris, to concert ideas and plans. He told me that, in anticipation of Italian entry into the War, I should go to Cairo for a month, to lay lines of communication to Poland and Czechoslovakia when those through Italy would be cut. When this was done, I was to use my discretion about my next moves. I told him about my undertaking to the Sudan with which he fully agreed; because, also, I had been the

MIR officer in charge of such plans as we had for Ethiopia. His last words cut into my memory:

'Go out to the Middle East. If the United Kingdom were to be overrun, keep outside the ring. Go to South Africa, Australia, Canada. Keep going, and in touch with Auxiliary Units in the UK. Remember it took the Greeks only six hundred years to get free from the Turks.'

Before I left, we had one final party. I told Wilkinson my sister had a girl-friend, of Polish-Hungarian birth, who might be in trouble if captured. We took her to dinner at the Perigordine and on to see Maurice Chevalier. While he went back to the Mission, I took her to her grandmother's flat near the Etoile; we crept in to hear the BBC news. At that moment the air raid alert went. We remained silent for fear Granny would come in; no one was allowed out on the streets. After the All Clear I had to walk home. Wilkinson, a well-trained soldier, slept with the door open and one ear cocked. Not having heard the alert, he merely turned over when I opened the front door, looked at his clock, muttered 'Sister's friend, my foot', and went back to sleep.

This illustrated the recurring difficulty of alerting friends and others to withdraw while the opportunity still allowed. Even when catastrophe was imminent, few would move until too late. In consequence, they were often condemned to years of virtual imprisonment, if not to transportation and worse in a concentration camp. When next morning a German fighter machine-gunned the airfield at Villa Coublay, I regretted that I had not been more determined. Back in London later, on my way to the War Office, I watched the lunchtime crowds in the parks, carefree and apparently ignoring the disasters occurring less than a hundred miles away.

I had no time to see my father and sister, to my infinite regret as my father was to die four months later before I returned from the Middle East. Neither did I have time for a proper handover to my replacement, Perkins. I received a message that, as he had not yet been able to go round the cavalry school training jumps at Weedon without falling off, he could not be commissioned. Certainly, in the best Polish tradition . . . My final task was to load six tons of 'toys' from the Magazine in Hyde Park for transport by flying boat to Egypt. There they were to prove their worth. Told there was a place for me on a Hudson aircraft, without any baggage, I left the War Office on 25 May, the day the Dunkirk evacuation was to begin. At four in the morning of 25 May I called in at the War Room. It looked touch and go whether many of our trained troops would get safely back. Only their hand-weapons would survive. All heavy equipment must be lost. In Britain there appeared to be only forty-two tanks left with units. Yet throughout this period I never met anyone who doubted that we would survive, although few looked far ahead, nationally or personally. To those who had tried to get activities moving, Churchill's taking office as Prime Minister on 10 May was a greater boost than any could describe. With so much to do, his example of 'no recrimination' set the tone. But I must admit, before take-off, wondering if and when I would ever see Britain again.

The Hudson I found at Northolt. It was specially equipped for long range reconnaissance; its pilot, Macphail, (known as 'Balbo', from a beard like the Italian Air Marshal's) was just back from a series of hazardous flights to photograph the routes the Russians might take on their southern borders if they were to attack in support of the Germans, as they had done in Poland and were to do all along their western frontiers. There were four other passengers: George Taylor, on his way to Cairo to set up a D-Section Office, and then round the Balkans, and to Yugoslavia to make the first proposals for the coup which, a year later, was to support King Peter against the defeatists and the traitors; Ian Pirie, on a similar mission to Greece; and two for Palestine, one of them Arthur, the brother of T.E. Lawrence. At our first landing, at Marseilles, we found much damage from German bombs, and we were lucky to get refuelled. Fearing it might be some time before we could again buy French cognac, we bought all the pilot would allow us to carry. After nightstopping in Malta, we reached Cairo the next day.

One day when all memoirs are written, someone will compile an account of those extraordinary months, May and June 1940, in France; of how, for example, General Spears could not get refuelled at Bordeaux when smuggling General de Gaulle to England, and how they flew the last hundred miles to Jersey with the fuel tanks registering empty. None knew General de Gaulle was on board. Had the aircraft gone into the sea . . .?

Chapter 8

Middle East and Cairo, 1940

No adequate account exists of the tremendous responsibility thrust upon the Middle East Command, on land and sea and in the air, under General Wavell in 1940. All had been ready for battle since the Ethiopian crisis of 1935. Contacts were as much with India, Australia, New Zealand and South Africa as with London. Although there were doubts about the immediate enemy, the Italians in Libya and Ethiopia, risks could not be taken. In the summer of 1940, Germany and Italy were to occupy or neutralise Europe from the Pyrenees to the Soviet Union. Britain was threatened with invasion. Bombing had begun. French colonies in Africa and beyond were of doubtful loyalty. Palestine had, until recently, been tying down more British forces than were available to defend Egypt. The Arabs had revolted against the inflow of Jewish unfortunates seeking the refuge that no other countries would give them.

The arrival of Australian and New Zealand (ANZAC) troops wearing their distinctive 'Digger' slouch hats had evoked memories of their presence twenty years before, and had helped to quieten local animosities in Egypt.

In June 1940 there was acute anxiety about the divided loyalties of the French, both military and civilian, in Syria and Central Africa. Marshal Pétain, voted into power by the rump of the National Assembly called together in Bordeaux, had the legal right to order an armistice. Many did not obey, and so were technically at fault. This was another 'grey area' for which, as later for the Resistance, there were no rules – but eternal honour to those who decided to carry on.

Wavell's first decisive stroke was to instruct Western Desert Force under General Wilson to drive the Italians off Egyptian soil where they had occupied Sidi Barrani. This British force, 30,000 strong, every man a volunteer and mostly professionals, was perhaps, despite its inadequate and outmoded equipment, the finest Commonwealth Army ever to take the field. Italian morale was so low and British so high that the attack was half way across Libya before communications and equipment became overstretched and a halt was required. This success lowered the morale of the 250,000 Italians in Ethiopia who had anticipated an early link-up across Egypt, and hastened their defeat.

Thus, in the Spring of 1941, the Germans came into action in the Desert to save the Italians. Their counterattack drove the British back. The earlier Italian attack on Greece, again requiring German help, had necessitated the diversion of British troops to help the Greeks. Yugoslavian military and political resistance, helped by British advice (for we had little else to offer), further delayed the German attack on Russia; and thereby gave time for General Winter to save Moscow.

Victory in Ethiopia was to release South Africans, Rhodesians, East and West Africans, two Indian Divisions and a strong French Brigade for these 1941 campaigns. In addition to Libya and Greece, Syria, Iraq and Iran were becoming increasingly dangerous. The rest of the Balkans were collapsing, even Turkey seemed threatened.

The entire area offered many openings for Special Operations. With the lack of preparations earlier, surprise is not at how little, but how much, was accomplished in the next five years.

All this lay in the future when I flew to Egypt in late May 1940. Cairo was another world, and was to remain so for most of the War. After recent weeks in London and Paris, it was odd to find that everyone wore civilian dress after lunch and played games and went nightclubbing as before the outbreak of war. There were 100,000 Italians, many of them Blackshirts, in Egypt eagerly awaiting the arrival of Mussolini. Perhaps the apparently unruffled attitude of the British helped sustain the bluff, to cover the lack of troops. News from the battle areas of Europe was scarce, and the intentions of the leaders in those countries which affected our future were unknown.

I reported direct to Lt. General Arthur Smith, Chief of Staff to Wavell, explaining the change in my appointment, my immediate (Polish Czech) mission, and my commitment to the Sudan. He told me to carry on accordingly, attaching myself to G(R) at Grey

Pillars, the headquarters building in the Garden City.

To the surprise of my aunt and my uncle, Major Alec Wise Bey, I walked into their house to stay. I had been ordered to tell not even my family where I was going or to be found. But the Wises could write to England 'Douglas here . . .'

We set to work at once. Roberts and George Green were my main colleagues and, soon to arrive, Guy Tamplin. A banker by profession he had, after service in the First War on the Lockhart Mission in Russia, lived in Riga. His initiative and vast experience of Eastern Europe helped immeasurably in the accomplishment of the first part of my mission, which was to switch the routes of Czech and Polish land communications through Italy to Greece and Turkey and beyond. I was to learn much from colleagues from these two occupied countries in Central Europe. They confirmed my belief that their spirit is indestructible. They have been so often overrun, yet have emerged unbroken. Gay and gallant, they could never resist a dare. In a lighthearted moment I said to one courier, 'Do bring me back a bottle of real vodka'. Six weeks later he placed one on my table. What the cost was in effort I shall never know. I did not risk such a jest again.

Tamplin's arrival freed me for other duties, sometimes at the personal direction of Wavell. A friend of my uncle's and a fellow Wykhamist, he would ask me to dinner at his house in the Gezira. Duly warned, I sympathised when on occasion he was somewhat silent at mealtime. He carried the heaviest burden against all those threats. Although there were some embryo groups for action in the Middle East, there were few individuals to be sent off on missions. GR and D Section were thus used for any special action which normal military and civilian facilities and personnel did not suit. We were sometimes regarded as superhuman, even supernatural – such was the general ignorance of capabilities which were, in fact, very limited. But we were unacknowlegeable and expendable – and were ready to have a go. It was difficult, and often a waste of time, to explain the realities of communications into and out of occupied territory, and of ungentlemanly actions. All senior officers were brave and honourable men, battle-tested in the First War. But we were fighting a very different war, much of which was to take place far from any sound of gunfire. In the summer of 1940 there seemed little else to be done.

I was kept busy. My first mission was to go to Palestine to discover the fate of some French armoured units in Syria which had wanted to continue the fight. I found that on arrival at the Palestine border they had been told to wait until permission was obtained from Jerusalem. As the afternoon break was still being observed as in peacetime, there was a delay before authorisation was received. Meanwhile, these brave French had been overtaken from Damascus and withdrawn. Many individual French remained with us, in particular, Colonel de Larminat and Captain de Kersauson, who was recommissioned as Captain McCulloch in the Royal Irish Hussars, until all seemed safe for his family in France. 'French Bob' became a great favourite everywhere. His bravery and energy took him into many a battle. He and others like him did much to maintain his country's high repute.

The next immediate issue arose over an Italian ship, the *Umbria*, which signalled her approach to Port Said some days before Italy entered the war. She was carrying 7,000 tons of bombs, which would double the stocks known to be in Ethiopia if she reached her destination. All agreed that she must be stopped. But how? Long discussions followed. What were the rules about international passage through the Suez Canal for neutral ships in war/peacetime? Would any delaying tactics aggravate the Italian attitude? What could be done?

While discussion continued, an ill-assorted group of four people from GR and D began to practise their school breaststroke in the Bitter Lakes on the Canal. 'Limpets' were strapped to their chests. These were devices, flown out from London on that flying boat; they were shaped like a steel helmet, each containing seven pounds of plastic explosive. They adhered to a steel plate, itself tied to the chest by a circle of magnets. On approaching a ship or other target, they could be detached, turned over and put on the side of the ship. They were detonated by time-delay fuses, codenamed 'pencils'. While practice continued, so did discussions. The *Umbria* reached Port Said. She passed through the Canal. The Royal Navy planned to hold her at Suez while willing but not-so-enthusiastic amateurs swam out in the darkness to do their best, timing the 'pencils' to go off when the ship was well out at sea. It was a great relief when the Royal Navy, perhaps mistrusting the swimmers' efficiency, decided to take the ship into Port Sudan instead. She was anchored off the reefs. At midday the next day observers saw her begin to sink. Later that evening Mussoloni announced that as from midnight, we were at war. So there, full fathom five, the *Umbria* lies . . .

When, on that Monday, 11 June 1940, Mussolini declared war on Britain, little did I imagine that, thirty-nine months later, I would play a small part in the ending of hostilities between our two countries which have so much in common.

Shortly after midnight the first bombs fell on Asmara in Eritrea. 47 Squadron of the RAF from the Sudan had shown the spirit of attack which was to prove so decisive. At the same time the first armoured cars went through 'The Wire' on the Libyan frontier. In Cairo we did not believe that they were doing much as the nightspots continued to be brightened by the cavalry's coloured overalls. Later we found that while two squadrons would be through the wire, the third, while its vehicles were being serviced, would return to their normal routine in the night clubs.

Already we had scoured the bookshops of Cairo in search of any copies of books like Michael Mason's, describing methods of navigation and travel through the Sand Sea in the Western Desert. He and others had carried out expeditions from Egypt to the Western Sudan through areas usually regarded as impassable. We feared the Italians might have found out the secrets of their success. This seemed to be untrue. Others, including Ralph Bagnold and Guy Prendergast, had already formed a secret unit soon to attain immortality as the Long Range Desert Group (LRDG). Once, detailed to instruct some New Zealanders in methods of destroying captured fuel stocks, I was able to go part of the way with them. MIR had sent out some explosive devices disguised as camel droppings, to be laid in the desert roads. By agreement, a New Zealand patrol of the LRDG were to organise for one to fall into the hands of the Italians. Thus alerted, news came back of Italian vehicles keeping to the few tracks as the desert was covered by real camel droppings.

General Wavell ordered me to make a short visit to Khartum to report on preparations for action in support of the return of the Emperor of Ethiopia. Before I left, we went through the details of provision made in London; the weapons, including the rifles and ammunition from President Roosevelt; funds of £1 million; and the Maria Theresa dollars. Smugly I told him about the order for two million a mouth, beginning in August.

'Why only two million', he asked, 'and why not till August?'

I saw little purpose at that point in enlightening him. Instead I felt it best to try to look inadequate.

In Khartum I found morale as ever very high. The Italians had come down to the Sudan plains at Kassala. Thence they could have motored across the desert to Khartum. The Sudan Defence Force with 5th Indian Division fought magnificently to hold the twelve-hundred-mile frontier. Later, when Italian troops had contracted much malaria, and 4th Indian Division arrived, they withdrew to the mountains. Such Italian tactics undoubtedly hastened defeat in Ethiopia and saved many lives on both sides.

My next mission was to try to destroy 11,000 tons of fuel stocks held in Jibuti, now at the mercy of the Italians. I had looked at these the previous summer when passing through Jibuti. Some secret talks had also been held with the French there. But in the confused circumstances of the summer of 1940, new plans for possible action seemed essential. I was sent off in a Hudson aircraft armed with a Boyes anti-tank rifle. My orders were to cross from Aden by night; shoot holes in the tank farm the next night; and hope to return. With me went Colonel de Larminat, a most gallant Free French officer, to cooperate throughout the War and later to reach the highest rank in the French Army. He was to help, as required, with the French authorities. In Aden the Governor housed us and the Air Commander-in-Chief listened to the plans. The RAF Reserve Officer detailed to be my sponsor had been, I learnt, 'on the table' of *Punch*. When he heard the plan, he laughed long and loud. We could never cross without the French finding out, nor destroy the fuel stocks as planned. In view of the unknown relationship between individual Frenchmen, I decided to visit Jibuti but, to his well-justified anger, not to take Colonel de Larminat with me. I was well received by General Gentilhomme, who duly lived up to his name on this occasion and later in North Africa. He assured me that the oil fuel, and other valuable reserves, would not fall into enemy hands. They did not. Shortly afterwards he joined us, by escaping through Somaliland.

Before returning to Cairo, I paid a visit to the Somali battle area. I flew in a Blenheim bomber to bomb Tug Argam, a range of hills which the Black Watch was defending against overwhelming odds. In Berbera I met Colonel Chater, a Royal Marine and former Commander of the Camel Corps in the Sudan, to see if there were any chances for special operations before the British left. Local District Officers, in fact, stayed behind unsupported, to keep the flag flying until the occupation ended six months later. I nearly met my end there. On my return flight I told the pilot that I had learnt to fly. We discussed 'angles of glide'. 'Let's see what it is on a Blenheim', he said. We just came out of the dive before hitting the sea.

On my return, I was sent to Jerusalem to call on the Jewish Agency, to see Moshe Shertok – later, as Moshe Sharett, to be Israel's first Foreign Minister and a good friend. I told him that we all seemed to be in considerable difficulties and asked what he could do to help.

'I will tell you on one condition', he said.

'What is that?'

'That you never tell anyone.'

I never have.

Finally, I went to Alexandria to call on Sayid Senussi, the religious leader of the people of Cyrenaica, the eastern part of Libya. I was to ask him, if Egypt was temporarily overrun by the Italians, whether he would prefer to go to Palestine or the Sudan. He was friendly, but non-committal. Later he became the first and last King of Libya. He was clearly a Reluctant Monarch and preferred being a Holy Man.

GR association with D Section was close. They helped me on the civilian side while I supported those in uniform. For the many problems and opportunities we were ill-equipped and untrained. Quick decisions of grave possible consequence were needed. Once, for instance, in a neutral country north of Egypt, a colleague spent a morning briefing a courier who was to return to enemy-occupied territory. Names and addresses were well memorised. He was due to leave at 5 pm. At lunchtime a signal was received, saying that the courier was a double-agent and must, on no account, leave.

At last, in September 1940, I handed over my Number 4 Mission duties to Tamplin. I arranged a code message with GR so that when my next project, in the Sudan, was accomplished, I would be recalled to London rather than to Cairo.

Before departure, I heard that Churchill had again been as good as his word. The first convoy with the promised reinforcements from Britain had arrived at Suez. Morale in the nightclubs and beyond was immeasurably raised by their safe arrival, especially by the news that the first units ashore were a posse of padres, a Mobile Bath Unit, and a Section of the Imperial War Graves Commission. All needs, present and future, had once again been foreseen by Churchill.

The activities so far related were, in fact, isolated 'coups de main', to be carried out without special training or equipment. Only in Norway had there been some pre-occupational work, and that had been swept away.

Not until July 1940, at the nadir of British fortunes, did Churchill direct Dr. Dalton to 'set Europe ablaze'. Dr. Dalton was one of the few politicians who accepted the ideological nature of World War II, and so of the possibilities of subversion and sabotage, of political and guerrilla warfare. The estimates and directives from the Chiefs of Staff in London, set out in the appendices of Dr. Stafford's *Britain and European Resistance 1940–45*,* were often unrealistic. The nature of clandestine survival and supply in face of ruthless Nazi/Fascist/Communist repression was little understood by those in high authority, and only just being discovered by those charged with putting the directives into practice who had to cope with the non-existence of adequate lightweight transmitters, of essential false papers, of aircraft in competition with demands from Bomber Command.

My colleagues still in London had been set to organising Auxiliary Units, equipped to operate behind German lines if invasion took place. They had little time, therefore, to do more than lay the foundations for overseas operations by the Spring of 1941 when I returned to London. By then the Balkans were being overrun. Only in Ethiopia had victory been achieved.

* Macmillan, 1980.

CHAPTER 9

Ethiopia, the first Victory, 1940–41

In Khartum, when I returned there in early September 1940, morale was high, despite the news from Britain. The Italians had not occupied the city. A thin but strong ring of regular Commonwealth forces had contained any Italian outbreak from Ethiopia.

The plans for irregular action were already set in motion, as conceived by the Sudan authorities, military and civil. The status of the Anglo-Egyptian Sudan has seldom been fully understood. The Sudanese, British and Egyptian officials all shared a common interest in the protection of the Sudanese and the defeat of the Italians. Their plans, coordinated with the Foreign Office and the War Office, had taken into account British efforts to keep the Italians neutral. When this failed, immediate action was taken, even before the end of the rainy season was to allow regular forces to begin operations.

Only one point proved controversial. It was one of timing, not of substance. The Emperor, as King of Kings of the many Amhara clans, was not universally acceptable, while the Amhara ruling race was unpopular with its dependent tribes. So it was felt that the Emperor's entry into Ethiopia could perhaps be more wisely delayed until his safe and swift arrival at Addis Ababa could be ensured. Flown out from London to a Khartum still under threat of Italian occupation, he was temporarily withdrawn to the Northern Sudan.

By September he was back in Khartum. The first phase of Special Operations had begun with the despatch of Brigadier Sandford, using an assumed Amhara name, into the Gojjam. His task was to mark the route chosen for the Emperor's advance, through my former Fung District, up the 6,000 ft escarpment, across the Gojjam, down and up the deep Blue Nile Gorge, and straight on to Addis.

The third phase of Special Operations had also begun. The

Frontier Battalion had been formed and trained by Hugh Boustead, a leader of exceptional quality and proven courage. These Sudanese troops, with officers from the Sudan Political Service and others of long experience in the area, were to carry out most of the organised, irregular fighting in the next few months. The Sudanese have always been among the bravest of the brave.

The first company, under Peter Acland, had already penetrated a hundred miles into Ethiopia, and the others were set to follow through the Dinder River Game Reserve where grazing was good for their transport animals and game for food abounded.

The arms and ammunition promised by President Roosevelt had arrived, despite the Congress and the reports from the American Ambassador in London; we felt we could count on the President even if Britain were overrun.

I took up my duties at GR at Headquarters British Troops in the Sudan which were in the Gordon College building. Reports came in that the Italian troops who had moved down from the mountains across the frontier from the Red Sea to the Blue Nile, were having much illness, especially malaria. The rainy season, at its height, had greatly decreased their mobility by vehicle and animal. Along this twelve-hundred-mile front our forces were meagre but, as in Egypt, most aggressive. General Platt was in overall command, with the small but highly effective Sudan Defence Force of some 5,000 men. 5th Indian Division had arrived, to be joined in November, after their contribution to the decisive victory at Sidi Barrani in Egypt, by 4th Indian Division. Among them were the Jammu Mountain Battery, but to our regret they had left their elephants in India. The Indian and Sudan mobile motor-machine gun units, used to desert conditions, patrolled ceaselessly and aggressively throughout the rainy season. Later, when the infantry and a few tanks were deployed, they were to win the great battle of Keren, one of the outstanding infantry achievements of all time; up a 4,000 ft escarpment, against some fifty unbroken Italian battalions, many of them Eritrean. These too were soldiers of valour whom the Italians had treated well and led well. Throughout these months the names Slim, Messervy, Briggs were often heard.

I was sent off along the whole length of the occupied frontier, and down to the Boma plateau in the far south, to survey and report on the possibilities of irregular action there. Parties of Ethiopians were coming in, among them some with whom I had tried to maintain relations in previous years; while loyalty among the Sudanese tribesmen was complete, as expected, thanks to their good relations with their District Officers, Sudanese and British. Although many of the Ethiopians were far from our proposed line of advance, they could guard our flanks and later join us once we were established on the Highlands of the interior.

On the Intelligence Staff in Khartum, under my former chiefs Jose Penney and Duncan Cumming, was 'Uncle Robert' Cheeseman. His experience and wisdom as a former Consul in the Gojjam were to prove invaluable. Our immediate task was to assess the reliability of local support, free from emotion. Cheeseman said that the people of the Gojjam valued their freedom from Addis almost as much as from the Italians. Though he judged that they would facilitate the Emperor's transit, they would not relish any increase in his authority over them, now made more possible by improved Italian roads. There were many 'shifta' (bandits) among them who could be unreliable if issued with arms. Despite these fears, we decided to call them 'patriots' for want of a better word and for the benefit of the world press. In the event, though many served loyally, early defections among those to whom the American rifles were issued proved the point. Very few rounds of ammunition were given to them till their loyalty was proved – while the use of any stolen .303 British ammunition risked destruction of the rifle.

The Operations Centres were now arriving. These were formed, each with an officer and four sergeants, from the regiments of the Cavalry Division in Palestine, and from the Australians. To each were added 100 armed Sudanese volunteers, taking with them 100 American rifles and 20,000 rounds of ammunition with which to form, with recruits from the Patriots, a guerrilla unit. The Australians led off, under Alan Brown, closely followed by 'Billy' Maclean, Basil Ringrose and Bill Allen. The Veterinary Department of the Sudan Government helped with the purchase of 18,000 camels, our first line transport. These were to carry their loads with customary patience to the Escarpment. Many struggled up it, though only some 300 arrived eventually in Addis. The whole route from the Sudan was strewn with animal remains. Good camel management needs conditions not found in the bush country, which required long daylight marches with unskilled loading and unloading.

I paid an early visit to the Emperor who received me with great courtesy, together with the Crown Prince and the Abuna, the Archbishop, and others who were all to share the rigours of the Long March to Addis. Andrew Chapman-Andrews, of the Levant Consular Service, with many years spent in Ethiopia, was attached to the Emperor's staff. He was to bear the brunt of the negotiations between Ethiopians, and British and Sudanese authorities. In a long and distinguished career later in the Foreign Service, he was never to play a more effective part, nor earn greater gratitude from his many admirers. The eyes of the world were on the return of the Emperor, and many difficulties were delicately resolved by Andrew.

There are numerous accounts giving details of those months – of the negotiations over the Emperor's return, and of his journey from Khartum to his capital city. I will not repeat these but add some points, from my personal experience, about methods and equipment and personalities, which were to be of value, or of warning, in the future.

My first duty was to explain to the Emperor how I had become connected with this campaign. He already knew about my efforts in the Fung; what I had tried to do to help his people, and to keep some hope alive in a distant part of his country. I also explained what we had tried to do in Khartum in 1938–9 and in London in early 1940. I gave him a personal letter from General Wavell with the latest news of further help coming from Cairo, amidst all other preoccupations.

To sum up. While the end of the rainy season was to allow the regular forces to begin their victorious advances, the irregulars were already on their way by October. At the end of the month an important conference was held in Khartum. Eden as Secretary of State for War, Generals Wavell and Smuts considered what further support could be given from East and South Africa and Rhodesia, whose forces were to play such a decisive part in the advance from Kenya to Addis early in 1941.

This conference also decided on the exact part to be taken by the Emperor. There had always been this doubt, as described, in certain circles about his acceptability, even to the ruling Amhara potentates outside the Highlands. There was particular doubt about the enthusiasm to be expected in Eritrea, a judgement to be confirmed by the separatist movement still active there forty years later. In 1941, however, once the Italian local forces had been broken in battle, the Emperor, as King of Kings, had a clear appeal to all within the boundaries of Ethiopia. These included the Galla and other peripheral tribes remote from Addis who had seen little of central government before the arrival of the Italians; and who might have been less welcoming to the Emperor had the Italian rule been less cruel. It was also politically essential that there should clearly be no hesitation at all in giving the fullest support to the immediate restoration of the Emperor. Eden had himself played such a prominent part in the whole tragedy of 1935 that he could be relied on to make certain that everything possible was done to expedite the campaign. For a while the Brocklehurst Mission, initiated with goodwill to ensure first the support of the tribes on the Kenyan frontier, created some confusion. Eden's personal intervention, however, quickly removed that diversion.

Thus, political difficulties were cleared away. Material shortages, however, remained. This was the result of a decade of delay. Insistent demands came from Regular Forces and the Home Guard in Britain, still facing the threat of imminent invasion, and from the outposts of Empire, of which the Sudan and Kenya were not the only high priorities. Churchill had swept aside recrimination, but could not conjure supplies out of the air.

At this moment he did, however, send Orde Wingate to assist us. In his excellent biography of Wingate, Christopher Sykes, writing of necessity subjectively, gives perhaps some impression that little if anything had been done to facilitate the Emperor's return to his country until Wingate arrived in Khartum. I have tried to show that this was not so. Inadequate though the preparations had been, and late their implementation, plans had been long ready, personnel and supplies were arriving, and all were moving into action.

At first Wingate was under Terence Airey who had formed the GR section in Khartum with Captains Muchu Chaudhauri and myself. Colonel Airey had wide experience of the Sudan and the Middle East. His exceptional administrative qualities were often to be disrupted by Wingate. Muchu was later to lead the Indian contingent in the Victory Parade in London, and to be Commander-in-Chief in India and High Commissioner in Canada. Most amiable of friends, I would salute him as taught at Windsor and say, 'Sir, you are the Boss. You can lock up and I will go home'.

Wingate told me that his first idea, when sent out from London to help organise irregular action, was to hide groups in the Jebel Akhdar, the 'Hump' in Cyrenaica, to observe and harass Italian communications. On his arrival in Cairo, he found the LRDG already at work; and he clearly had no chance of taking over command from such experienced leaders. So his next idea was to come to Khartum and try to take action in Ethiopia. He had served in the Sudan Defence Force on the Eritrean frontier, along which regular forces were now in action. He had once led a patrol south through the Dinder Game Reserve, but had no knowledge of the southern areas, nor of Ethiopian affairs. Having served more recently in Palestine, he had learnt that the Emperor was also styled The Lion of Judah. Wingate had the greatest quality of leadership of a type for which he was to be awarded the DSO three times. He would always lead from the front.

Perhaps I lived too close to him to take him entirely seriously. He was always trying to provoke a dispute, usually after dinner, as a mental exercise. With others, I preferred different forms of relaxation. There was enough mental anguish before dinner. When he became specially aloof, Muchu or I would say, 'Come on, Orde, you are not Napoleon yet . . . nor even T.E. Lawrence'.

He had some claim to be a relation of the Lawrence brothers, and one evening confided to me that perhaps one day T.E. would be called 'The Wingate of Arabia'.

Whenever he became more than usually offensive, I would remind him that I was only in Khartum temporarily, and could go into the field or back to London and tell them what a so-and-so he was. This had a calming effect. He was believed to hold a personal letter of instruction from Churchill. But I was in charge of all his papers and knew this was untrue. After my training in the Sudan and at Windsor this was an odd way to treat a senior and distinguished officer. But I could find no alternative.

It had been agreed that once the GR section had been set up I was to go into the field as my training and inclination required. Such was the hostile atmosphere created by Wingate at Headquarters that when later he went himself into the field to command Gideon Force, he told me that I must stay in Khartum since he trusted no one else to ensure his requisite support. I said this was completely untrue; that all had been set to support the venture long before his arrival. He still demanded that I stay. I showed him a note he had made on my record, 'He wants to fight. He should be allowed to do so'. When General Platt took the same line as Wingate, I had most unwillingly to agree. I was thus to spend most of the next five months in Khartum, with forays into the field. It proved most valuable in the event, as it brought home to me the essential requirements of signals and supply in special operations; and the importance of confidence from the field in those at base.

Again we made reconnaissances. In an exceptionally skilful and hazardous feat of flying, the first I was to organise into enemy-occupied lands, Flt. Lt. Collis landed Wingate in the Gojjam to consult Sandford. My task was to visit the frontier districts on either side of the Emperor's proposed line of advance, to see what degree of support my Political Service colleagues believed might be mustered to protect the flanks. In the north and centre it seemed to promise well. In the far south, on the Boma plateau, the war had not been heard of.

On his return in November 1940 Wingate was summoned to Cairo to report on the possibilities of Patriot activities. He was given ten minutes. A senior officer later told me what had happened. First Wingate said that with the personnel, arms and money already available, he would lead the Emperor back and rot the Italian Empire from within. Beyond the military value of this, the Red Sea would be cleared of the threat from Ethiopia, which would allow American ships to come to Suez. While the Red Sea remained a war zone, the American Neutrality Act forbade their coming thus far north. Wingate then went on, uninvited, to give all the Highest Commanders in the Middle East a twenty-minute talk on Grand Strategy.

'Keep 5th Indian Division in the Sudan, and the African Forces in Kenya. Take 4th Indian Division, all South African and Rhodesian Forces and Transport units and the French to the Desert. Drive through to Tunisia without delay. Having thus cleared North Africa, forces must be put into Greece, for in the Spring of 1941 the Germans will be in the Desert and in Greece. I will have cleared Ethiopia by May. I will then come to Palestine where we must be ready to face an attack through Turkey'.

The main fault in this forecast was that, even with all those forces kept in the Sudan and Kenya, the threat to the Red Sea was not removed until June 1941. Without them, it is doubtful whether this would have been achieved for another year at least.

In private Wingate would say that from his experience with his Special Night Squads in Palestine, formed from Jewish irregulars to anticipate Arab attacks, he could raise two divisions of first class fighting troops. He believed that with them he was destined to defeat the Germans on the Plain of Megiddo.

'I suppose that the mantle of the prophets would then descend on you . . . Elisha . . . Elijah . . . Orde?' I would comment irreverently.

As a first step Wingate sent for some of the Jews who had served him so well in the Night Squads. One in particular, Avraham Akavia, was to become a valued colleague in the next six months. For competence, courage and devotion to the Allied cause he was outstanding. Told by Wingate to write a citation for an award for gallantry for him, wearing a British Captain's uniform, I could trace no record of his having ever been formally recruited into the British Army. Such were the oversights and formalities which throughout the years of special service were to deprive so many of just awards.

One night at dinner with the Emperor we discussed the problems of administration which would face him later. The Italians had put in a network of communications, roads and airfields, which had unified the country as never before. This should facilitate efficient administration, but who would be there to carry it out? Almost all educated Ethiopians had been killed by the Italians. I had just read in a report of a shipload of illegal Jewish refugees, bound for Palestine, who had been caught and diverted to Mauritius for the duration of the War. The Emperor was styled the Lion of Judah. Would these refugees not be able to find work and safety with him? The Emperor expressed great sympathy with the idea and said it would be given close attention if put to him officially.

So, later in 1941, when back in London, the proposal was sent to six friends. Next an enquiry came from the Private Office at 10 Downing Street, asking how many of these I had put in. I had taken the precaution to warn No. 10. They waited until four of the six had reached the Prime Minister, with differing degrees of support. I heard that in the event the Jewish authorities had rejected the idea, understandably from their point of view. Any such second class solution, even into a friendly country with such potential, could never take the place of a sovereign state into which could be brought all and any refugees if a fresh persecution, such as that of the 1940s, ever occurred again.

On his return from Cairo, Wingate sent me to try to establish better contact with Peter Acland, commanding the first company of the Frontier Battalion to enter Ethiopia. Wingate had flown over it and believed that an aircraft, even without notice, could land there. I set out in a Battle, a single-engined aircraft, as rear-gunner with a Lewis gun firing only single shots. We wore the usual twenty-four-foot parachutes. These were so small that if required to drop on to the plateau which was 7,000 ft high, the wearer would break both legs. This would make escape from the Patriots impossible and emasculation by them the more likely as they could and did not differentiate between friend and foe. I still have my identity card, personally signed by the Emperor, ordering them not to do so. My faith in it was strong.

Before leaving I asked Wingate for a message to be dropped if we could not land. 'You must never anticipate failure' was his characteristic reply. We had trouble in finding a village near Belaia, but saw no signs of the company. We dared not drop a message giving any real information in case it fell into enemy hands. So we dropped a hastily written message of general goodwill and encouragement to what appeared to be a signal fire. Such indeed it was; later I was asked what had been the purpose of the flight, and why we had not dropped at least some newspapers and supplies. I made a note for the future.

Following this failure, we made another reconnaissance up the Dinder River, seeking the best route, and method, for the Emperor's march in safety. The Frontier Battalion's trail was slow and tedious. From his visit to the Dinder River, Wingate believed that it would not be too difficult to get wheeled vehicles through to the Escarpment. Led by an experienced Canadian, Captain Le Blanc, and carrying Alan Brown's first, Australian, Operational Centre, we crossed from the Blue Nile to the Dinder. Striking south-east, we found the river bed impassable. The Dinder was fed by streams with banks up to thirty feet high. Our guides warned us that many miles of such country lay ahead. So we turned back with the vehicles, with barely enough petrol in hand. More seriously, the Australians had already run out of tea! They were to add distinction to the ANZAC reputation for bravery and endurance, and to return safely home.

I had only one other difficulty with them. Months later a letter arrived from the Game Warden's Office, saying that they had shot, without a licence, a giraffe with a Bren gun and an elephant with a Boyes anti-tank rifle. The fine was £Ex.

Wingate worked very well with the Press. That is to say, he would, from time to time, disclose to them the likely timing and course of future operations. In those early months such disclosure was strictly against the rules, until a better system was worked out. These journalists were an experienced group of colleagues, as we regarded them, who had seen much of troubled Europe in past years. I had met some in Central Europe and Spain, Alan Moorehead, Alexander Clifford and Richard Dimbleby among them. Freddy Palmer of the *Daily Mirror* taught me much about camera angles. Although my place was far to the rear, my friends in Britain were often impressed by pictures of the Emperor in which I always seemed to be closest to him.

Until the battle of Keren began, our lesser affairs were the more spectacular and of world interest. From these Press friends came much valuable advice and help on the presentation of the Emperor's support, and from their experience, on ways of increasing it. On one occasion their help was critical. After a visit with me to Gallabat, they wrote pieces describing the scenery. These descriptions were so phrased that they fitted similar scenery at Um Idla where the Emperor was to enter his country. Indeed, all the area is much the same. The stories were to be filed at home some days before his entry, and duly released when he was across the frontier. This would ensure that they would soon reach enemy eyes. The Italians would deduce that the point of entry was near Gallabat and concentrate a search there rather than at Um Idla, one hundred miles away to the south. This duly happened. The stories were released. The Italian air and ground search was made to the north while the Emperor marched in further south. He was safely up the Escarpment, in Patriot-held territory, before the enemy found out the truth.

There was a price to pay, of course, for the information given to the Press from time to time by Wingate. As these disclosures were irregular in every sense, he would hold his 'conferences' in his bedroom in the Grand Hotel. I would go along to keep an eye and ear open. I treasure the memory, once so well described in *Life Magazine*, of the faces of half a dozen journalists, sitting in a row, watching Wingate as he lay on his bed, wearing only a shirt, brushing his lower anatomy with his hairbrush. Luckily for me, I could sit facing the other way. All the journalists came to give a good send-off to the Emperor when making his formal re-entry, after nearly six years' absence, into his own country; the first, and we prayed not the last, such restoration we would witness. Landing by air on a roughly cleared field, the party walked down a path cut in the banks of the Dinder River. This may not have been the exact frontier, but it gave the best photographic angles. The 2nd Ethiopian Battalion, brought from Kenya to guard the party, provided a Guard of Honour. Then the Imperial party set off to the south-east. The Emperor, indomitable and dignified as ever, led the way. Next went Wingate, clutching as usual his alarm clock. Then the Crown Prince, the Abuna, the Archbishop, Andrew Chapman-Andrews, Akavia, and many others who were to suffer great hardship and considerable danger before we all met again in Addis three and a half months later. I returned to Khartum, despondent at missing what I had worked for for five years.

In January 1941, the Allied armies were advancing on Addis on three fronts, General Platt with the two Indian Divisions, the Sudanese and French forces, from the north; General Cunningham, with South, East and West Africans from the south-east. Gideon Force took the most direct line, through difficult but friendly country where the Italians were restricted to the only road.

My sole concern with these regular operations was to help Oliver Corvedale's propaganda unit operate near Keren, to weaken the Italian morale and seek recruits for the Emperor's army. Richard Dimbleby's BBC van had microphones at the end of long cables, to record the sound of battle. With Richard's agreement, Oliver and George Steer, his assistant, reversed the process. Creeping up near the front lines, they played recordings to the enemy troops, in particular appeals, in the Emperor's own well known voice, to the Ethiopian levies to rally to him and the Allies, now advancing victorious; to come over in the darkness, bringing their arms with which to fight for the freedom of their country. Many would be found the next morning, around the spot whence the voice had come. One error had an unexpected result. Oliver, a music lover, would borrow records from friends in Khartum. In the darkness, so he said, it was hard to see what was what. One morning he was sent for by the General Commanding who said 'Oliver, I agree that you are producing results, but I am damned if I see why I should be woken up at night by the overture from Aida'. Later, an Italian taken prisoner at Keren told me,

'It made many of us think, "there are other things in life . . ." '.

The four months of the Emperor's progress to restoration in Addis in May have been chronicled often before, particularly by W.E.D. Allen, an Operational Centre commander. The ten Centres, with the Sudan Frontier Battalion and the 2nd Ethiopian Battalion, were the fighting nucleus of Gideon Force. Formed under Wingate's overall command, this Force's first task was to escort the Emperor; its second to rally Patriot groups and Italian deserters to form units under Mesfin, once again Commander of the Emperor's Bodyguard. From these units would be formed an Ethiopian Regular Army. As the advance continued, many groups and organized units, for example those whose first loyalty was to Ras Hailu in Debra Marcos, came to swear allegiance. Others were no better than bandits, hoping for money and arms. Their main use was to guard the flanks, and give warning of enemy action.

Supply was the greatest problem. Although the direct air route from Roseires to Addis was but 150 miles, the land route was over 250. The first sixty miles lay across featureless savannah country; then up the 4,000 ft Escarpment, on to a plateau of fertile farmlands; across this to the Blue Nile Gorge; another 4,000 ft down, across the only bridge, and up to the highlands on the final approach to Addis. One unpaved track made the use of wheeled vehicles possible, but there was no way to get them through from the Sudan. Camels remained the sole method of transport of ammunition and food. Local stocks were scant. An occasional airlift was to show the possibilities of air-supply to light forces making deep penetrations, and for the support of locally entrenched resisters. This was to prove as valuable an experience to Wingate later with the Chindits in India as it was to me, later that year, helping to organise the first air-supply into occupied Europe. Never were there enough aircraft; there probably never could have been, as the demand was to increase as victory came nearer.

Valuable experience was also gained in the need for easily portable weapons, using when possible captured enemy ammunition. Later, to meet this need, the Sten gun and the PIAT, a small anti-tank weapon, were developed. Meanwhile, the Bren gun was to prove the 'heaviest' weapon suitable, but available only in small numbers.

It is beyond my experience and competence to evaluate the relative merit of the contributions to victory of Wingate, Boustead and the many brave leaders of individual actions. The part played by the Emperor himself should not be underestimated. The route taken was not only the best tactically, but meant that while Italian forces were concentrated to withstand the two main Allied attacks, many local Ethiopian groups could visit and give allegiance to the Emperor, thus further undermining Italian morale. The Emperor's standing underwent a marked change. Until he left Khartum, he was entirely under the control, militarily and politically, of others; he often felt that his country's interests were subordinated to factors beyond his ken. Once back again on his own soil, however, the position changed, the more so as his final victory approached. Local resources were limited, but known – and could be used at his discretion. He was a world figure and all except the enemy rejoiced at his restoration. He had always been treated with the greatest deference and consideration by the British authorities, both for his position and his character. There were some difficulties, but not due to his personality. Later this 'change of gear' was to occur time and again as military forces freed Occupied Europe. Warnings were given, although not always heeded, of the need for realistic political decisions to anticipate disagreement, at least until the lines of communication were safe.

I visited Wingate as air transport offered. There were some difficulties which could not be sorted out in radio messages which all read. Exceptional efforts were made to supply him, but he always wanted more. There were comic moments also. One officer, believing special service signals came to my desk alone, sent a series of messages about his love-life. When he saw these, the General exploded, 'What sort of officers have you brought . . .?' Written messages took weeks to arrive by mule. Meantime his requests multiplied; until a signal was sent, in the General's name, if not by him, ordering the officer to place himself under arrest. As he was alone apart from a radio operator, he 'got the message'.

Another typical Wingate episode followed an argumentative dinner; as a Gunner to a Grenadier, he told me how best to throw a grenade, learnt during his operations at night in Palestine. To prove his point, he led us, a small assorted group, to attack an Italian post. Grenades were thrown in from all sides and next day the post was found abandoned. The methods seemed to me as hazardous to us as the enemy. I told him this and said if I was allowed to join Gideon Force I would go with Boustead rather than with him.

It is hard, many years after these events, to recall the circumstances in which we operated. We were under pressure to bring the Ethiopian campaign to a prompt and successful conclusion in order to release regular forces sorely needed in the Middle East where further defeats still threatened. All available methods were employed to speed our victory. Some quick thinking occurred after the capture of Burye. The telephone rang in the Fort. An agitated voice from the next Italian post down the road asked what was happening. Grabbing the nearest Italian-speaker, Wingate told him to say he was advising his hearer to withdraw without delay. This he did. It did not occur to Wingate to consider that the journalist he grabbed was a non-combatant and a neutral, at least in theory.

The fabled victory at Keren in the North, an infantry triumph perhaps never to be repeated, and the spectacular advance of hundreds of miles from Kenya, brought victory within reach by early May 1941. By this time Gideon Force, with the Emperor and Wingate, were across the Blue Nile Gorge and approaching Addis. General Cunningham's forces were already there, and began making due arrangements for the Emperor's triumphal entry. At last the day came. With his proud, if battle-and travel-worn companions, and many fresh adherents, he came to re-enter his capital. The day chosen was 5 May, exactly five years since Marshall Badoglio had ridden in his 'triumph' into Addis on a white horse. Wingate had decided that it was appropriate that the Emperor should make a similar entry. As the procession approached the city, General Cunningham sent cars for the Emperor and his party, to greet him and ease his journey. Gratefully, the Emperor climbed in and went off to Army Headquarters. Not to be thwarted, Wingate climbed aboard the white horse and himself led the Victory March into Addis.

I had been sent up from Khartum to arrange the details of the transfer of responsibility for the Emperor from General Platt's to General Cunningham's theatre of operations. Later that evening I was sent for; 'For heavens' sake get Wingate off that horse and bring him to dinner'. It was a memorable occasion.

The campaign had not quite ended. Aosta had withdrawn to Amba Alagi in the most mountainous region of the North. There his surrender came a few weeks later. Final defeat was not accepted until months later by a few isolated posts; but this did not delay the rapid redeployment of the regular forces to the Mediterranean to meet new threats; while American ships could now come all the way to Suez and thus save scarce Allied shipping.

Aosta had been held in the highest regard and respect by all who knew him, by friend and foe, by Italian, Ethiopian and British. Another born leader, he combined the widest political vision with profound humanitarian sentiments. These his actions proved. Had he been appointed to Addis earlier, the reconquest would have been the harder. He was to die the next year in Kenya – perhaps partly of a broken heart, for all knew how depressed he had been by war between our two countries, by political tyranny in Europe, and by suffering inflicted on Africans. He was an Italian patriot and a good European. He did all he could to lessen the impact of war, especially on the Africans. Typically, he sent Jack Maurice, a Political Officer at the Sudan enclave in Western Ethiopia, back to the Sudan instead of interning him. He also arranged for any Allied pilots shot down (he was a magnificent pilot himself) to be quartered in the Italian Air Force Mess where he paid their mess bills himself.

Thirty months later I helped to get some of his most co-operative staff brought back from Kenya when the Italian Armistice was signed. Had he been alive he would most certainly have given the Italian monarchy a better chance of survival as a non-political national rallying point. He was untainted by Fascism, and might even have succeeded, however reluctantly, to the throne.

After dinner on 5 May I bade Orde Wingate farewell, never to see him again. I was to leave at first light, to catch the courier aircraft back to London. I congratulated him on his success in leading the Emperor's forces victorious into Addis. I thanked him for his forbearance to me as an amateur; and hoped that whatever the future might hold for us all, I would be able to make use of the methods, suitably adjusted, which had been so usefully applied in this campaign. At that moment he was riding high, little aware that he was soon to be returned to base as a major instead of the colonel's rank he held in Gideon Force. While many paid tribute to his positive qualities of courage and leadership, his waywardness could be disruptive. Even the Emperor who owed so much to him felt, so his staff told me, that the atmosphere might be calmer if Wingate left.

It is not for me to try to assess his true merit, or his place in history, though in the past seven months I had seen him in so many moods. At his best he was a real leader. He went in front, physically and mentally, regardless of consequence. Had he shown more thoughtfulness for his professional colleagues he might have achieved more, but he might not have been followed so keenly by all ranks in the field. He put forward ideas, strategic and tactical, and tried to be the first to lead the way. Although the details were not known, his first DSO, won in Palestine, had earned him a reputation for successful valour.

At his worst he would seem to disregard the judgement and good intentions of others. Every one of those going into the field with him into Ethiopia was an experienced volunteer of proven determination. There was no need to question their individual application. The same applied to those overtaxing themselves, both at base and on the line of communication, to get supplies forward to Gideon Force. But his behaviour was sometimes wickedly and foolishly offensive; as when he told two staff-trained officers in front of me, 'You are only here because you are trying to avoid leading your troops in the field'. I stood up, placing myself alongside them and said, 'Me too, Sir. When can I go back to my Regiment?'

On more than one occasion I was sent for by Brigadier Scobie and told, 'The General and Wingate have had another row. Both have resigned. You must bring Wingate back to work this afternoon'. Time would be spent in calming Wingate down.

A third Wingate I saw when alone with him on a few occasions. When I refused to rise to a series of provocative remarks, he would become a good companion, confiding his hopes of doing something to make a better world; in which he had an acceptable ambition to BE SOMEONE. In the Sudan Defence Force he had been a keen Arabist. This changed during his service in Palestine. His Zionist beliefs were well known in 1940, but never appeared excessive.

On occasion I am asked for a summary of his character for a proposed film of his life. I reply that I could only tell of the various sides of his character which a good actor would have to portray.

My flight home was, for those days, remarkably swift. The first night in Kano; through Lagos to Freetown and the second night in a flying boat, landing at Lisbon in civilian dress. The third, night-clubbing amid the bright lights, I met von Rheinbaben, the SD agent from Prague. I was restrained from assaulting him. We reached England, again by flying boat overnight, on the morning of 10 May, to see the last big 'Saturday' Blitz before the Germans turned east and, a month later, attacked without warning their ally, Russia.

On the way I had sketched out the lessons to be learnt from Gideon Force. The campaign in Ethiopia had been wider than Wingate's contribution although his personality made the most impact. There were to be innumerable occasions when experience gained there was to prove of value in the next four years. There were few activities which were not be repeated or developed from this first successful irregular campaign. The first principle was that while sabotage could be carried on ceaselessly, guerrilla warfare could only succeed in support of regular operations. A charismatic leader was essential, such as the Emperor or General de Gaulle. We so often failed to understand their frustration when outside their own country, entirely dependent on a foreign power, often with different aims; and the consequent rebound when back on their own soil with their own resources. Such a leader needed to make the widest internal appeal while allowing for local sentiment. When the Emperor entered Debra Marcos at the head of a few hundred troops he was faced by several thousand men, Italian-equipped, under a local king, Ras Hailu. Assuring the Ras that he was only passing through, he went on in safety. Three and a half years later in Athens, the Communist group ELAS was not so restrained. But for British determination, with troops to secure it – just – the returning government would have been overwhelmed.

There was always latent conflict between those who maintained resistance within occupied territory and those who, mostly for the best reasons, worked from exile to sustain them. This conflict was to affect plans to use local resisters to guard the line of communication and screen any remaining enemy posts while the regular forces pursued the main enemy. These local groups often had political aims different from those of the returning government, and had to be restrained until victory was won. The retention of British officers with patriot forces thus became on occasion a matter of judgement. Did they help or hinder co-operation between the conflicting groups? The slight conflicts in Ethiopia were to be magnified in North Africa and Europe, especially in Italy and France and in Greece.

The Operational Centres had proved to be of great significance. Small, well-led units, radio-linked, had served as magnets for local resisters to join. They were formed later by SOE as missions in the field, in the Balkans and Italy; and to support immediate military operations as Operational Groups and 'Jedburghs' – teams of three – in France.

Experience in Ethiopia had also highlighted the urgent need for lighter-weight signal sets, weapons and explosives, and secure codes. Limited parachuting, airdropping and 'pick-ups' had shown the possibilities of air supply and communications. Indeed, without them there would have been no supply into Europe. SOE's research and development in the next year were to produce methods and equipment which were to transform airborne operations by regular forces.

Propaganda field units had served a practical purpose. Deception in embryo form had been practised – a foretaste of the support later given by SOE to Brigadier Dudley Clarke's brilliant work in the Mediterranean. His was perhaps the most cost-effective of all special activities. In my future responsibilities my orders were to report all mistakes and failures to him. They would then be turned round so that the enemy could well believe that they were planted.

On my return to Britain I was told to give some private talks on the success of this 'irregular' campaign. The talks were soon discontinued. Later I found out that South African pressure had been brought to play down the victory of mainly non-white troops over a largely white army. Certainly there is little trace in available United Kingdom records of this first successful 'Liberation' campaign.

Chapter 10

SOE London, 1941

The morning of 10 May 1941 was spectacularly fine, as it had been that Whit-weekend of my departure nearly a year before. The spectacle of devastation in London, after eight months of bombing which was to culminate that night, was surpassed by the spirit of resistance. Even the voice of Churchill could not convey to us abroad the spontaneous feeling of united determination which inspired all. I was immediately involved. Reporting to Wellington Barracks I was put in command of a platoon guarding Churchill's shelter at Storey's Gate against possible parachute attack. The Guardsmen were joined by some charming young ladies from South London who kept us all in high spirits. Despite the bombing it was 'cheers, and not tears' all the way. The dropping of an estimated 350 tons of high explosive and incendiaries in seven hours made me wonder, again, if I had been wise to leave the sunshine of the Sudan. One could only respect German endurance in face of Allied air attacks, dropping 15,000 tons in an hour, later in the war.

Next morning I found Gubbins at Baker Street where Norgeby House was to be my constant home, often for days and nights on end, for the next eighteen months; he was to be my effective Chief until VE Day four years later. He had summoned Peter Fleming back from Greece, Peter Wilkinson from Crete where the German parachute attack was just beginning, and me from Ethiopia. I was the first to arrive. Gubbins briefed me.

'You saw last night. With American aircraft now arriving for the RAF, we will one day be able to hit back even harder. For the moment, counter-attacks with clandestine action, subversion and sabotage which have been so successful in Ethiopia are to be our main efforts, until Russia is in the war . . . there are already signs of her entry, and later, perhaps, the United States'.

It is now common knowledge that the 'Enigma' intercepts of

German signals had alerted us to their switch of forces to the east.

'We must redouble our efforts. You have seen one campaign through to victory. I want you to take on the organisation of air and sea transport into and out of enemy-occupied Western Europe. There are few facilities available, but more will come as production allows. Without a reliable transport system – each sortie of which will be a military operation – none of the tasks allotted to SOE by the Chiefs of Staff can be carried out . . .'

A study of the Chiefs' and Planners' Reports and Directives as set out in the Appendices of Dr. Stafford's *Britain and European Resistance* shows the attitude towards Special Operations becoming more realistic from 4 September 1940 onwards, but paradoxically as the number of air and sea craft increased, so did reluctance in some quarters to make sufficient available for the directives to be carried out.

Although the evaluation in these Staff papers is realistic, few except the Regular officers in MIR had firsthand experience of the ruthlessness of ideological clandestine action, as they had witnessed in revolutionary Russia, in Ireland in 'The Troubles', and in Palestine. The practical problems of organisation in occupied territory where no previous preparations had been made, and of maintaining security, were outside the experience of most people. The willingness in the early years in Occupied Europe to risk appalling reprisals was found among only a very few; only when there appeared to be hope of final liberation did substantial numbers come forward. With such risks to family and friends and livelihood, it is not for those from countries which have never been occupied to criticise. While the Blitz was bad enough, occupation was the more demoralising as well as materially damaging. So while the early staff suggestions of mass secret armies declined, the usefulness and practicality of subversion and sabotage, in support of liberating armies, became better understood.

Even less comprehended were the techniques of clandestine activities in the field. SOE itself had to learn, experiment and develop the methods needed to ensure a supply of food and to survive capture; the production of false papers, so widely used; radio and code security; 'silent killing'; sabotage targets, especially the *insaisisable* or unaccountable; above all the selection and training of individual men and women, called by the RAF

'Joes', suitable and willing to undertake the unknown and unimaginable hazards.

Following the German attack on the Russians on 22 June, the Recommendations of the Joint Planners for SOE set the first priorities:-

'(a) Subversive activities should be given preference over secret armies.
(b) Sabotage should be chiefly directed in accordance with the bombing policy aim.
(c) the secret armies . . . order of priority: Northern France, Belgium, Holland, Norway . . .'

Several accounts have been written about the top level organisations and personalities in Whitehall in the war years. The conflicts of interest between the Special Services concerned us little at the lower, operational, levels except as they affected availability of supplies and, on occasion, permission to operate. Dr. Dalton and Lord Selborne as our Ministers, Gladwyn Jebb from the Foreign Office and Sir Frank Nelson and Sir Charles Hambro as our Chiefs, each, in his different turn, made major contributions.

Thus far, as I have described, my work had been mainly paramilitary, in uniform, apart from time spent in Central Europe and in Khartum. This was now to change. I myself, without an adequate knowledge of any language required, was not qualified to survive in the field in Western Europe in civilian dress; for from May 1941 until the final stages of the War, SOE's operations there were carried out by individuals not in uniform.

Two men in particular were to transmute these high level directives into useful action in the field. I have already told of Gubbins' personal qualities and of his brave words on my return to Baker Street. He was an inspiring leader, as brave as Wingate and endowed with the additional ability to maintain an atmosphere of friendly respect and loyalty with his subordinates and superiors. He carried, also, the burden of day-to-day cooperation with the governments-in-exile. All of these had differing political aims which did not always coincide with the British. None strove harder than he to reconcile these shorter and longer-term legitimate needs, and few had such success. In the necessarily secret conditions of his work he seldom got the credit that was his due.

Little did he care except when it limited his later capabilities. Myself an amateur, I could see his professional military colleagues regard him as 'too political', while the politicians and diplomats looked on him as 'too amateur' to be in a position to take, and often to be taking, decisions which they regarded as rightly theirs. Later I was in a very minor way in the same position as a Mission Commander in the Mediterranean. I came to realise then the pressures in such a position, stretched between political and military, short and long term; and what effect our judgement would have on the future fortunes of Governments and individuals. Those to whom communications were given and supplies sent were often the de facto authority in their area on liberation. Luckily we were not plagued by these thoughts in those early months when the struggle was still for national survival.

The second leader was Colonel Dick Barry. We had last met fourteen years before at Winchester. I was to serve under him directly or indirectly for the rest of the war to my great advantage. After the next twelve months organising the Staff Operational work in Baker Street, he went on to plan the Allied landings in North Africa in November 1942, and then to be Chief Planner at Allied Force Headquarters (AFHQ). His early SOE experience made him aware of the possibilities and limitations of Special Operations. He was not only to allow but to suggest and coordinate SOE's preparations and actions with regular operations, to the profit of both.

These two briefed me on the situation. The first, or Secret Intelligence phase of operations was improving. The Secret Intelligence Service (SIS) had been virtually wiped out in Occupied Europe as Himmler had announced in a speech in 1941 which was not made public in Britain. But we were increasingly benefiting from intercepts of messages, the value of which I had known in the Middle East. There was a specially accurate one whose true source I did not seek, on the 'need to know' basis; this later became known as Ultra.

I was then sent on a week's leave to Oxford, the first of two I had in the six years of war. After my father's death in 1940 during the Battle of Britain when he was serving in his third war as a Medical Officer, our house was requisitioned and I moved to Buckinghamshire. I took the chance to call on Jan Masaryk who was in Oxford for part of the War, and heard the latest news from Prague. The situation was still one of apathy, of shock felt after the events of 1938 and the dismemberment of the country in 1939.

Back in Baker Street I found cheerful new colleagues among the handful at work. There were three main groups in the Organisation which, when it was closed down four and a half years later, was to number many thousands. First was the nucleus from MIR and D Section whose varying initiatives had come together at last in Baker Street. They were to be the spark plugs, as it were, of most of the political decision-taking as well as of the supply services to be built up. Recruiting, as always for secret work, was difficult. Training expanded relatively to the increase of knowledge of conditions in Occupied Europe, and with it the availability of false papers, money and clothing; at home, radio sets and codes and signals were being developed as well as explosives, delay fuses and 'toys' of many ingenious types; the finding of targets and the determining of priorities were being established; and the selection of men and women dedicated to the requisite meticulous attention to detail at home on which so often the lives of the brave men and women in the field would depend. It was a slow process to recruit and train, and sometimes to reject, suitable candidates.

The second group was formed by those who provided the transport facilities by air and by sea from the RAF and the Royal Navy and included many foreign nationals from occupied countries. These 'transport' operations were of a hazardous nature requiring special skills.

The third group, the Resistance in the field, was the most vulnerable. By the spring of 1941 loyalties were being sorted out and organisations taking shape. Before that time only the Communists had been prepared for clandestine activities and had made some pre-occupational arrangements. The Soviet authorities had been giving them some assistance before, and more after, they themselves were attacked in June 1941. Cleft between their agreement with the Germans and their long-term aims for world communism, their actions differed in each occupied country. In Britain they were telling their supporters to give the minimum help to the British war effort against the Germans.

This attitude was to change, at least for two years from June 1941 until the tide turned after Alamein and Stalingrad. After those victories their activities were aimed not merely at survival but at post-war expansion. I had heard enough of what the Russians had done, especially in Poland since 1939, to strengthen my determination never to help them establish their form of tyrannical dictatorship over other peoples in place of the Nazi/Fascist form.

Under Barry in the policy and target-setting section were first Arthur Nicholls, later to meet a hero's death when winning a George Cross in Albania; and next Charles Harington, one day to be Chief of the Army Staff. The skill and vision of these three ensured that action was properly directed, short-term to sabotage targets and longer-term to support of liberating armies. Their tasks were clearly set out in the Joint Planners and Chiefs of Staff directives of 9 August 1941 and 12 May 1942.* These were issued after the Russians and later the Americans were in the war with us.

My section's duties lay in arranging transport into and out of occupied Europe, from North Cape in Norway to St. Jean de Luz – of happier memory only two long years before – and through Gibraltar to the French Riviera. In depth we reached out to Poland and the Non-Occupied Zone (ZNO) of France. The sea coasts were restricted by Brittany being reserved for SIS, who also had priority on aircraft. Derek Dodson had already set up the section. The last Briton to graduate from the French Military Academy at St. Cyr, he was soon to leave to win two Military Crosses in Greece and later to give outstanding diplomatic service for Britain. Picquet Wickes was, if a little unpredictable, a gay and helpful colleague, later to join the Free French (RF) Section to cooperate with General de Gaulle's Special Services.

Resources to carry out our tasks were limited. Despite directives from the Chiefs of Staff and Churchill's personal interest, there was considerable resistance in practice to SOE's obtaining the means necessary to implement them. From published accounts it is clear that Air Marshals Portal and Harris believed, as they were entitled to do, that every aircraft diverted from bombing

* Cf. pp 240–6 of Dr. Stafford's book

was wasted. So, in the summer of 1941, only one Flight, 1419, had yet been made available for dropping 'Joes' and containers. Half a dozen twin-engined Whitley bombers had been converted, for the 'Joes' to drop through a hole in the bottom of the fuselage, with the containers to be released from the bomb racks. They operated from the racecourse at Newmarket. There were also some ex-Army Cooperation Lysanders which had proved quite unsuitable for their designated role; they were to prove beyond price to us. To increase their range and that of the Whitleys, Tangmere, on the South Coast, was often used as an airfield.

For sea transport there were two converted French 'tunneymen', each fitted with extra engines, which had come from France in 1940. Their operational method was to sail from the Helford River in Cornwall, under an air umbrella to speed up their engines during darkness, to mix with the French fishing fleet by daylight. There they would exchange passengers, or set down underwater containers marked as lobster pots for later collection by the Resistance. The sailors under Holdsworth's command would man the dinghies and folkboats used to put ashore and pick up individuals from Royal Naval craft.

All air operations were carried out of necessity by regular RAF crews, although on occasion SOE personnel would accompany them. Sea operations were usually led by SOE sailors, a small group of unusual experience. Gerry Holdsworth DSO was in command; a film producer, a D Section member who had served in Finland, he was later to make a unique contribution to Italian Resistance. His second in command was Brooks Richards who after designing yachts while at Cambridge and small boats for Combined Operations, was to win two Distinguished Service Crosses, one for minesweeping cross-Channel and the other for holding the coastal flank of British First Army, a lighthouse, with a posse of Free French, in Tunisia. He, too, was to make a unique contribution as head of the political section in Massingham, the SOE base in Algiers which became the link with the Free French operations into France from the Mediterranean. After these six years of intensive effort, he passed another third of a century in many arduous posts in the Foreign Service. The two other officers were of a very different type, both also of exceptional courage and amiability. Geoff Marshall had commanded a Loyalist ship in the Spanish Civil War, while John Newton was the most successful smuggler in the Channel Islands. Together they were a boatload of modern-day pirates regarded with the highest admiration and affection by all who worked with them.

SOE was still, mainly, a British Action Service. It was to evolve, within two years, into an Allied Service, using techniques mostly developed by SOE, often based on Continental experience and later on American supplies. It emerged slowly from the shadows, putting on uniform and growing into the paramilitary wings of Anglo-American and national regular forces.

The operational state in May 1941 was hardly encouraging, either in Baker Street or in the field. Most of Europe lay stunned under Nazi/Fascist/Communist oppression. The Balkans were still being overrun. Gubbins had said, 'Resistance is just beginning, encouraged by continuing British endurance'. Recoil in the Desert and in Greece, and a month later Russian withdrawals with huge losses, checked this reborn faith. Indeed, until victory in North Africa two years later, Resistance was of limited strength. It grew as occupying forces weakened and the threat of Communist occupation drew near. Not until hope turned into certainty, in late 1943, was it to wax strong; with many joining the few who had kept hope alive and built and rebuilt organisations in the darkest years.

In those three years from the summers of 1940 to 1943, the few were very few indeed. My great privilege was to meet many of them, though seldom knowing more than their code names. Communists certainly played a considerable part at first, being almost the only groups trained and ready in 1939. Any attempt to ascribe credit or blame to those who resisted or did not, democrat or communist, would be sterile at this or any later stage. Traditional Russian imperialism, although masked in the guise of economically ineffective Marxism, by its behaviour was being revealed as a greater and more immediate threat to Eastern European freedom than to the Anglo-Saxons.

All country sections were to face this threat in due course, but, at first, made use of anyone prepared to fight the existing German tyranny. To this purpose each country section was charged to find resisters inside each country and to find nationals or British outside, to be trained and put in to organise and act. In this search I was not to be directly involved until the end of 1942 in Algiers.

France was clearly the first consideration. The failure of attempts by the Poles to hide radio sets before the occupation had been caused by French interference. In 1966 Professor Michael Foot in his *SOE in France* gave a very fair account, from the official records then put at his disposal, of the stages of French Resistance. Without any such records, I will not try to cover the same ground. I will attempt only to fill in some details from the general 'operational' side, in those unrecorded months from 1941 to 1943 when despite all setbacks, spirits were beginning to revive.

Before May 1941 a small *coup de main*, 'Josephine B', in which two Frenchmen blew up a transformer near Bordeaux, had been the first of many such coups. It was deliberately leaked at the highest social levels. Thus soon at lunchtime in the Best Clubs whispers of 'Josephine B' floated round. Subsequently, our requests for further facilities were more sympathetically heard, apart from the RAF; 'Something has been done' – little though it was.

The head of the French Section (F) had not yet been finally chosen; but several good individuals were at work. F was still – and was to remain so until the paramilitary stage was reached – a British Section composed of British and some French who were prepared to act against the 'legitimate' Government of Vichy but did not, at first, approve of de Gaulle. Soon after my arrival in London, a large individual with a heavy moustache came into my office.

'You don't know who I am' he said.

'You look just like Jacques de Guelis' (an Oxford friend), I replied to his concern. He had hoped the moustache disguised him during the twelve months that he had taken to get to England after serving with the Canadians in France. He was to head our French section in Algiers in 1942 during those months when we were not allowed to 'know' the Free French. Jacques' views, well to the right of Louis XIV, suited him admirably in the few contacts officially allowed there among the non-Gaullists. After the political change came, he returned to Britain to support the re-entry into France. He was to be killed in a jeep accident just before the war's end. As a true patriot, his services to France, even if his views were a little outdated, were conspicuous. My only difficulty with him was on occasion when he could not understand why I, rather than he, was in a position to take decisions affecting France. I had considerable sympathy with him.

I welcomed back, from the first 'blind' drop, André Simon. Shortly afterwards he called in.

'Do you think you could help me to get back into France', he asked, 'It's not much fun being chased round there, but the food here, and the wine . . .'

I was to feel duly humble when Captain Ben Cowburn, returning from his second visit to France, winning his second Military Cross, congratulated me on my promotion to Major. My admiration for the spirit and panache of André and Ben and their like remains unbounded.

In the autumn of 1941 the decision was taken to set up a Free French (RF) section. The arguments for and against close co-operation with de Gaulle were not for us. Told to help establish the Section, to be completely separate from F, I was to find myself on occasion in between the two sections when there were insufficient aircraft available. Colonel James Hutchison DSO was put in charge initially. He carried out his duties to the satisfaction of all; but inevitably, and to his credit, a note duly arrived from de Gaulle's Headquarters at Carlton Gardens . . . Instead of returning to home duties as his First War Service allowed, he chose to have his face lifted to escape identification if caught; while the delay in finding his fishing rod dropped with him into the Morvan is still remembered there.*

Our main Free French colleague was the famous Colonel 'Passy'. He was Chief of de Gaulle's Special Services where all took as noms-de-guerre the names of Paris Metro stations, to protect their identity and their families left behind in France. 'Passy', after the war to resume his real name, Comte André de Wavrin, was to win every French decoration and the British DSO, OBE and MC. He was at first, understandably, not very forthcoming;

* See *That Drug Danger*, J.R.H. Hutchison DSO, re-published as *Danger has No Face*, Arrow Books, 1978

but slowly both sides came to see that in all our interests and for the sake of those in the field, our cooperation must be ever closer. Thanks to him and his colleagues and to Jim Hutchison and 'Tommy' Yeo-Thomas, a good working relationship was soon established.

General de Gaulle was urging all in France to come out and join the Free French Forces. This made good political sense but was clearly not practical. There was not enough space on the escape routes, nor by air and sea to Britain. As the few original organisers in France were being contacted by more and more who were becoming active there, it seemed best to keep them in France and send in supplies and communications.

Such became the accepted pattern, the scale of which has seldom been assessed. By May 1941, a year after the Battle of France, only two drops, both 'blind', had been made into France, and one Lysander pick-up. No Reception Committees had been organised, and no radio links. Who could at that time possibly have foreseen that, by June 1944, three years later, it was estimated that in response to radio messages on the BBC or Algiers Radio, over 4,000 Reception Committees could be alerted to receive a drop the same night. This was in France alone, not counting all the other countries. This required large-scale organisation, with minute attention to detail and intense concentration. Precious lives, and worse torture, were at stake. The work was largely carried out by women, civilians and uniformed members of the FANY and the Women's Royal Air Force (WAAFs).

My first enquiries in May 1941 had been for my Polish and Czech friends. No. 4 Mission had been absorbed into SOE where good use was being made of their contacts and proven techniques. Poland was still occupied by Germans and Russians who had partitioned her in 1939, for the third time in two centuries. Such partition had produced clandestine international networks which were to continue functioning until VE Day, made hollow for Poles by the Yalta Agreement of February 1945, which accepted their being 'in the Soviet Zone', entailing continued Russian occupation under a tyranny worse if possible than the German. One sortie only had been flown, in February 1941, by John Austin, an epic 14-hour round trip in a two-engined Whitley. Four-engined aircraft were essential for such long flights, but not until the winter would the necessary hours of darkness be long enough. Until then land routes, through neutral countries and over 'green frontiers', would maintain some communications. Their spirit remained as ever indomitable.

The Czechs were different. As Jan Masaryk had confirmed, they still lay stunned by the events of 1938 and 1939, transformed from the most democratic country in Central Europe into a serf nation. Pieces of their country had been nibbled off by their neighbours, Teschen by the Poles, the Sudetenland by the Germans, Ruthenia by the Russians . . . they seemed friendless. Their leaders, now in London, were deeply pessimistic. They had left behind a good team, to organise clandestine communications and action. Against whom? and for whom? After enduring another spell of occupation by aliens, Russians as well as Germans, it was to take longer for their spirits to revive. Throughout, their leaders were convinced that, like the Poles, they would one day re-emerge a free society, within a truly democratic Europe.

Some tentative connections by land had been made into Scandinavia and the Low Countries and Belgium. The Shetland Patrol could operate into the long Norwegian coastline with some success; but in the more closely inhabited countrysides to the south, dropping from the air 'blind' or even to Reception Committees was to prove much more hazardous.

Demands from the 'customers', the country sections, were growing steadily, if only for blind drops. Aircraft availability was to improve but never fast enough. Until we could show conspicuous success of an immediate and military kind, the authorities, especially those disliking SOE, could aver, with some justification, that aircraft would be better used in bombing. Indeed all the Special Duty aircraft were added to Bomber Command to help form the first Thousand Bomber raid on Cologne. We had heard all these arguments in East Africa. In Britain they were to prove stronger, offset by the essential need to keep up the morale of our numerous friends in the field.

Sabotage, therefore, seemed the high priority; *insaisisable* and if possible within the Geneva Convention rules, although in the event this was to make little difference for anyone caught. It has been claimed that the Hotchkiss factory, making 300 tanks a month in 1940, had seen its output reduced to a fraction of that number without anyone being caught. As for those tanks which went into battle, it was said that their tracks often broke under operational strain; while the variation of the 'heat treats' for armour plates resulted in the plates not being resistant when hit in battle.

The Research and Development of 'Toys' was expanded with great verve by Colonel Wills at his factory in the Ace of Spades, on the Barnet Bypass. Working closely with Colonel Millis Jefferies in research and development, many were the ingenious devices made there. Among the most popular of the new weapons, in parts of France, was itching powder. Fed into blankets and underwear for use on the Eastern Front, it made them unusable when issued, usually too late to be replaced so far away. In Greece, I heard, stink bombs were popular for use in cinemas used by the enemy. These were manufactured by a leading perfume firm, using mostly the usual ingredients.

The most effective action was undertaken, long before support was given from outside, by the *cheminots*, the railway workers, members of the Second (Social Democrat) International. I had experienced their work in Prague in 1938, and had used them to send material into Germany in 1939. One easy trick was to put a handful of gravel into the axleboxes at night in the marshalling yard, to produce a 'hot box'. As the type of gravel could lead to discovery and consequent reprisals, a better way was found. The destination cards on waggons were changed, to other waggons two or three down the train: the subsequent disruption of delivery was substantial. One of the most effective and sustained operators with the French *cheminots* was Tony Brooks, who was awarded two DSOs before his 21st birthday.

Many of these practices were suggested to us by Communists who also helped to prepare the handbook on guerrilla warfare. This was based on up-to-date experience in the Spanish Civil War. It was of particular value for those who went into the field to prepare, among other tasks, for the day when they would organise groups to support liberating armies.

Another method used to demoralise the enemy was through the spreading of 'sibs', false rumours in which we helped another Special Service by sending the same 'sib' on our radio links. They were the more effective when linked to a degree of truth and became current simultaneously all over Europe. It was all part of the campaign to spread alarm and despondency among the enemy and those who collaborated with them. The consequences of this were to be long-lasting. Many, especially the young, learned to disobey and frustrate their governments, officials, teachers and sometimes their families. Perhaps this was later to lead to a weakening of social discipline.

It was clear that so much would depend on good radio links with the field that training and equipment must be greatly improved. This subject requires a book on its own. Three points stand out. First, the lack of a good lightweight transmitter required operators, often girls, to carry 35-pound sets from one unsafe house to another and so to run the constant risk of being checked. Second, the brilliant work of the coding section under Leo Marks. I believe that no-one was caught in the field through a failure of coding but only by disregarding the rules. More difficult was to persuade the writers of signals to keep them short. Many were caught through having to transmit a long-winded message. Thirdly, the system of 'fingerprinting' whereby the instructor of a radio operator could tell by listening to a transmission if it was truly his pupil and whether he was transmitting under duress; in due course, it was possible to set the incoming message against a prerecorded one to verify the above facts automatically.

In always hazardous circumstances, signals and codes proved most reliable. They were the life blood of Special Operations. I repeat that I do not know of a case of SOE codes being broken if the rules were obeyed. From post-war books, however, it would seem that, through lack of inter-Service coordination, more time was spent by all sides in breaking the enemies' codes than in protecting their own.

To illustrate the often haphazard nature of our work; I had met in 1937, lunching in Hollywood with Joan Crawford, Spencer Tracy and Judy Garland, a film director, Clayton Hutton. He later joined MI9 who were also much concerned with the development of small-scale equipment. Forbidden to meet officially, we met at a pub in Beaconsfield to exchange ideas and samples of items like small-scale radio valves. We were both sure this worked to the general good.

Two special operational activities beginning in 1941 were to expand in spectacular manner, when we moved from the clandestine into guerrilla warfare. First was the Small Scale Raiding Force, under Gus March-Phillips DSO and 'Apple' Appleyard DSO. They advocated unremitting action and in the highest tradition did their best always to lead it. They had already achieved a success in West Africa. 'Postmaster' was designed to cut out, in true piratical manner, two Italian merchantmen lying in Fernando Po in Spanish West Africa. Though forbidden by the High Command to do so, with junior Nigerian District Officers and others they brought out the ships and added them to the Allied merchant fleet. The anticipated Spanish reaction did not result, so all was well. Brought back to Britain, they advocated small raids nightly on enemy posts between North Cape and the South of France; arguing that these would continue to damage enemy morale and stretch their forces while our resources were being mustered for larger scale raids. They were to carry out several small raids before March-Phillips was killed and the others absorbed into bigger units.

The second was research and development into air supply, based on the SOE training unit under Ray Wooler at Ringway where even the Baker Street staff, led by Gubbins, 'went through the hole'. Wooler, a Canadian who had fought in Norway, worked out himself the methods and skills of this new technique. He always tested any fresh idea himself, usually at considerable risk. His experience was put at the disposal of the embryo Airborne Division on the head of whose first Commander, General 'Boy' Browning, a Grenadier, I first saw the Red Beret. So SOE's experience, tested in early special operations, was to spread throughout Airborne Forces. Even today equipment used at air dropping displays will recall his experiments. None deserved better than Wooler for his skill, courage and good cheer. Despite an airman saying that parachuting was an act contrary to nature, many were persuaded to do the course; the worst moment was waiting for the parachute to open when jumping from a balloon 600 ft. up the dark. The last in my stick jumped before making certain he was hooked up, so we all jumped again quickly to keep our nerve.

Survival training – living off the countryside – and unarmed combat were mostly taught at Arisaig, from a house belonging to a friend. Feelings ran high when a trainee put a grenade in the best salmon pool and, worse still, put in the game book '34 salmon'!

In the New Forest other methods of surviving were taught such as avoiding personal detection when moving round in occupied lands. Again, only untiring attention to detail could save many from being *brulé*, burnt or detected.

Our section began in early 1941 in Baker Street with a unit of two secretaries and two drivers. At first each officer would himself prepare the 'operation', drive the Joes to the airfield, await the return of the aircraft and hear the result and return to London. Soon it was clear that, for the sake of security and continuity, we needed allrounders. So I asked for three secretary/driver/companions; after the initial shock, three FANYs appeared. They were the first of a dedicated group of FANYs who were to serve SOE so splendidly in the field as well as in operational supply. Many, as the memorial at St. Paul's Church in Wilton Place testifies, were to pay the supreme sacrifice, some in indescribable circumstances in concentration camps, others in the course of duty at home and abroad. No words of mine can ever pay adequate tribute to their contribution to the cause of freedom, in so many roles throughout all theatres of war.

Near the airfields – first at Newmarket, with occasional use of Stradishall and Lakenheath, and in 1942 close to the permanent base at Tempsford – a Despatch Station was formed. Joes would come there before final departure. Its main purpose was as a point for the concentration of stores for the field, for their packing, and provision of parachutes for stores as well as for Joes. Containers were devised that could be dropped from the bomb racks, and packages for unbreakables to be pushed out from the hole in the fuselage. Other packages were attached to the rigging of the parachute, or to the leg of the jumper; on impact these helped to break his fall. The shock of landing was estimated as the equivalent of a jump from a fourteen foot wall with the speed of the wind added – quite a strain if the wind was strong.

Until navigation aids came into use later, air operations could only take place during moonlight periods. This meant intensive activity, usually day and night, for twenty days a month, with ten days preparing for the next period. Our section, joined by Philip Rea and 'Van' Van Maurik in July, would prepare the priorities with the country sections, sometimes strongly supported by governments-in-exile. The Air Ministry had to be consulted about areas within possible range in the hours of darkness, which varied each month. Finally, each day's operations depended on weather conditions.

There were two further aids to be considered for each operation. The first were homing pigeons. To home on a loft in, of all places, Wing House opposite St James Church, Piccadilly, was their instinct. A pair would be strapped on the parachutist's chest, fitted with containers for messages, often precoded. One or both were to be released directly it was certain that all was well. On our return to London it was not uncommon to find that, helped by early daylight hours, the pigeon was already at Wing House, having beaten airplane and fast car from a point in Northern France. Sometimes only one pigeon had arrived. We would wonder if the other had made a good pie.

The second aid was the S-phone. This device allowed a country section officer to ride in an aircraft and have a short conversation with the Reception Committee. Of limited range, it allowed a quick check also on the reliability of the reception, and on occasion whether they were under enemy control.

The use of Lysander aircraft was becoming of vital importance in the summer of 1941, not only to bring back Joes but to take in some whose age or physical condition did not allow them to parachute. S/Ldr. Farley had had one success by then but the techniques of pick-ups had not been expanded. John Nesbitt Dufour and 'Sticky' Murphy were the other two original pilots. Barry took me to Tangmere for my first operation. So secret were our activities that, as we wore brown uniforms, we had to be described as 'beam-benders' who were reputed to be able to bend enemy air-guidance beams away from their target aims on our main cities. We felt flattered. We used The Cottage, on the far side of the airfield, where John Hunt, a pianist of international repute, would while away our hours, waiting tensely for the aircraft's return. The Lysander waited while the pilot and the Joe agreed plans. Off they would go to fly perhaps over 300 miles into the ZNO of France; to land, set down and pick up one or perhaps two passengers; and fly back, all in a single, unarmed aircraft with no guidance aids.

Hugh Verity, one of the most skilful of the many brave pilots, has written a full account in *We landed by Moonlight*,* as has Michael Foot in *Special Operations Executive in France*.† But records only began in late 1942. Before that date Station war diaries and pilots' log books only say, 'Operation, X hours, completed'. This does not disclose the hazardous nature of those experimental early flights.

My responsibility in those early months was to help persuade the Air Ministry that each pick up was essential; and that the pilots were being given a fair chance by adequate training of ground reception. At first Farley and I together began this training on a disused airfield at Sawbridgeworth. Having given the local authorities some warning, we would take the Joe, in daylight, to pick a point free from road traffic or likely observation; the ground to be smooth with no obstructions in either direction of the planned flight path, which was an inverted L with pocket torches marking each corner, pointing up wind. Later, to avoid leaving traces behind, three torchlight bulbs, linked by wires, took the place of the torches. The pilot, navigating alone, had first to find a single flashlamp signalling the recognition letter; to switch on his landing lights on his approach; to touch down on the bottom point of the L; to run forward the few yards to the top, turn back again to turn to face into wind for takeoff. The outgoing Joe would climb out, while the incoming would identify himself, load any cargo, and wind the light wires round the tail skid.

In training, the aim was to take only two minutes from 'wheels-on' to 'wheels-off'. At first Joes were trained to arrange their own pick-ups; but later specialists were given the task.

On occasion I briefed some RAF colleagues who had not had the full MI9 (escape) training, giving them a few key words in French in case they were grounded. This would enable them to contact one of the main groups of helpers; the village priests, the

* Ian Allan, 1978
† HMSO, 1966

garagistes, the bistro-owners and the mesdames of the bordellos. The last were reckoned to be the best bet. It was said that the Gestapo never interfered with anyone 'on the job'. So, 'put your uniform under the bed, and keep going . . . indefinitely, in the best traditions of the Service . . .'

These four groups had organised themselves more or less spontaneously. Sometimes an enemy would 'get on to a line' and report back on arrival at the Pyrenees. The whole line would then be rounded up and shot out of hand. To this day I do not know of any more liberty-loving groups.

At first, operations were few. I had excellent relations with the RAF. They knew I had been trained by them at Oxford, and had just had some initial experience of air supply in Ethiopia. So jokingly a pilot would say to me when I had made no arrangements, 'You wouldn't be prepared to fly with us? There is room tonight'.

If I came prepared to fly, however, I would be told, 'why should we take extra weight just for a joy ride?'

On the few occasions I did fly, my training in map reading from the air was useful. I would lie in the perspex nose trying to help distinguish the target point. Chateauroux, just within the ZNO of France, was a favourite area; well lighted, at the centre of a number of straight Roman roads, it was yet difficult to distinguish the right road, and to find the flashing light.

We only had Michelin road maps which we had managed to collect in secrecy. With no official anticipation of operations except along the 1914/18 Front, only a black and white contour series of maps of the rest of France were to hand which proved useless. But again the navigational skill of the pilots overcame such difficulties. Their practice of low flying helped, as at 1,500 ft when crossing the coast, the aircraft would be above the low flak and below the enemy radar.

Innumerable books have been written about operations whose real risks and action only began when the parachute opened. It is not for me to chronicle the later activities of the scores, hundreds of men and women whose transport we arranged, and whom we saw off and sometimes welcomed back. At the time it was difficult to give an adequate send-off to them. Even to venture into enemy territory was a very brave act. We never exchanged names nor tried to say much. The French salutation on departure, 'Bonne chance . . . et merde' was the most acceptable – and has remained so, long after, among those with whom we worked. Many were never to be seen again. It has been an enduring honour to meet many survivors in many occupations. Courage and dedication were their uniting attributes. Usually unwilling to discuss the past even with former colleagues, they are still to be found giving a lead, taking a grip, running a risk – for others.

Each operation had a codename, used by SOE for those in the field as well as for their air or sea transport. SOE was to use more codenames than all other services put together. They were issued from a central office, not always with tact. I did not even refer before changing Bastard to Dastard. To this day some codenames will strike a chord. I give half a dozen of the most noteworthy, burnt into my memory.

MOONSHINE/OPINION was the first air operation of which I was fully in charge, in May 1941, and the first into Belgium. I drove the two Joes to Newmarket. The radio-operator had asked to see a priest before departure and this we managed to arrange. Then the pilot, John Austin, said casually, 'You can come too if you want. It is only a short flight'. I handed over my wallet with security passes and climbed aboard, sitting in the nose with the navigator. Our target area was in the Namur/Dinant part of Belgium, for a blind drop. We crossed the coast south of Boulogne without incident, looking nostalgically at familiar points. As the drop began, I was called up by the pilot as I was not on the intercom.

'The first Joe is alright', he shouted, 'but the second has got caught up on the tail-wheel'. He was trying to shake him off. He failed to do so, luckily as it proved.

'We must return to base; but with the Joe, spinning round a few feet behind and reducing our speed, we may not make it'.

The despatcher studied the possibility of lowering me through the hole but the harness was not long enough to let me free him. I then had to take the decision that we must on no account risk dropping someone, by now almost certainly dead, and disclose our then MOST SECRET operations, false papers, radio set and codes. Less important, I was not keen on finding myself in

Occupied Europe, in Grenadier uniform, without any cover story or the escape equipment provided later. I had only my L tablet.

John Austin remained imperturbable throughout. We plugged steadily on, nose well up, wondering if we would see Home and Mother again. Flak near Boulogne turned us back, to cross further south. Over our own coast we were fired on; we fired the (wrong) recognition signal – and firing stopped! John put the Whitley down with the shortest run ever but too late. The Joe must have died, of cold and suffocation, very quickly. I was glad we had found the priest.

The first Joe, not seeing his radio-operator follow him and then watching the aircraft fly off, finished his mission and being without a radio, walked back through Spain. It took him a year.

Later I was told to report to M. Spaak, the Foreign Minister of the Belgian Government-in-exile, on what had gone wrong. He listened sympathetically but only said,

'I am sure it will be all right next time'. Honouring me by asking me to stay to dinner, he discussed the future. One remark was to inspire me ever after.

'When we have won this war', he said, 'we must unite Europe. We cannot afford any more civil wars among our nations or we will destroy our civilisation'. Brave words indeed in May 1941 when neither Russia nor America were yet in the war.

Another codeword which recalls a more lighthearted colleague is MOUSSE. While held at the Despatch Station awaiting departure, he was given chocolate mousse by the FANYs to celebrate his codename. Safely established in Belgium, he sent in due course for a container of supplies. In memory of his last dinner, a FANY slipped in a packet of chocolate for a mousse. Caught later and imprisoned, he managed to escape. He duly found his way to North Africa. There he told me the one thing above all which kept him hopeful was the knowledge that someone cared enough about him, a complete stranger, to have put in that chocolate.

With the coming of autumn, longer hours of darkness allowed more distant flights. One acute difficulty arose when Stalin asked Churchill personally for help. This was to put two German Communist agents into Germany from the West as the range from Russia was too far. This was an unpalatable request but in the circumstances of the autumn of 1941 was impossible to refuse.

Gubbins took me to 10 Downing Street where the Prime Minister told us that we two alone were to know the identity of the Joes; and that I was to carry out all detailed arrangements myself.

With the help of the head of the NKVD, the Russian Secret Police in London, I arranged dropping points and all the normal details of checking clothing and equipment. The two German nationals were already well equipped with documents, showing the degree of penetration of German security already achieved.

On the night agreed, the two-engined Whitley, still the only aircraft available, heavily laden for a long flight, crashed on take-off, killing one of the Joes and the pilot – whose name was Boris Romanov. The other Joe's face was very badly burnt. After prolonged plastic surgery, which he said cheerfully had made him unrecognisably handsome, he was keen to have another try.

By then it was March 1942. The hours of darkness were shortening. The RAF said, fairly enough, not knowing the importance of WHISKY, its codename, that it must wait until autumn, even though a four-engined aircraft, a Halifax, was now available.

Great pressure was brought to bear. S/Ldr. Farley, by now commanding 138 Special Duty Squadron, said he would go himself; in the most lethal post of rear-gunner was F/Lt. Pulton, 'Pullthrough', who had been with us on Operation Moonshine and was, in happier days, a member of the Magic Circle. I urged that I be allowed to go too as Despatcher but was told that as every pound of extra weight counted, I could not. I saw them off – on a flight of No Return. A report of a single aircraft being shot down over Mannheim confirmed that they were on course. Only forty years later did I hear that they were all buried near Munich.

As far as I know this was the last, and only, attempt to put Russian-trained Communists into Germany. By the autumn of 1942 the Eastern Front had been stabilised and the long haul back from Stalingrad had begun. No further requests from the Russians came my way. After the first eighteen months of defeat had brought some signs of cooperation, they were to withdraw into solitude and longer-term plans for post-war expansion.

As related, the longer hours of darkness and the hopes of four-engined Halifaxes becoming available held out promises of more distant flights, to the further parts of France and Norway, and to Poland and Czechoslovakia. The Czechs were a high priority and were nearer. There was a good organisation lying low, sending intelligence and waiting orders, hopefully from the West. Despite the shattering blows of 1938 and 1939, their special services remained effective. But by late 1941 they were surrounded by hostile territory, and the population felt betrayed by their Allies, in the West and in the East. After the German attack on Russia, I had visited Jan Masaryk and Dr. Benes. They were not optimistic about the course of the war, nor of the chances of their country regaining its full freedom at its end. They feared Russia as much as Germany; something must be done, they stressed, to revive their country's latent patriotism and love of freedom and democracy to make a more positive contribution in the struggle against the Nazi/Fascists; primarily by slowing down the output of industry and cutting German communications.

The immediate and most spectacular aim was to remove Heydrich, the Gauleiter of Czechoslovakia. He might well be said to have been the worst of a monstrous gang. Hundreds of Czechs and Slovaks were being murdered, shot without trial. The Czech staff in London were to plan the attack. The SOE codename for the air transport, ANTHROPOID, has survived, to honour some very brave men.

I was told that this operation would be high on the list as soon as a four-engined Halifax was available. On Boxing Day 1941, a FANY drove me to Tangmere for a routine visit. There I found a message to say that if the Joes for Anthropoid could be ready by 6.00 pm that evening, for take-off by 7.00 pm at the latest, the operation was on. Golly Foulds, my FANY driver, became an Operations Room while I set out to collect all the necessary papers from London. I drove out of Tangmere at 3.00 pm with just three hours in hand. The distance was 75 miles each way. I did not know the road well. Darkness fell about 4.00. The headlights were mere blacked-out slits. I reached Porchester Terrace where Capt. Keary met me; he unlocked the flat, a room, a cupboard, a safe; found and checked with me that all requisite papers were there . . . I refuelled at Robin Hood Gate, and drove into Tangmere airfield at 6.00 precisely . . . to find the Halifax had not even arrived. On landing the pilot, another imperturbable, Ron Hockey, sensing the importance of the operation said, 'Of course

I am going, even if I have to come back in broad daylight' – which he did, after dropping the four Anthropoid members safely despite atrocious weather conditions, losing his trailing aerial on a mountain top. I was never happier to see a safe return.

The rest is history. No news was heard of the group until May 1942. A headline in an evening paper, 'Heydrich Assassinated' told the world of their success. They had been trained to use the Sten light machine-gun invented by SOE to use captured enemy ammunition. Used operationally on this occasion for the first time, it jammed. A follow-up grenade proved lethal.

The group got away, but were later betrayed and cornered and killed in a church in Prague. These brave men died as they well knew they might, in removing one who was perhaps Hitler's closest colleague. They were fighting as soldiers in the only way left to them by Nazi methods. None could have imagined the ruthless brutality of the reprisals that followed. The destruction of the village suspected of complicity, Lidice in Bohemia, will remain for all time a blot on the repute of Germany, with other such atrocities as Oradour and the Vercors in France, committed as acts of pure terrorism against women and children.

The Poles were in little better order. Partitioned thrice in two centuries, they had a worldwide organisation of exceptional efficiency. I had been allowed to glimpse a little of this when I was involved in some of their pre-occupational work in 1938 and 1939, as a political friend rather than a special service officer. From late 1938 they were at work doing all they could to leave behind a patriotic organisation against the day, perhaps years ahead, when they would again be able to determine their own destiny. Such élan has carried them through the centuries ever since 968 when their king sent a message to the Pope asking if they could become Catholics.

Having helped in the summer of 1940 to keep their communications working through Eastern Europe, I was delighted to find myself again trying to improve these links; but this time it was to be by air. The first flight, fourteen hours in a two-engined Whitley, had been successful in February 1941. The next was not to take place until February 1942 when four-engined Halifaxes were available. These went first from Lakenheath in East Anglia, the nearest point to Poland. The route lay over Denmark, and only some fifteen minutes were allowed over the target area before the return flight had to begin; in that short time the dim hand-torches had to be found. An immediate result of this was an urgent development by British and Polish technicians of Rebecca/Eureka, the first radio beacon. This allowed flights to be made with greater accuracy throughout the whole of the long winter months of darkness, and not only in the moonlit periods. Later these devices were used in cooperation between the Allied air forces and the Resistance, to guide aircraft more certainly on to the targets. Many years later, at a government reception in Warsaw, a man came up, clicked his heels, bowed and said,

'My Rebecca is still working well. When will you send me some more arms to help drive out the enemy?'

He was away, in true Polish style, before I could grab him. With such verve, freedom of the spirit will always survive in Poland. A fuller, though it can never be complete, account of this co-operation is given in Jozef Garlinski's *Poland, SOE and the Allies*.*

Among the many Poles I was honoured to know in those early years was Josef Retinger. He had first come to London as interpreter for Josef Conrad, just before World War I, so he had a wide circle of friends in Britain as well as in Poland. He was most energetic and gallant, being parachuted twice into Poland. He seemed to be the most effective link between the Polish Resistance and the duly constituted Polish Government-in-exile in London. Caught between their two traditional enemies, Russians and Germans, Polish clandestine action was widely and effectively organised, despite the most savage suppression by both foes, as the murders at Katyn by the Russians when allied to the Nazis were to show. Later, SOE officers like Peter Kemp witnessed in the field their hopeless but undaunted struggle against occupation on one side and the threat of worse on the other. But always they fought with the utmost élan.

There were, of course, many experienced Polish aircrew in Britain during the Battle of Britain. They had escaped through France in 1940. Later they were retrained on Halifaxes and were to prove themselves in the highest class in Special Operations.

* Allen and Unwin, 1964

In face of growing demands from other Services and other countries, they were determined to put their national needs first as was understandable. They were to suffer as much as and longer than any. But they were always most pleasant to work with, even when they felt I had given undue priority to others.

One such occasion was on New Year's Day 1942. REX, I was told, was a most important Frenchman. I was to take greater precautions than ever that all should go well. The first plan, to land him from a Lysander, was changed for a drop into the South of France, to a Reception Committee. I went with him to Tangmere, and was at once struck by his personality. His bearing and demeanour showed that he was a person of great authority. He was Jean Moulin, the first Chairman of the Committee of National Liberation in France. His story is an epic of French Resistance. In 1954 I was to attend the unveiling of his memorial at Chartres where he had been Prefect. After landing safely in France, he was caught and met his end after terrible tortures endured without making any disclosures. He is the only Frenchman of World War II buried in the Pantheon in Paris.

Little progress was made in establishing air and sea links into the Netherlands and Denmark during this early period. Land routes through Spain had first to be set up. The first parachutist dropped into Denmark 'Roman-candled' – the parachute failed to open – and alerted the enemy to the initiation of links with the growing Danish Resistance. Lines through Sweden made co-operation easier, while the running of gunboats through the Skaggerak, bringing ball-bearings to Britain, provided another link.

These were a few of the highlights of those interminable months from the spring of 1941 to the summer of 1942, as techniques were developed, and organisation expanded – on which the success of later years was so much to depend. The original small group of 'Believers' continued to work together, although often in different branches of Special Services. We were always on the lookout for new ideas and techniques, while our field workers were on the lookout to send back enemy equipment. But I drew the line at some impossible visions. Early one morning, returning through Hatfield from a night flight operation, my FANY driver said,

'Look. There is an aeroplane without any propellers'.

'Nonsense', I replied, 'You are seeing things. Late nights are no good for you. If you imagine things like that you will have to give up this work. Keep your eyes on the road'. She lowered her eyes. But we had seen one of the first jet-propelled aircraft, of which rumours had reached us.

So much for some of the development of outward bound traffic by air. Incoming passengers and freight were also on the increase. Hugh Verity, in the top class of a most skilful and gallant group, has given details in *We landed by Moonlight*.

It speaks well for their skill, and the care taken by those arranging the landings, and luck, that all these operations were completed with so little loss. In 1941–2 when I was in charge, one of us always went to Tangmere for each sortie. Philip Rea returned one morning to recount how 'Sticky' Murphy had come back from the Ardennes with a bullet hole through his neck. The Germans had surprised the Reception Committee, and on his approach the pilot was suspicious. Most bravely, he landed in the next field without any aids, to give the passenger a chance. But all he got was a hail of bullets and was lucky to get back alive. Such was the spirit of the pilots to which we landlubbers were the only witnesses.

As traffic built up, two Lysanders were sometimes sent, one to land shortly after the other. Thereby the second stood a risk of the enemy being alerted. One day Fielden, who commanded 161 Squadron as well as being Captain of the King's Flight, said to me when a double Lysander was being planned,

'I don't like double Lysanders'.

'Nor do I', I replied, 'but this is urgent and there is no alternative'.

'I've got an aircraft', he went on.

'But there is no aircraft which the Air Ministry doesn't control which is suitable'.

'I've got the King's Hudson'.

'But you couldn't land a Hudson on a Lysander strip'.

'I could, old boy . . .' and land it he did – bringing back half a dozen passengers and, it was alleged, a case of champagne and some perfume, and starting a fashion.

For one afternoon I was rung up by Leslie Rowan, a Private Secretary at No. 10.

'Today the King gave his weekly lunch to the Prime Minister. He offered him a glass of wine, 1941 vintage. If you wish to continue to get the 100% support from here that you have always got, you had better do something quickly'.

It took me some six weeks for the Prime Minister, when returning the King's hospitality, to be able to offer a glass of a 1941 vintage red or white. This is the first chance I have had to thank the Tempsford Squadrons for their help over this.

I can give no evidence for the events described above. By order, the minimum was put on paper or in log books, the more the pity. 'Mission completed. 7½ hours' gives no indication of the skill, bravery and often historic importance of some of the early sorties. When aircraft took off and went over the Channel, only we knew where they went, whether they landed, or only flew round allegedly 'bending enemy beams'. Certainly no-one was thinking of providing a historic record to be studied half a century later.

Our sea operations across the Channel were somewhat restricted as Brittany was reserved for other Services. Despite this, Holdsworth and Brooks Richards carried out a number of important operations on the French coast from the Helford River. So successful were they in fact that their cover was wearing thin when Operation Torch, the move into French North Africa, was being planned. Without hesitation the two ships sailed out to Gibraltar two days faster than the fastest convoy. Later in the Mediterranean they were to achieve some of the most effective action of all.

The enemy-occupied coasts of the North Sea were almost impenetrable. To my knowledge only about three sorties, to land passengers, were tried. I happened to know Commander Robert Hichens, the legendary small-boat fighter who when killed was the most highly decorated of any Service. I had rowed behind him at College and had learnt, at '7' behind him as stroke, how dauntless he was. He agreed to try to land two on the Dutch coast. With Dick Laming I went along for the ride, seen off by Prince Bernhard whose support was always unfailing. Weather as well as an unfriendly reception made the attempt futile.

In the Far North, Jack Wilson had organised the Shetland Bus Service, using fishing boats and other unlikely craft to sail across to the Norwegian coasts. They worked most closely and amicably with the Royal Navy with the minimum of contact with the Admiralty and Baker Street.

In all these operational techniques much use was made, of course, of the experience of smugglers, so many of whom joined in our operations. And as far as I know many may still be at it. Indeed, many years after the War, one of them arrived to see me.

'Sir', (I could never stop him saying that) 'Best French brandy, £15 a case, landed at Chelsea Pier, any good to you?'

I, of course, became very pompous – but reminded him as a precaution to observe the wartime rule of having any cargo labelled 'To the Prime Minister at No. 10'.

By the summer of 1942 circumstances had changed beyond the hopes expressed to me by Gubbins in May 1941. He had foreshadowed the entry of the Russians (with some indication of Nazi intentions gathered from the Enigma code-breaking) and of the Americans into the conflict. With these two countries involved by the end of 1941, the survival of freedom in much of the world including Britain was now assured. I had never met any who doubted that we would survive, but at times, if pressed, it would have been difficult to describe exactly how and when.

Russia had been treacherously and ignominiously attacked, and for more than a year had moved rapidly backwards, suffering immense losses of men and material. Only in the Moscow and Leningrad areas had the innate patriotic tenacity of individuals held the line. Until June 1941 pro-Russian supporters in Western Europe, including Britain, had been passive at best and subservient to the Nazis at worst. After June 1941 they became more active in Europe, using their proven sabotage methods wherever possible. Later, in my experience, after the tide had turned with the defeat of the Germans at Stalingrad in October 1942, the national Communist parties became more concerned in helping the Russians and in preparing to seize political control in their own countries after liberation from the Nazis, than in co-operating to drive the Nazis out. Our reports from Occupied Europe, in particular from Poland, confirmed the belief that the Russians had plans to occupy as much of Europe as possible, using Marxism/Leninism as a smoke screen for their age-old imperial expansionist designs. Fears in Occupied Europe of another foreign, totalitarian power replacing Fascist/Nazism were to affect all Special Operations for the next three years.

The second change had been the arrival of the Americans. Hitler and Mussolini had made the unexplained and inexplicable decision to declare war on the USA. Without this decision, there had been a fear that the mood in the USA would have led to making revenge for Pearl Harbour a top priority. None could then have foreseen the result of a year's possible delay in D-Day in France, thereby leaving Britain open for a year to V1 and V2 bombardment. Instead, the first American reaction had been to propose an assault landing on Western Europe in 1942, which was as unrealistic as the 1940/41 British Chiefs of Staffs' ideas of arming secret armies. While these plans were being readjusted on the top level, the American Office for Strategic Services (OSS) under General 'Big Bill' Donovan went into top gear.

Donovan had paid a visit to some of our establishments in the summer of 1941. He had been second to none in the previous decade in doing all possible for the cause of freedom, and more recently of Britain in particular. It was one of my greatest privileges that for the next three years he was to share with Gubbins the dubious honour of being my boss, in the Mediterranean. It was to be of inestimable value and encouragement to me. We were never to disagree on aims. Sometimes, as I will describe, I had difficulty in reconciling his priorities with those of the American part of the Allied High Command, especially when he had, as I did, responsibilities outside the theatre of operations.

Meantime David Bruce had come to represent Donovan at the Embassy, with Warwick Potter and James Lawrence as direct liaison officers. All four were to remain lifelong friends. To none did we owe more for their support in the difficult years ahead. At that time Averell Harriman had set up his Mission under the same roof. He was close to the President, a 'dollar-a-year man' and Chief of all the Joint Supply Boards. In his Mission, as one of its first members was, unbeknownst to me, my future wife.

Among the earliest American arrivals were two who were to prove most valuable allies in the difficulties ahead, Charlie Saltzman and 'Abe' Lincoln. We had rowed together at Oxford and kept in touch since. Lincoln was, after helping to set up the Supply Organisation, to return to head the Operational Planning Division in Washington. There he was able to help from time to time when our joint operations came to notice. Saltzman became Deputy to General Al Gruenther, Chief of Staff to General Mark Clark. He was to save me in the future when things went wrong in North Africa, by saying that I was well-intentioned if sometimes out of step. I can never repay what our Operations owed to them.

When Donovan came to inspect the Operations sections in Baker Street, we could show him the groundwork of a Europe-wide organisation. Country sections, for organisation, recruitment and training; Operations, to indicate targets; research and development; codes and signals; air and sea transport, and the 'taxi service' to bring them back – which even the Foreign Secretary was unaware of until 1943, such were the enforced security limitations in those early years. All was clearly set out on the maps in the Operations Room, centrally placed without windows. On the walls, carefully curtained so that only one could be visible at a time, were maps indicating radio sets, dropping and pick-up points, targets of special importance when the day came to interdict enemy movements.

While a few gallant individuals had gone into Occupied Europe in the past fifteen months, the results would not have repaid the efforts required but for the spontaneous resistance groups now beginning to appear, despite the merciless reprisals taken against any suspects by the occupying enemy. Resisters had doubted the possibility of their liberation until North Africa had been cleared. They then became over-optimistic. The problem thereafter was to restrain them from too daring action, laying them open to attacks which could not be countered from outside.

By the early autumn 1942, we were too intent on the future, perhaps, to think over much of the past, but with hindsight great credit must be given to those in the field whose faith and spirit never wavered, and to the airmen and sailors who carried men, women, and material and hope in and out of occupied countries. Without the patience, research, and action of these comparatively few, the great resistance organisations of 1943–5 could not have been built up, supplied and directed to play such an important part in final victory. For many the defeat of their armies in

1939–40 by a treacherous and better-prepared enemy was more than offset by the contribution to victory made by their resisters, men and women of every class, type and occupation.

In the late summer of 1942 I told Gubbins that I felt my usefulness in this sphere was now ended. Regular Royal Navy and Air Force officers had come in to take over their specialised activities. I asked to be considered for any task in the coming phase when we would begin to move forward again. My inadequate knowledge of any European language precluded me from going into the field in the clandestine phase. My experience with regular forces and The Ungentlemanly in Ethiopia could be of value. So Gubbins appointed me to be Operations Officer in the Mission being formed to undertake any action that might prove possible from North Africa into the south side of Occupied Europe. Little did I think that events would leave me, more than somewhat precariously balanced, in charge of Special Operations on the Western, later the Central, and, finally, in limited ways, in the whole Mediterranean, helping to support the revival of freedom from Greece to France, and from Italy to Poland.

PART TWO

. . . . the better to spring forward

CHAPTER 11

Clearing the path: Algiers 1942

It may be useful to set down here, in brief, the changing situation in the Mediterranean in which we were to be involved for the next two and a half years, as a background to the description of the range and purpose, military and political, of our Special Operations.

After a short and victorious campaign in East Africa in the spring of 1941, the battle lines were drawn in the desert west of Egypt where the Italians had been defeated and demoralised by General Wavell's Western Desert Force. This victory, with the coup in Yugoslavia in March 1941 and the successful Greek resistance to Italian aggression, had necessitated German intervention in Greece and in the Western Desert. The Nazi attack on Russia was thus delayed six weeks – a delay which may have saved the Soviet Union from complete disaster, since winter weather closed in before the capture of Moscow could be achieved.

In December 1941, the Japanese attack on Pearl Harbour had brought the United States into the War. The immediate American reaction was, naturally, to concentrate on the Pacific. But the Combined Chiefs of Staff ruled that the Atlantic/European War should come first. Until the Americans came fully to realise the problems of an opposed seaborne landing, they proposed to mount an attack on Western Europe in 1942. The Dieppe Raid underlined the difficulties. As second best, the assault was put off until 1943, and later again until 1944. Instead the clearing of Axis forces from Africa was substituted, with the British Eighth Army coming from the east and British First Army and an American corps, under overall American Command, from the west (Torch). This assault was launched in November 1942 on French North Africa.

The political situation, made the more difficult by finding the collaborationist French Admiral Darlan in Algiers, was finally resolved. Wet weather and long communications slowed the attack from the west. It was not until May 1943 that North Africa was finally cleared by the surrender of the Axis commander to Eighth Army.

From that point the decision was taken to advance through the Central Mediterranean by assaults on Sicily (Husky) and Salerno (Avalanche). This should knock Italy out of the War, and keep Anglo-American troops fighting the Germans until the main assault across the Channel was ready in 1944 (Overlord). Considerable forces, land, sea and air, were to be kept in Italy, including, at first, the Canadians, though they were withdrawn later for Overlord. Many landing craft, always in short supply, were also to be withdrawn, so a series of sustained landings behind the enemy lines was impossible. In August 1943 an Armistice was granted to the Royal Government under Marshal Badoglio, following the fall of Mussolini. This left an Italy divided between the neo-Fascists still working with the Nazis in the north, and the patriotic Italians, non-communists and communist, in the south. These latter were to play an increasingly important part as they were organised and supplied while the allied regular forces were reduced in 1944–5.

In the Western Mediterranean, Corsica was liberated after the fall of Mussolini. It became an advance base for movement into and out of France. In August 1944, an assault on the South of France (Dragoon) linked up with Overlord in north-east France.

In the Balkans, it was impossible to implement plans to put in regular forces to support the guerrillas in view of the decision to keep all available troops for Italy and Overlord. More decisive action, to harass the lines of communication of the German armies in Russia, and to give local governments a chance to re-establish themselves before being overwhelmed in the tide of Russian imperialism, was thus frustrated.

With hindsight, miscalculations on moving into the Western Mediterranean proved even greater than feared. There were no certainties, even probabilities, on which to build; the attitude of the Vichy authorities towards an Allied landing; the strength of the Gaullist groups; the temper of the local population; the potential of any enemy reaction, tied down as they were at

Alamein; the worth of American valour and equipment, finally so decisive, less than a year after their entry into the war; the chance of establishing air and sea control over the Eastern Mediterranean.

Many accounts have been written of those early months. I can only add some details. One day an historian will gather all accounts together and define a more coherent pattern of a most confused period. The full facts may never be known.

SOE Gibraltar provided effective support in the preparation of our reception by known pro-Allied groups in French North Africa. For obvious reasons, especially the deep resentment caused by the unavoidable British shelling of French naval ships at Oran in 1940, all contacts and operations were to be carried out under the Stars and Stripes. With the assault forces an SOE Mission landed to organise any irregular action found possible in Algeria and Tunisia.

A third Mission, code-named Massingham, to which I was appointed as Operations Officer with wide but undefined duties, was to establish a base for later operations northwards, into France and Corsica and possibly into Italy, whose secret police, the OVRA, were the most effective of any in Europe. We were to recruit from the many refugees in North Africa, among them tens of thousands of 'Loyalist' Spaniards who with others feared further enemy persecution. The Mission was under the command of a Regular Army colonel, with two merchant bankers of international experience to carry out intelligence and supply duties; it was equipped with a signal link to work back to Britain until posts were established in enemy-occupied territory.

David Keswick's daily reports, sent direct to London, proved brilliantly perceptive, but led to resentment in political circles, even to threats of suppression of the signal link, since they so clearly showed up the mistakes of Allied actions. 'Mouse' Glyn meantime organised a good dinner table, in addition to an excellent administrative base, which enabled us to entertain many of the leading French, like General Montsambert, with whom we were forbidden officially to consort.

I reached Gibraltar by air the day after the landings. There Saltzman got me a lift on a 'Flying Fort' of the American 96 Squadron, despite the lack of a parachute for me. After a leisurely flight to Algiers, we came in to land. Defensive ditches had been dug short of the runway, and one of these we struck; after nearly nosing in, we all but stalled on getting the nose up, but the great skill of the pilot saved us. With our undercarriage useless, we were re-routed back to Oran. To lighten the load we threw out the astrohatch and machine guns, and we all lay against the bulkhead for the crash-landing. Staff Sergt. Sullivan, who had just won the Air Medal, was put on top.

'In we go', all called out – we pulled up in twelve feet from a speed of some 120 miles an hour. I stood up, and, being best placed, gave a hand to lift the others out through the astrohatch before fire broke out. Being last, I could find no foot-hold.

'Get out of that goddam aircraft you goddam fool' cried a bewildered voice, at the appearance of a strange cap. Somehow I got my head down and fell at the foot of a man whose face later became famous as Supreme Commander, Larry Norstad.

After an uncomfortable night in a French barracks which had just been captured that day from the French Foreign Legion by the American parachute troops, I got a lift to Algiers. There I arrived at headquarters, the St. George Hotel, just as the curfew sounded. I went in search of friends. On the first floor I found a door labelled 'Generals Doolittle and Curtis'. I did not enter. Next door I found an RAF Group Captain pinning up top secret maps with the help of an Algerian maid. Next, two British Colonels who, being unable to decide who should sleep in the double bed, had unrolled their bed rolls on the floor. Next, in a big double bed, was an American Staff Sergeant asleep – alone. So it went on. Glyn had already secured a villa ten miles east of Algiers from where, for the next two months, we worked. Glyn also obtained the use of the Club des Pins, a few villas fifteen miles west of Algiers on the beach over which the main assault had come in in November. Its location and its facilities for training of all kinds and for housing groups in secure conditions were ideal.

My first visitor was M. Pauphilet, who had commanded the reservists organised to arrest Admiral Darlan when he happened to be in Algiers when the Allied landings took place. Pauphilet knew, of course, that the Americans were making the plans, under Robert Murphy. On the night of the landing his group were told to go to the Darlan villa, saying that Allied ships had been seen offshore and that they were to take over from the normal guard. At 2.00 am, as instructed, they entered the villa, and went to Darlan's bedroom. On knocking a voice said, 'Come in'. They entered, to find Robert Murphy sitting with Darlan. Being ordered out, they left in bewilderment; later that day the group were rounded up and some of them shot. To my knowledge Pauphilet was never employed again, by Americans, French or British.

I made early contact with the American consuls who had organised the landings so bravely. When going to see Robert Murphy I thought, 'Heaven help us, Irish, Catholic, Milwaukee . . .' In the event he proved the staunchest of allies right up to our last official cooperation in 1956. Without him we would never have made the progress we did in the Mediterranean jointly with the OSS.

But we were not welcome in general, as a Special Service, British, with known Gaullist links. It was clear that little could be done operationally until the Darlan involvement with all its consequences was sorted out. General de Lattre had set up military resistance to the German occupation of the non-occupied zone of France and had ended up in prison. He sent messages that as long as Darlan was known to hold any position in Algiers, French Resistance would cease. 'He is as great an enemy to everything that France stands for as he is hostile to the Anglo-Saxons – and to the Royal Navy'. Later, de Lattre was rescued from prison and came to lead us all.

Frustrated in Algiers, I accepted an invitation from Springs, the American consul in Tunis, to accompany him to help there. In a few civilian cars we took the coast and secondary roads, to rally resisters on the way. At Al Ouina airfield on the outskirts of Tunis we found German troops already landing. The local French Command had not tried to resist, but many individual French, in uniform and not, were fighting in the dark trying to stop the air landings. I believe there were some British armoured cars there. But we only had the ammunition we carried, which was soon expended. By morning all had to withdraw. Many of the French returned to Tunis, after making arrangements to keep in touch as soon as radio and other links could be set up. I made some useful contacts, there and on the inland road back, telling reliable men how to get in touch for future action in North Africa or France – or Italy, or Greece.

The next six weeks gave us a chance to assess the possibilities for action. Jacques de Guelis proved skilful in sorting out 'patriot' from 'Vichy'; David Keswick moved elegantly among the political elite and provided his valuable assessments; while I worked up some London/Gaullist contacts which proved of value later.

The High Command was, of course, Allied, but the influence and decision-takers were predominantly American. It began to appear that the general intention was to maintain good relations with the French officers and bureaucrats in office on our arrival, and not to replace any of them. This was in part due to President Roosevelt's antipathy to General de Gaulle, a sentiment shared by many including Churchill. General 'Papa' Giraud had been brought out of France to be built up, if feasible, into an alternative leader. This proved impossible. A brave and charming man, he lacked the essential fire of political inspiration. Six months later all accepted what had long been clear to those working with the Resistance; de Gaulle alone could rally support in France. Meantime recruitment of agents improved steadily. Two and a half years earlier Colonels Rivet and Villeneuve in the Deuxieme Bureau in Paris had done all they could to eject the British 'Polish/Czech Mission' from France. Entering the headquarters in Algiers, I found them still at work. They were unlucky that I alone in North Africa knew of their past.

There were in existence several organisations formed under Vichy auspices like the Chantiers de la Jeunesse and the Corps Franc d'Afrique, from which we were able to recruit many excellent young volunteers. Their ranks had included many genuinely cloaking their patriotism until a real chance for action offered.

The greatest luck was in finding Captain Colonna d'Istria, a Corsican gendarme serving in Algiers. Code-named 'Cesari', he organised and led the original, genuine, Maquis in Corsica. This was the first great act of liberation by the French Resistance, virtually unaided by any regular forces from outside. It can only be regretted that this success is not properly acknowledged in the Musée de la Resistance in the Invalides. The reason given is that it was not achieved under the Gaullist banner, although de Gaulle had no more loyal supporters than those who rallied to carry out this operation from November 1942 until September 1943.

To support this first venture a number of volunteers were trained by Massingham. Among them, as instructors, were Capitaine Sabatier and Lieutenant Réné Bonnier de la Chapelle. Initially we had little material to work with, but I issued the two instructors each with a .38 pistol from the few brought out from Britain. As the Head of the Mission was back in Britain, David Keswick signed the authority to issue them.

One episode underlined the growing impossibility of the British position in North Africa. A message was received from British sailors who, cast ashore from sunken ships, had been imprisoned in Biskra and other places in southern Algeria. Weeks after the Allied landings, they were still being held in prisons, and only released when two of our officers went to inspect. This was typical of the continuing impasse. Generals Mast and Bethouart, who had helped the landings, were held back. It is difficult sometimes for Anglo-Saxons, especially when they have not been put to the test, to understand the conflict of loyalties between the clear national interest and an oath given to a Head of State. Most accepted that there had been a case for reaching an accommodation with Darlan, to secure our landings and the accession of the rest of French North Africa with the minimum of delay and conflict. But when December came, there seemed the likelihood of some kind of permanent 'Darlanist' regime being established. This was quite unacceptable to all those French who had helped in November, who had seen their colleagues killed and their killers decorated by the regime. Many escapers from France, by November 1942 wholly occupied by the Germans, came straight to North Africa. All confirmed that as long as Darlan was in high authority, resistance would be minimal. It was clearly inevitable that unless the Allied authorities acted quickly by changing the regime, others would take drastic action. On Christmas Eve it came as little surprise, then, when walking into the Aletti Hotel to take our car back to base, I noticed several officers wearing the forbidden Gaullist Croix de Lorraine.

'Why?', I asked.

'Darlan has been shot', I was told.

'By whom?'

'By Réné Bonnier de la Chapelle'.

That evening our villa at Cap Matifou was surrounded by French and American security police. Surveillance continued for several days. Out of respect for Christmas, Réné's court martial had been postponed until Boxing Day. We heard that he had pleaded guilty, defending his action as a patriotic duty. He was condemned to death, but pardoned by General Giraud. The Darlanist influences round the General had worked on him until late into the night, and persuaded him to withdraw the pardon. The young man was then, contrary to all custom, taken out and shot before dawn, before any effort could be made to help him.

His colleague, Capitaine Sabatier, sought our assistance. He was taken to safety, pending any further judicial enquiry – which was never made.

All these weeks the Comte de Paris, the Pretender to the French Throne, was in Algiers. Some believed that he might make a compromise leader until the future was clearer. But the Americans were as usual anti-monarchist (even without reference to the President) and few others were interested; while the Comte himself seemed disinterested in the idea. It is certain that he had no part in the removal of Darlan.

This event gave a chance of recasting the structure of Massingham. The High Command was, and remained throughout, befogged about clandestine operations. The Mission in Tunisia under Colonel Anstruther and Brooks Richards was making an effective contribution working into Tunis and Bizerta and in the open country towards the south from which the British Eighth Army were soon to arrive.

Massingham, looking across the Mediterranean from Algiers, seemed top heavy with three colonels – at least until the de Gaulle-Giraud impasse was cleared. The accuracy of Keswick's daily reports to London, sent through our own channels, was still causing resentment in certain Intelligence circles whose information and judgement had not proved so correct.

Major-General 'Jock' Whiteley, the senior British officer at AFHQ, under whom I had served in Cairo in similar conditions in mid-summer 1940, told me that he would recommend my appointment to lead the Mission, but on conditions that he would set, to operate on the lines of our work in Khartum rather than in Cairo.

In early January Gubbins arrived from London, and Donovan from Washington. Gubbins showed me my terms of reference which he said had been approved, for an Allied Theatre of Operations, by Selborne, our Minister, after clearance with Churchill. After a discussion with Colonel William Eddy, the American Marine who had organised the landings in November, we four went into Eisenhower's office where he received us, attended by Bedell Smith and Whiteley.

Gubbins read out my terms of reference. Little else was said as few really comprehended the potential for special operations at that moment. Eisenhower said that OSS and SOE should work closely together; that Eddy was to be the head and I was to be his second-in-command. Clasping his hands, he said to us all, 'You must work together like this. You must have no secrets from each other'. We all agreed. Eisenhower, like Alexander later, inspired devoted loyalty.

Before leaving Algiers Gubbins said, 'Your terms are much too secret to be left lying about at Algiers. I will look after them in London'. I was never to see them again. In effect I had carte blanche, knowing that if I went too badly wrong, I was expendable; hoping that others would not be too much harmed by my mistakes; and knowing that, as I had learnt in principle in the Sudan Service, I could rely entirely on his support as my chief.

CHAPTER 12

Building the Springboard: Massingham 1943

Before leaving, Gubbins told me that AFHQ had agreed my promotion to Lt-Colonel. At the same time we moved our base to the Club des Pins. Not overlooked, set back in the sand dunes away from the road, it was to prove an ideal location for training and security. I was given the best villa, with a spare room which was to house many a distinguished guest.

Settled there, I suddenly realised that all the experience of the past seven years had culminated in this unexpected challenge. Little did I then think that this base would grow to the size it did, and its activities spread throughout the Western and Central Mediterranean. First, and fastest, I had to set up Massingham – the codename for the formal Inter-Services Signal Unit No 6. It must provide the full range of facilities as developed in Britain, to be available to Americans as well as French. Recruitment was good, despite the prohibition about Gaullists. We had no independent French, though we supplied F Section parties already in France. On the working level all three Allies were to cooperate admirably in the immediate tasks. I published my war aims: 'Chasser l'ennemi et chercher la cuisine Française' No-one quarreled with these aims and politics were precluded. As described, I did what I could to discourage Russian imperial expansionism. As we became increasingly the transport, supply and signal communications for Allied government-in-exile, I found that our aims were usually the same as theirs. But in addition to the flood of French now arriving from France, there were many refugees from other European countries. These were put in touch with their own authorities and often trained and went back into Occupied Europe.

A full training section taught 'survival', signals and coding, guerrilla and sabotage action. Donovan sent us an invaluable parachute training unit under Major Rucker. Flying from Blida, a few miles south, the drops were made into the sand dunes near the Club. Unique in North Africa, Rucker's unit worked with Ray Wooler who joined us later in Italy, to develop even further the operational use of parachuting, our experience being of value in the first airborne operation into Sicily. The opportunities, and the limitations, of air supply were further demonstrated by this splendid 'jump happy' group, who persuaded unlikely volunteers at the Club, including many FANYs, to savour the thrills of jumping.

To put into practice this training, a Flight of 138 Squadron came out from Tempsford each moon period, under 'Mouse' Fielden himself. By the summer of 1943 full RAF facilities were established at Blida.

Our own naval vessels had sailed out from the Helford River; to these Holdsworth added locally hired schooners, and fast craft. He also trained men to use small boats for going ashore on enemy-occupied coasts, landing agents from submarines and picking them up. HMS *Maidstone*, under Capt. 'Barney' Fawkes, provided additional transport unsurpassed in verve. Our debt to them, running so many risks for us outside the normal line of danger and duty, was immense. Our only loss was one FANY, married to a submariner. The French put at our disposal their submarine *Casabianca* under her famous Captain L'Herminier. At first it was a little disconcerting to find oneself discussing operations in the wardroom under pictures of Petain and Darlan. But however deep the dislike of the 'sales Britanniques' and the bitterness left by our unavoidable attack at Oran in 1940, all aboard were dedicated to France and freedom. Cooperation left nothing to be desired, with bravery and competence of the highest calibre.

Our radio station under Bill Corbett was soon working into Corsica and France, as well as keeping essential links with Britain and Tunis. Most of the work of signals and coding was carried out by the FANY.

The 'Fannies'. I have told how I claim to have been the first to bring them to work with us in Baker Street. A party of ten had come out in November 1942 in the ship *Scythia* which had been torpedoed but had limped into Algiers. Others arrived in 1943 until a total of some 250 were serving in the theatre. Their uniforms and rank badges were unusual, so they were all, rightly, treated as officers. All spoke at least one foreign language. I can never adequately express our thanks and respect for what they did, in all the varied activities found at the Club. Several sent into Occupied Europe from Britain met savage but gallant ends in concentration camps. As circumstances loosened up in 1944 some dropped into France from Algiers but all survived. They worked on every duty, from parachute packing to top-level staff duties. Indeed, it soon became the practice whenever special equipment was needed from AFHQ, to send in one of the girls with a written request. I cannot recall their ever failing to bring back a satisfactory result; occasionally the benefactor was brought to dinner also!

Scores of books have been written about the many brave men and women who carried out the real work of resistance, in the field; others have described the highest political and military discussions and plans to use clandestine action to help the regular forces to liberate Europe. Few have told of the minute application, the meticulous attention to detail, needed to put these top level ideas into practical action. It was little understood at the time. So began a series of invitations to the top decision-takers to explain the possibilities and difficulties of clandestine action, and the likelihood of mistakes of judgement if risks were to be taken and early results achieved. We were expected to operate in all enemy occupied territories – to support Allied landings in some places and to help Deception in all others. It was a big assignment. Eisenhower and Bedell Smith came out to the Club one afternoon. Clearly, and understandably, doubtful at the few obvious facilities, they were always willing to support us when things went wrong, and, in due course, especially after 'MONKEY', described later, were to expect the impossible from us.

Later on we organised bigger demonstrations. After an inspection of our various facilities, dinner in the mess and coffee with the Fannies, visitors would watch a parachute drop in which at least one FANY would take part, followed by a small boat exercise over the beaches. One difficulty in writing this account is to avoid its becoming largely a dropping of names – of these many top decision-takers, military and political, who came to see and so often afterwards to help.

At first there was not much to show. It was only in mid-1943, as Europe saw the tide really turning, that the resisters began to take stronger action. Our task from then onwards was, while encouraging sabotage, to persuade them to keep their powder dry and to resist the coming temptations to rise prematurely before rescue from the outside was near. In this we were too often unsuccessful.

We would not have progressed so quickly in Algiers but for the personal support of three men: Saltzman with the Americans and Whiteley with the military; to them was added in January 1943 Roger Makins, as senior British diplomat. I had been his 'clothes fag' at school; from then until now my regard for him has ever increased, as valet to master. Apart from personal friendship, these three knew of my track record in the East African campaign; the first, and until then the only, successful through-run from secret intelligence to clandestine action, from guerrilla and regular warfare to liberation. We were now in the action and the guerilla phases in Europe.

Throughout the next two years I could always count on these three, and on the unfailing support of Gubbins and Donovan. Once the band-waggon had begun to roll, some highly competent 'commercial' recruits believed that it would roll the faster if they were put in command. I was kept informed of these ideas. Their greater skills were duly employed in other ways; but they had not had the chances to establish relationships of trust that had fallen to me. My job later proved to be to keep touch with the senior decision-makers at AFHQ, while others organised the operational units from day to day, in Algiers and Italy. Our future was to depend so often on favourable top level decisions on radio frequencies, or availability of aircraft, or access to captured enemy arms.

At the same time I kept in touch with the political elements of each unit with all of which I had worked operationally. The French gave me accommodation in Algiers while I was always found a welcome at the other units, as I will describe. Each unit became increasingly under the control of military Commands as they moved into the final phases of liberation, Massingham under the French Command and the others under 15 Army Group.

I began by going to the Anfa Conference at Casablanca where President met Prime Minister in late January 1943. Churchill's staff had long taken helpful interest in our work. When I heard that de Gaulle was to come, I went out to the airfield to meet him. There I found little sign of a true welcome. Leaving my car to help his staff, I withdrew. A quarter of a century later he told the Dutch Prime Minister, 'A deliberate insult. French and American Guards of Honour for Roosevelt and Churchill. Not for me, even though it was the first time I had set foot on French soil since 1940. Not even a car . . .'

Back in Algiers, still under the de Gaulle ban, the first step into Europe was taken when Cesari set out for Corsica, carried by the French submarine *Casabianca*. The success of this operation was due so much to his leadership; his friendship lasted until he came to see me a decade later to 'ask permission' to leave Germany and return to North Africa.

Mr. Harold Macmillan arrived at this time, to head the British Political Office at AFHQ. There had been a British Minister of State at the British Headquarters in Cairo for some time. Such an appointment to an Allied Headquarters was a novelty, one which could be helpful, particularly to us, but, with all the political overtones following the Darlan and de Gaulle controversies, could make things worse. Macmillan worked with great skill. Realising that 'politician' was a dirty word to Americans, he found that the British Service attitude was little better. Many had witnessed the close-run disasters of the past few years. Macmillan had been one of the few to support Churchill in Parliament, but he had seemed ineffective. His undoubted success in the Mediterranean in the next three years has been little acknowledged. His books give little idea of his skill, first in getting together with the Americans, being half American himself; second, taking on the French; and, finally, taking part in political action affecting the many countries whose problems came to AFHQ. He was particularly helpful to us. It was his ill-luck that after spending six months supporting the anti-de Gaulle attitudes of Churchill, supervision of French affairs were taken from him when the policy changed. But de Gaulle never forgot. Added to the belief that Macmillan was the main advocate of committing Britain to the Suez venture and the first to demand it stop, it was unlikely de Gaulle would welcome such a 'perfide' colleague. This surely affected de Gaulle's attitude when in 1961 he rejected Macmillan's effort to take Britain into the European Community. Far ahead though that time was, this hostile sentiment was to affect our efforts, but not to the disadvantage of those fighting for freedom in France.

A welcome development in those weeks was the spontaneous agreement by the British Special Service heads in Algiers to hold a weekly meeting. We had all seen the difficulties flowing from inter-departmental jealousies in London and Cairo. None of us had professional careers to advance. Agreed approaches to our Allies were vital, first to the Americans, then to the French, and later to all the others. So SOE's voluminous Intelligence was made over to MI6. Priorities over use of aircraft and submarines were agreed between us. As and when our operations went wrong, we informed Brigadier Dudley Clark whose Deception achievements will never be fully known. Through his ingenuity the maximum effect was caused by the minimum effort. He could turn round a failure so that the enemy would wonder if it was a failure, or a plant.

I paid several visits to Tunisia where we had set up a radio station to work into enemy-occupied Tunis. Many had joined our irregular groups, under French Command. Their enthusiasm was often greater than their skill. Mickey the Greek took an antitank shell, put its nose in a crate to open it, and hit the other end with a hammer . . . From others who survived we found many good future field workers.

Returning one day I took a short cut through the mountains from Constantine to the coast through the Aures Mountains. My political-officer antennae alerted me to the unfriendly atmosphere. Later this was to be one centre of resistance to the French occupation. Such hostility made operations in Tunisia doubly hazardous. Given a burnous as I lacked an overcoat, I was warned that anyone so dressed would be shot if captured. Little reliance could be placed on any but the proven friend among the locals. Liberation to so many meant getting rid of the French, or the Italian settlers in Tunisia, even more than the Germans and Fascists.

On the coast at Djidjelli I found Michael Mason training on landing craft. An original member of D section, he had eluded capture in the Balkans and was more than willing to try to help clandestine landings on the north coast of the Mediterranean.

While I was gathering the threads together, the first contact was made by our irregulars with Eighth Army coming from victory in the Desert. Many units were those to whom I had shown some methods of demolition in the summer of 1940. Never have I seen men so fit, with such high morale, with such confidence in their leadership at every level. The immediate contact was with the Long Range Desert Group whom G(R) had helped at the start. The Special Air Service (SAS) and Popski's Private Army were also there.

David Stirling, the original SAS commander, had been taken prisoner, but his brother Bill had taken over. They were to prove a wonderful link between SOE and the regular forces. Our methods were increasingly the same, the difference being that SAS operated in uniform while our fighters wore civilian dress. Later in France this had little relevance, since by Hitler's direct orders anyone found behind lines in uniform or not was to be shot out of hand. Through this order many of the brave SAS were to meet their end. Meanwhile, after their Desert triumphs these private armies began to consider their new operations techniques. We were all using the same small lightweight equipment, little of which was yet available, for the massive American production was not yet in top gear.

While North Africa was being finally cleared, Donovan paid a visit to Algiers. He asked me to dine at his villa, where I found myself alone with him. I always found 'Big Bill' most sympathetic. I had met him first in the summer of 1941 before the USA were in the war. He had just completed a tour of the Balkans where his observations had proved invaluable to us. At dinner he told me that he believed that he must build up an independent, all-American Special Service, to work on the long term; while in the short term he must have all-American projects, despite Eisenhower's orders that all should be joint. Otherwise when he met the President and could only report that he was reinforcing British initiatives and projects, he would not get the necessary full support. It was unnecessary to spell out the President's anti-British sentiments, beyond victory in this war and the independence of the United Kingdom. I replied that I could only concur with his views. As for the President, I felt that it was due to his advocacy of Lease-Lend and to certain naval action that, under Churchill's leadership and with the fighting qualities of the Commonwealth, I was sitting at dinner as a free man.

I added that I was certain that if freedom was to continue, the USA must bear a larger share of the burden. Britain and the Empire would be bankrupt and unlikely to be able to carry on as before 1914, or even 1939, while it was surely now clear to almost all that isolationism had led to near-suicidal unpreparedness and divisiveness among the democracies. I would certainly do all I could in both the short and long term; but I must do all I could to obey Eisenhower's orders. These were already made the more difficult by the lack of any American equivalent to our Official Secrets Act; while an occasional attempt by a junior American officer to take over a project disclosed to him by SOE had resulted in crossed wires; and, for example, the OSS use of lines into Occupied Europe which were known by SOE to be in enemy or hostile hands had led to embarrassment. It was virtually impossible to operate thus without another Ally finding out. Such failures had on a number of occasions been referred to the High Command, as showing lack of coordination between us. I had been sent for by Bedell Smith, to be told off – twice by Eisenhower himself. I took my punishment and apologised. It was clear that they knew who was responsible, but found it easier to remonstrate through me.

It was all part of the operational hazards. Like most of us the Americans had been trained in the strict use of official channels. They found it difficult to be told by Donovan that he would be having breakfast with the President in two days time and would report on what a fine job they were doing. Later the British suffered in much the same way when Members of Parliament appeared and sought to short-circuit the delicately balanced political and operational supply guidelines. Despite moments of exasperation, all had the highest regard for 'Big Bill' and realised that he was doing his utmost to help. We met regularly during the next two years. Cooperation from Algiers into France was to work excellently thanks to the quality of the OSS officers sent out. In Sicily and Italy it was not so good. I would have cause to wonder if some of the operations there were any better known to Washington than to us. Rumours persist that the Mafia dates its revival in

Southern Italy to those days. Indeed, some of the brave American field workers I was to meet there seemed more suited for such activities than for candidature for the Senate of the United States.

Temporary social embarrassments were a daily hazard. On one occasion a voice on the telephone asking for transport announced that Hugh Verity, piloting a Hudson operation into the Rhone valley, had been chased by a night-fighter and had arrived at Algiers. His passengers included Henri Frenay* head of the great *Combat* Resistance Group, and one of the D'Astier de la Vigerie brothers. Delighted to have reached another part of French soil, they announced that they would visit the town. This, with considerable mixed feelings, I had to resist, pointing out that their public appearance contrary to the existing orders could well endanger all we were working to achieve. Eventually, with dismay, they accepted, hoping that before long all such constraints on joint action would be removed and full cooperation would be achieved.

This fulfilment came soon after the fall of Tunis in early May, bringing the whole south coast of the Mediterranean under Allied control. Prime Minister and President had accepted that, whether they liked him or not, De Gaulle was the strongest runner in the Jeanne D'Arc Stakes. We could all now cooperate openly with the Gaullists. De Gaulle arrived in Algiers. Jacques Soustelle became head of the Action Service, with a seat on the Committee for National Liberation. Manuel, Pelabon, and later Willie Widmer became our main links. Some were later to have controversial careers, but for the next two years all were to prove good allies. With Soustelle and Réné Massigli, Gubbins and I agreed that all operations into France would be coordinated with their officers. There were to be no separate operations; but the French realised how the necessity for these had arisen in 1940, and perhaps independent operations into France of a short term nature might still be necessary on occasion. On their side additional orders were sometimes given besides the official *ordres de mission*. These sometimes led to misunderstandings which had to be sorted out. One of our tasks was to explain to the decision-

* *Night will End*, pp. 250–2 by Henri Frenay: Abelard-Schuman, 1976 and *We Landed by Moonlight* by Hugh Verity

makers that whereas military objectives were short-term – the liberation of territory – Resistance movements were basically political with longer-term aims. Targets for sabotage and disruption of communications, to support landings later, could all be agreed. But few surely wished to replace Nazi totalitarianism by the Russian variety. As described, the Communists were the only ones to have clandestine networks in place in 1940, and were now in touch asking for support of all kinds. The French authorities were left to sort out their priorities, though we all urged them to consider the need to have clear lines of communication when our regular forces moved through France, and ensure that there should not be political strife. They fully agreed. The circumstances in Yugoslavia were different, but in Greece and Italy the same difficulty was to arise. As in France, British support helped to save those countries also from undue disruption.

To meet the changed situation Massingham was reorganised. In response to my request for a senior administrative officer to take overall charge of the base, Gubbins sent John Anstey, staff-trained and with an impressive commercial record. He was to prove an outstandingly effective organiser, as our work became increasingly paramilitary in support of the coming landings. Before long I split my command into two or more parts, many of the experienced men and women going forward, leaving Anstey to train and expand in Algiers. Because we habitually obeyed our orders to destroy records, no trace of Massingham's contribution survives. It has been estimated that some 40% of the supplies into France went in this period from Massingham. For security and political reasons neither the French nor London were anxious to give full credit to Algiers.

Several of our best officers were impeccable French speakers. This could lead to their expressing views on French politics which required their removal. Jacques de Guelis naturally was one. He had carried out his duties splendidly, but the time had come to change to one not connected with the recent anti-de Gaulle period. He was succeeded by Brooks Richards, who had just been recommended for a Military Cross for the defence of a lighthouse for several months in Tunisia, but as a Naval officer was given a bar to his DSC. His contribution to Anglo-French relations in the following years cannot be over-estimated. As country section, political head of Massingham, he got to know all the military and political French leaders. His fighting record for freedom and his personality were, as Duff Cooper told me, of significant value in later years at the Paris Embassy.

On the American side a change took place also. Colonel Eddy, as I have described was the first head of our joint OSS/SOE unit. By June, however, he told me that he preferred a more limited sphere of activities than the future seemed to hold in Algiers. Perhaps he also sensed that action was being taken behind his back. One of the very few Americans who spoke perfect Arabic, he was posted to Jeddah as Ambassador. I lost a good friend and colleague. In his place I was put in charge with, as second in command from OSS, Russell Livermore who in the changed circumstances proved excellent. We were lucky in those men whom Donovan sent. Their lasting friendship proved that it was not just a short-term association. In the work we did, mutual confidence was essential. It can only be regretted that accounts written in the USA by academics have been published which imply some disreputable motives. Under the accepted rules, no account has so far, to my knowledge, been published on the British side. This is one reason why I have written this. I recognised with respect some who disliked the British. We were fortunate in working with the many who got on so well together in the fight for freedom.

While the base and the Alliance were being strengthened in Algiers, I spent much time in Tunisia. Instructed by London, I went to seek a new base for air operations to use for sorties into the Balkans, Central Europe and Poland. All these areas were outside Eisenhower's theatre of operations. I had to enlist the support of American as well as British political advisers. I pointed out, with due diffidence, that SOE had been helping to organise worldwide, for nearly four years, clandestine and economic warfare as well as paramilitary action. The latter was of paramount importance to the military. Our support in occupied territory came from the politically conscious and the nationalists, and not from some form of military call-up. All were volunteers. Disruption, tying down of enemy forces, attacking their morale and keeping our friends going until liberation – opportunities were possible and necessary all over Europe. Murphy, Julius Homes, Reber gave great backing as did Makins. Air Generals Eaker and Curtis and Air Marshals Slessor and Coningham were eager to help as invited, without lessening their normal air operations.

Huge quantities of captured weapons lay in Tunisia. Possibilities were immense. I called on General Alexander at 15 Army Group, introduced by General Airey, my chief in Khartum, and 'Maori' Coningham whom I had also known there. Between them all a proposal was put to Eisenhower who, without hesitation, put at our disposal all we could pack and land by air or sea into enemy occupied territory. Donald Hamilton-Hill was put in charge. He has written a good account which, characteristically, fails to do full justice to his dedication and energy in collecting so much in Tunisia which had no sooner been collected than the base was moved to Brindisi. Nevertheless, nothing was lost. Stores were loaded on to local schooners manned by Holdsworth's matelots; and brought in due course to Italy or Algiers. To this treasure was added more captured in Sicily.

An abandoned enemy airfield south of Tunis had been allotted to us. We sent a party to organise this for flying use when all was ready. An RAF party came from Tempsford and one from Cairo to help. For four months they laboured. When all was ready, the advance into southern Italy gave us a base nearly 600 miles closer to the target areas. Once again their efforts were not wasted. Under Hamilton-Hill they had sorted themselves out and were able, without delay, to transfer the unit to Brindisi and Bari and expand into the largest Special Operational supply organisation of all.

While these preparations were being made, the High Command was discussing the next steps. The Americans were in favour of limited operations into Italy, and holding operations only in the Balkans, while the main thrust from North West Europe to the heart of Germany was being mounted in 1944. Few could envisage the possible scope or expansion of special operations – or the limitations of techniques and supply. But our political judgement over Gaullism had been proved right, and we were consulted on future possibilities. While the plans to assault Sicily were being made, we were asked to help prepare Deception activities in Corsica and Sardinia. I warned that Corsica, although being well prepared, must be dissuaded from premature insurrection until prompt support from outside could be given. In Sardinia, thanks to the efficiency of the Italian Secret Police, virtually no action was possible. A message had been received from Lussu, a Communist married to the sister of a British colleague, that he would deliver Sardinia to us immediately we landed a strong force provided we then declared Sardinia independent from Italy. I did not feel it lay within my terms to give such a guarantee, nor was a strong enough force immediately to hand.

It was becoming difficult to keep our clandestinity virginal, so we stressed the paramilitary nature of operations since so many private armies had come from the Desert. Among several who joined us at that time was Douglas Fairbanks whose imagination and gallantry in operations with SOE was to earn him a good British DSC. Such recruits added greatly to our social standing. Taking up a wager, I led from the Club a route march which included men and women from so many services and nations that it created a security alert and was not repeated. The Fannies more than any others had raised our prestige, and through them and other recruits we found many in North Africa ready to operate in occupied lands.

Best of all was an unexpected event which gave immense encouragement to us all. In late May the telephone rang in my room.

'Wing-Commander Fielden's compliments. He is coming out to bathe and bringing General Lyon with him'.

'Delighted to see the Wing-Commander,' I replied, 'but no Generals unless cleared by our Security'.

Five minutes later a word from a somewhat bewildered Duty Officer. 'General Lyon is your Colonel-in-Chief. They are on their way'.

Alerting Security, I leapt onto my motor cycle and reached the gates half a mile away as the King drove up. His Majesty had arrived that morning. He had flown in operational conditions across the Bay of Biscay where night-flying German Condors were still shooting down our aircraft. After a bathe we sat for a while in the spare room in my villa. From the conversation I gathered some idea of the strain of the last few years, and how much the support of the family had meant. This was the first time they had all been parted.

The King was to visit us on four afternoons during his stay. All had been trained at base to carry on regardless of any visitors. They demonstrated to HM their work in detail, in all our facilities. It was clear that HM had considerable knowledge of our activities, while his testing of captured enemy weapons showed the skill of an expert and his ideas on the use of stink bombs, itching powder and other unacknowledgeable 'toys' revealed operational experience.

When he came for the last time, I asked if our troops could be allowed to turn out and give him a cheer. This was gladly agreed. When we came out from my villa we found double ranks of indescribable variety; men and women, British, American, French, all Services, and others. At the end the King spoke to a very old man. No reply. He tried in French. Still no reply. I led on. The ancient was a Spaniard. Beyond them stood a taut Royal Naval group – Holdsworth, Brooks Richards and Cesari. They had been taken by surprise when conferring in a submarine off Corsica and had to return to base, arriving that morning.

I watched with a little apprehension when the order to cheer was given, wondering what the Spaniards might do. I need not have worried. They threw their caps as high as any. Yet the next morning, when I received a request to receive a delegation from them, I thought that perhaps a mistake had been made. On the contrary.

'We wish to say how proud we are that we should have been allowed to join the parade yesterday with our friends and allies. And what an honour to be able to cheer the King. Now if *we* had a King like that . . .'

This was significant coming from these representatives of the two hundred left-wing refugees who were making it possible to maintain the services in the Club. They had been recruited by a Royal Naval officer who had commanded a 'loyalist' ship in the Spanish Civil War. No breach of trust was ever found among them. Without them it would have been the harder, if not impossible, to maintain our camp services for the hundreds now living and training there. They all said the same thing:

'If Hitler comes down through Spain, we will go back and attack his communications. But we beg of you not to restart the Civil War. We realise, now, that a million Spanish have died, men and women, fighting not for Spain but against Fascism and Communism, against Germans and Italians and Russians, none of whom do we want in Spain'.

These contacts proved invaluable as we strengthened our escape routes through the Iberian peninsula. Official hostility in Spain was still considerable, and the German presence formidable. But the growing flood of escapers from France and countries north was the easier to bring in after the German occupation of all France in November 1942. Whereas Vichy France had been hostile, all French authorities were now united in helping the Resistance, and in facilitating well hidden operations.

In May 1943 the decision had still not been taken on the direction of the advance to be made after the assault on Sicily, to support the plan to knock Italy out of the War. The exact methods needed to achieve this and its results were still unclear. I paid a quick visit to Cairo to seek information on the state of action, and the potential, in the Balkans. It was just three years since I had flown out to Cairo with Taylor and Pirie on their way to prepare for action in Yugoslavia and Greece. Resistance was growing, though riven by official dissent. Throughout the Balkans, politics were becoming polarised between authoritarian, semi-Fascist governments dominated by the Nazis/Fascists, and some Communist groups who alone had any clandestine capability. As liberation approached, with the Allies now moving north from North Africa, the former groups looked for Allied help to save them from Russian imperial expansion disguised as Marxism, while the latter hoped the Russians would arrive before the Allies. This race was to be the dominant political factor for the next two years. In Greece the Allies won. In Yugoslavia it proved, in the long-run, a dead heat. The rest were to find the Russians the victors. But the final result is still to come.

Meantime, until liberation by the Allies came within reach, advice was given to do all possible to sabotage the enemy war effort, but to 'keep your powder dry'. Little else could be said until Sicily was cleared and the next steps decided. Malta could, however, now be used for air operations, nearer to the Balkans and Central Europe.

Back in Algiers we pursued instructions to expand action in Italy. I explained to the High Command the difference between Resistance in Italy and in the Balkans. In the latter some pre-occupational arrangements had been possible; but in Italy the only known resistance was some slight left-wing activity in north Italy which had proved ineffective, such was the power of the Italian Security Services. I explained to those concerned in Algiers that we could not create an effective resistance organisation without a political base; and after twenty years of suppression, little existed to work on. The decision-makers, AFHQ and 15 Army Group, needed immediate action, to support assault landings by cutting communications. This the OSS were best placed to provide, with *coup de main* groups of Italian-Americans, backed by the growing supply of equipment which OSS generously shared with us.

Chance was to provide us with a great opportunity three months later. Bill Corbett, our Signal Officer, insisted on doing his parachute drops, to show willing to go that far with the many field workers he was training. Being of considerable size, with consequent risk of injury on landing, it was decided to try a drop into the sea. All witnessed the immense splash and Bill's emergence with relief – perhaps it was the first drop ever made into water. Shortly after it was decided on the basis of this experiment to drop Dick Mallaby into Lake Como, blind, as a lesser risk than onto land. Unluckily he was seen on landing and taken prisoner – a disaster, we thought at the time, but soon to prove a godsend.

June and July were a period of intense activity, making preparations for ever-increasing evacuation through the Iberian peninsula from France and North West Europe and from Poland and Central Europe through the Balkans. Gubbins gave us great support by sending out qualified officers versed in the political and military backgrounds of these areas. Much would now depend on the amount of air transport which the decision-makers could make available. We had done little so far to show what we could do, as there had been little Resistance in North Africa, such as could be expected in Europe.

About this time we received the first feeler from an apparent German source suggesting some cooperation against Communism. As instructed after the declaration from Casablanca in

January, of 'Unconditional Surrender', this was referred at once to London. Other contacts made later were similarly referred. An attempt was made by one of our Allies to follow up such a contact in Switzerland, and it was quickly known to the Russians. They need not have feared that the Allies would compromise with Nazism as the Soviets had done in August 1939. Nor need they have feared at that time any real wish by a significant military group in Germany to come to terms or to show signs of contrition. The Generals alone had the capability of bringing the war to an end. They were only to consider overthrowing Hitler when defeat and Russian occupation over-hung them. Even then they lacked the patriotic courage, to the bitter end, to take any effective action.

For the attack on Sicily, Massingham put all its resources and experience at the disposal of the British 1st Airborne Division under General 'Boy' Browning. Ian Collins, the Operations Staff Officer, took with him to take part in the drop, Appleyard, one of the earliest and best of Special Operation officers. He was lost, shot down by our own side. Such losses were inevitable since many working at base, although against orders, went on operations if there was a spare place in an aircraft or a ship.

At this time I called on General Alexander as the senior Brigade of Guards officer in the theatre. He told me to come direct to him if I needed help in the future. I took advantage of this invitation right up to the time when we served together in Churchill's last administration. He gave unfailing support. The only secret I kept from him was over an Alfa-Romeo racing car which had been 'liberated'. It took four Military Police to start it with a push, followed by a huge bang. I heard that Alexander gave orders to find out who drove it, but the Police feigned ignorance. Years afterwards he told me he had only wanted a ride in it.

In retrospect, the most effective Supreme Command was, at least in the eyes of junior officers, formed by Eisenhower as Supreme Commander, Alexander at Army Group, Montgomery for the set piece assault, and Patton for the end run as found for Husky. Allied cooperation was at its best among those who had grown up together in Algiers, welded together by the political and military difficulties experienced there. All were 'interleaved',

American and British. Cooperation had been made the easier by the threat, in case of any known expressions of 'Goddam British, Bloody Yanks', of being sent home . . . on a slow convoy, across the seas still not clear of submarines.

The campaign in Sicily drew to an end in late July, with no sign of a break on the Italian political front. Their troops were clearly unhappy but the German grip kept them in the battle. Then, one evening, we heard the dramatic news that the Fascist Grand Council had withdrawn support from Mussolini and he was under arrest.

CHAPTER 13

MONKEY, the Italian Armistice

The part played by SOE in the Italian Armistice negotiation in July-September 1943 was codenamed MONKEY. Eisenhower ordered that knowledge of MONKEY be kept to minimum. Our two senior officers and Signals Officer knew whence the messages came. The two officers and three Italian-speaking FANY coders alone knew their contents. On the completion of the operation I sent the file back to London (I might as well have kept it) as the only record of an historic episode. I have failed, despite the help of a former Prime Minister, to get access to the file, to check exact dates and times. So, once again, I have only my memory to rely on.

Eisenhower himself, in *Crusade in Europe** has described the event. 'Then began a series of negotiations, secret communications, clandestine journeys by secret agents, and frequent meetings in hidden places that, if encountered in the fictional world, would have been scorned as incredible melodrama'.

Following the withdrawal by the Fascist Grand Council of support for Mussolini, the King, helped by Marshal Badoglio, arrested him. They then began to seek ways to contact the Allies to discuss peace terms. Their task was made trebly difficult by the presence in Italy of eighteen German divisions and by the many Fascist sympathisers whose whole future depended on the survival of Fascism.

Badoglio therefore sent General Castellano to Spain, to contact the British Embassy. Castellano has given an understandably curtailed account of his very embarrassing mission. He implies that all talks took place in Spain or Portugal. As the one most directly concerned with the arrangements of the next five weeks,

* Heinemann, 1948, pp 202–6

I can vouch for the accuracy of what follows.

About 10 August a message 'decode yourself' arrived from London. It told of an apparently genuine attempt, this time by the Italians, to discuss peace terms. Utmost secrecy was vital. Next morning I was sent for by General Strong, Director of Military Intelligence. Impressing me with the need for the utmost discretion, he took me to see Bedell Smith.

'The Italians have sent an emissary to Lisbon to discuss an Armistice'. I concealed my foreknowledge.

'We two are to go to Lisbon to collect him'.

Among other requests, could we help with civilian dress and passports? One eyebrow was raised as we provided a genuine American passport for 'Mr Smith'.

With the flow of extraordinary visitors through the Club, there was no problem in meeting the request to house the emissaries and arrange the meetings. I allocated my villa. Signals and Fannies were alerted. Messages, with no copies, were to come to me alone. Few senior regular officers had experience in the finer points of coding or signalling into Occupied Europe. The skill of the signallers and coders, and the courage of those in the field, tended to give the impression that it was little harder, and no slower, than sending a telegram at home.

All arrangements had been made when a message arrived to fetch the two Italians from Maison Blanche, the airport. After a good dinner, the negotiating group arrived. In addition to the two Generals, Macmillan and Makins represented Britain, and Murphy and Reber the United States. They set to about 9.00 pm, and worked through the night. I had microphones installed in my bedroom which the Italians used when withdrawing to confer. Their conversations were listened to by the Fannies who translated them and sent in the typescripts with jugs of coffee.

I make no apologies for this action. I was employed to do everything possible to bring the war to an end, with the quickest check to the killing of Allies and Italians, and to the destruction of Italian territory. 'Ungentlemanly' no doubt, but surely justifiable. General Castellano carried out his task, the most distasteful that could befall a career officer, with the greatest courage and dignity.

At dawn I was summoned. Terms had been agreed. The

Italians were to return as soon as possible, by the same route as they had come by. How, from Rome, were they to communicate the result of their discussions with Badoglio? The reply must come quickly and with the utmost secrecy. I thought at once of Dick Mallaby, languishing in an Italian prison, under threat of execution and being ill-treated in ways in which the Fascists were expert. It was at once agreed that his 'music box' would be used. He would be brought to Rome and set up in complete safety. A signal plan was agreed with the Italians. On their way through Lisbon they collected another set sent from London, and a revised code plan most ingeniously woven into the original, which might have been broken. Both sets were recovered from the Quirinale when we reached Rome in June 1944.

One military difficulty, as Eisenhower had described, was to keep the security of Allied intentions. The Italians had asked for the immediate landing of large forces. At that stage the plan was only to occupy the airfields at Foggia, and take Naples as a supply port. Combat loading for this operation was taking place in ports as far apart as in North America and the Indian Ocean. The assault could not be brought forward from 9 September.

So we waited. Then about 6.00 one evening Mary MacIntyre, the FANY coder, came in with a look of excitement and a rather scruffy piece of paper. On it was a message in Italian, accepting the Armistice terms, ending with, for security reasons, the single initial 'B'. Contrary to standing orders and discipline, I kissed Mary.

'Ring AFHQ and tell Bedell Smith that I am on my way with a good message'.

As the quickest way, I took my motorcycle, with the precious piece of paper in my battle-dress blouse. It would have been unintelligible to any other who might see it. On arrival at his villa, I found Bedell Smith at dinner. Reading the message, 'This is very satisfactory', he said. 'We must go and tell Eisenhower'. His staff car took us the few yards to the next villa. He went in alone, taking the paper. On coming out, 'The General is very pleased' he said, handing the paper back. A man of deep understanding, he wasted few words. Back at his villa he thanked me again and went back to his dinner. On my way home, too late for my dinner, I reflected that in the United States I had always been told to tip the

Western Union messenger boy.

During the next few days a number of messages were exchanged. These were kept to the minimum, and concerned arrangements made for Italian representatives to fly to Sicily to sign the Official Armistice terms; exact details of which have never been published. Macmillan refers to them in his *Memoirs.** With the contents I was not concerned, but only with the security of the communications on which so much depended as the date for the landings at Salerno came nearer.

All seemed well set. A slight check had been caused, we heard, by the decision of Eighth Army to postpone its assault on the mainland until 3 September, the fourth anniversary of Britain's entry into the war. This was to put them behind schedule when coming to support the landings at Salerno which got into some difficulties. The British signal 'Hang on. We are coming' was said, in the circumstances, to have caused some rude remarks at Salerno. A year later, when Montgomery was in some difficulty in Normandy, Alexander, from a thousand miles away in Italy, allegedly repeated the signal, 'Hang on. We are coming'.

Meanwhile the Advance Headquarters of AFHQ had been set up at Carthage in Tunisia. Before they departed from Algiers, I had been given a message to be sent to Badoglio giving him notice that the landings were to take place within twenty-four hours. This was at his request, to allow action to be taken in many ways, but in particular to get the royal family and other colleagues out of Rome and away from possible capture by the Germans, who were present there in some strength. It was left to my judgement to decide the exact timing for the despatch of the message. The Italians had asked for six hours notice, to allow for coordination of Badoglio's announcement of the Armistice from Rome, at the same time, 6.30 pm, as Eisenhower's broadcast on Algiers radio.

With our signals and coding staff, I had decided that the message, encoded early, should be sent off at 10.00 am on 8 September, the day before the landings. This should allow enough time for decoding and passing to Badoglio by midday. Dick Mallaby had been 'direction-found' to be operating from the Quirinale in Rome.

* Macmillan, Vol. II, 1967, p. 386.

Just before 9.00 am on 8 September I was handed an emergency message from Badoglio. He said that he believed that the Germans had found out about the Armistice, and the whole project must be abandoned. Ordering the despatch of our signal to be held up, I sent a message to AFHQ that I was coming in with an emergency signal. Strong was ready. I showed him the signal and asked for instructions. He rang Eisenhower in Carthage while Kenneth Keith, his Military Assistant, once again kept up our morale.

Then Eisenhower, from 700 miles away, came on the telephone. His first question was 'Are you sure your codes are secure?'

I thought of the thousands of troops now within a few hours of the beaches at Salerno, at the extreme range of fighter air cover, with so many friends among them. Were they sailing into a trap? We had, of course, always kept this aspect of security under continuous consideration, one of the permanent worries of clandestine operations. In this case London as well as we had taken especial care. So I replied, 'I have no reason to believe that our codes are in any way compromised'. It was, perhaps, the most important snap reply I was ever to give.

Years later we were able to confirm that, in fact, our codes had been secure. But from records captured in Berlin, and from the witness of a German officer in Rome at that time, Von Plehwe, the Germans had some idea that negotiations were underway. This knowledge came from the Roosevelt–Churchill transatlantic telephone conversations which the Germans were monitoring until the end of 1943.

On receiving my assurance, Eisenhower dictated to me a message of intense emotion and authority.

'Italy, her honour already twice . . .' was among the phrases. The full text is in the MONKEY File. I was ordered to go back to base and despatch the first parts of the message. The last part would be sent to me at once. About 11.30 am the first part and the original message were sent off. The last part did not go until about 1.30 pm. The young officer told to bring it urgently had stopped to have lunch on the way. We sat and waited until 6.30, the hour set for the two broadcasts.

At 6.30 Eisenhower's announcement was made by Algiers

radio. Nothing from Rome. 6.45 . . . 7.00 . . . 7.15 . . . 7.30 . . . nothing. Fearing the worst, and helpless to boot, we went into dinner. About 7.40 I was summoned to the telephone. It was Colonel Charlie Sloane of AFHQ, clearly the better for his dinner;

'It's OK, B has spoken'.

We were up most of that night, making plans in case the Germans had found out and our forces were going into a trap; and, belatedly, making plans to follow up a successful assault, now we could bring in others once the Armistice was general knowledge. Next day I was sent for by Eisenhower, to come to Carthage on my way to Italy. He was very generous as always in his remarks, although the general situation was still critical.

'You have been the leading anti-Fascist. Now you must be the leading pro-Italian', he said. 'You will go to see Badoglio and the King. Get them to help you find any Italians willing to help throw the Nazis out of Italy. And try to find any others who may be there, including the many prisoners-of-war who should be free. We do not know what will follow the Armistice, but we hope that the Italians will at least arrange to free our prisoners before the Nazis grab them. After that we must see.'

Eisenhower repeated that if SOE needed airfields and accommodation in Italy, the Bari/Brindisi area alone was available. Foggia to the north and all facilities on the west coast were needed for regular operations. The needs of Special Operations in the theatre could be considerable, while shorter distances to the Balkans would mean more demands from Cairo – despite these countries being outside his authority. Bedell Smith gave me written authority to requisition such facilities as needed. This was reduplicated, and later Holdsworth and I nailed a hundred on as many doors between Bari and areas to the south and west of Brindisi.

CHAPTER 14

Back into Europe: Maryland

The decision to try to knock Italy out of the war after the clearing of North Africa has been mentioned already, to be followed by the limited objectives of occupying the airfields at Foggia and Naples as a supply port. This would bring closer support to Resistance in the Balkans, and more importantly, keep more Axis forces involved in fighting in Southern Europe. One strongly held view was that only a rapier thrust from Britain straight through the heart of Germany, from the Ruhr to Berlin, could be decisive. It had been agreed, however, that from the estimates of forces, training and equipment needed, it would not be possible to launch this attack until 1944. Meantime the Russians must not be left fighting alone on land.

So Italy must be the arena, but without any clear decision being possible in the summer of 1943 on how far an advance might reach before forces had to be reduced and returned to Britain for the main assault in 1944. Nobody could foretell at that moment how Italy would divide between the patriots rallying round the King, and the Neo-Fascists and the Communists; nor that the Germans would be able to sustain for another two years with undiminished vigour yet another battle front added to those in Eastern Europe and the Balkans.

I had been questioned about SOE's capability, if any, in Italy. I repeated that resources made available to penetrate Italy had been necessarily restricted; the Italian OVRA had been the most effective Secret Security Service with the exception of the Japanese, and so the hardest to circumvent. They had been organised for longer than others. Italy, also, had not had the great influx of foreign workers which in Germany had made it possible to organise some action. There were a few links through neutral countries. Alfredo Pezzoni, of the Credito Italiano, was one of the earliest and the bravest, being head of the Committee of National

Liberation in 1941 when the future looked blackest. From Milan he led a non-Communist group which did magnificent work. Even today little is known of the success of the many non-Communist resisters in Italy. This is in part due to the unwillingness of British authorities to give access to such records as exist. Charles Mackintosh's belated record* of his brilliant success found an Italian, before any British, publisher.

We had in the Mediterranean only a small Italian country section. Some contacts in Italy, mostly of a political nature, were known, but effective action had to be organised from outside. Malcolm Munthe, whose home was in Capri, had already proved his worth in Norway. Until seriously wounded at Anzio, he was tireless and unequalled in sorting out the recruits who came to Naples. Max Salvadori was of Anglo-Italian stock. Freed from a Fascist gaol, he had become a teacher during the long years of appeasement. Later he joined the ranks of the fighting academics who added such lustre to SOE, winning a DSO and MC in northern Italy.

The capture of Sicily had brought no immediate advantage except by adding to the stock of captured enemy weapons. The OSS provided some second generation Sicilian-Americans who had given effective paramilitary support to the armies.

I had warned Holdsworth of the bare facts of MONKEY. Following the assault by regular forces elsewhere, he was to take one of his small ships into Brindisi. He would find some friends there in due course, as a result of the main landings some distance away, at Taranto and Goia del Colle. These points left little scope for any immediate special operations. Across the Adriatic, however, lay the Balkans with all their resisters. An air base was planned at Foggia, for the strategic bombing of Germany and other targets in occupied Central Europe. We hoped to be able to take advantage of this air base to supply our friends in the whole area, especially in Poland, whose sustained attacks on the German lines of communication into Russia had proved so valuable. We must await developments in Italy, and see what reliable groups would turn up.

All this I had discussed with Bedell Smith before MONKEY, but as

* *From Cloak to Dagger*, William Kimber.

most of our target areas were outside Eisenhower's theatre of operations, he told me to discuss these plans with Alexander, who had come to Carthage to command 15 Army Group with authority over all operations in Italy, though his authority over operations from Italy were as yet undefined. Alexander was willing to discuss, encourage and support as far as he possibly could. He was at first a little doubtful. He was aware of the formidable difficulties found with SOE in Cairo – political disagreements among the politicians in exile, and among the various groups in occupied countries – and the much larger-scale supply problems for guerrilla groups in the Balkans. The behaviour of some SOE base workers in Cairo had brought undue unpopularity. Thanks to Whiteley's advocacy, however, and the role we had been able to play in MONKEY, Alexander agreed to help, but said he must be careful since he had not heard of any agreement between the Americans and the Russians on Balkan cooperation.

I had been ordered to remain in Algiers until the final stages of the landings had been completed and until Badoglio, it was assumed, would have taken refuge somewhere in south Italy. Following my visit to Carthage, I was given a ride by British 6 Airborne Division to Goia del Colle, in the heel of Italy, which had just been captured by them with the loss to a sniper of their commander General Hopkinson. The division was heading north to Foggia, while my aim was Brindisi which I reached by my motorcycle, a delightful trip free of any sign of war. There I found Holdsworth and his well-trained crew. For the first time we were in ex-enemy territory, and felt justified in 'liberating' any government property which might be used to advantage – that famous four-masted sailing ship, the *Amerigo Vespucci*, two Mitropa sleeping cars in the station . . .

I went straight to the local hotel which many will remember from sea and air journeys through Brindisi. There I found General Max Taylor, the American Commander who had paid a clandestine visit to Rome to explore the chances of an airborne assault. I told him of our plans.

Next I called on the King and Marshal Badoglio. We had a very frank discussion, during which I asked for help in finding individuals to go north to link up with any groups of patriots known to them. Our immediate aim must be to disrupt enemy communications, to slow down German concentrations in the Naples area. I said we must use every agency, monarchist and all others willing to fight the Germans, until the threat to our regular forces was cleared. They explained the delay in issuing the announcement on Rome radio, claiming that, as our message was later than wished, they had had to wait until certain people had been able to leave for Ancona where a cruiser was standing by. They did not mention their attempt to call off the Armistice. But they had remembered to bring Dick Mallaby with them. He was awarded an immediate Military Cross.

The next few weeks were to bring home to me how inadequate had been my preparations for the countless opportunities which offered. The tightness of security and the uncertainty over the outcome of MONKEY were little excuse, nor was the endless time-consumption in other immediate tasks such as Corsica. The most urgent need was for trained individuals with radio sets to go to selected points. Later from this experience were formed the Jedburghs – teams of three, a leader, a radio-operator and an instructor – who contributed so much behind the lines in France in 1944. The SAS were not to hand in strength; their techniques and initiative would have been ideal to meet the challenges, for it was said that between the forward elements of 6 Airborne at Foggia and Berlin there were no enemy troops. But in Italy in early September 1943, few of these irregulars were available. Our needs, made more intense over MONKEY, for security on clandestine operations had led to neglect as we moved into the para-military, guerrilla phase when most could wear uniform. With the Ethiopian experience behind me, I had only myself to blame.

All this I explained to Holdsworth. I said that with Gubbins' agreement, AFHQ accepted that he was best qualified to take command of SOE's affairs in Italy; a most experienced officer, from Finland onwards, with imagination and initiative, he had just been awarded the DSO. At first he demurred, saying that he knew nothing of high policy, nor about 'Pongos' – the nautical term of endearment for soldiers. My task, I stressed, was to keep in close touch with AFHQ, now divided between Algiers and Tunisia, and soon to move into the Naples area. Anstey and Richards were now running Massingham, and he was needed to build up the Italian Mission on the same lines, while I kept overall supervision, and looked ahead for the many opportunities which would arise. He would be given an experienced team from Algiers and London, with good back-up from Cairo. His acquiescence was finally achieved by agreeing to codename the Mission 'Maryland' in honour of his wife.

Thus began one of the most successful organisational and operational missions in SOE. In addition to the normal practice of giving little publicity to Special Operations, there were unusual factors; working with ex-enemies, in ex-enemy country, and with a hated Badoglio under a discredited monarchy. Cooperation with Badoglio seemed to many to resemble the cooperation with Darlan. Until, however, the battle front was stabilised, and liberated areas of southern Italy secured and organised, it was essential to use as a rallying point those who had carried through the Armistice.

Many patriotic Italians came forward, to be trained and later sent to the north where they performed outstanding feats of gallantry. The great majority of Italians clearly detested the Fascists as well as the Nazis, and were glad to have a chance of showing it by making a fighting contribution to the liberation of their country. They lacked the early clandestine organisation which the Communists had managed to keep going through the years of Fascism. The greater credit was due to the non-Communists, therefore, for all they did. The more was the pity that the rest of the world does not know the contribution made to freedom by those non-Communists, as well as by the Communist Resistance.

As I have explained, I had made copies of my authorisation to requisition buildings and facilities required for Special Operations. These Holdsworth and I took when we set out in his jeep to reconnoitre the coastal strip from Brindisi to Foggia. We drove north through welcoming crowds until we met the 6 Airborne units already occupying Foggia. In three days we managed to inspect and nail requisition orders on some hundred buildings. I regret that from this time onwards SOE had the reputation for getting the most desirable properties. The charge was justified; but then SOE usually got there first, if not ahead of the game.

Later Special Operations (Mediterranean) (SOM) was set up at Bari and Monopoli under a Major-General. Its prime purpose was to supply the growing irregular forces in the Balkans. In our area demands were to increase, for Italy and Poland as well as Central Europe. Phil Macpherson, Bill Harcourt and Ian Henderson, its mainsprings, arrived quickly.

On my return from Foggia, I called on the new Duke of Aosta, the younger brother of Amadeo, Viceroy of Ethiopia who had died recently in Kenya. The former, usually known as the Duke of Spoleto, had committed the social solecism of accepting the Crown of Slovenia from Mussolini. This empty distinction had now vanished. Of more importance at this moment was his nominal command of a motor boat squadron. He was persuaded to tell Commandante Parigi to bring the Squadron from Taranto to Brindisi where, under the orders of Cmdr Morgan Giles and Holdsworth, it was to operate very successfully.

The following month was, in many ways, the most confused period for SOE in the war. Eisenhower had estimated that there were some 30,000 Allied prisoners-of-war in Italy. Many had broken out of prison. The Red Cross had lost touch with others. The release of Mussolini from captivity and the organisation of a neo-Fascist government in the north had further weakened such authority as the King's Government had. In the north neo-Fascists and Nazis were employing the most ruthless methods to sustain their position and supply the rapid German concentrations against the Allies at Salerno. Loyalties were divided more by fear than by favour, for Nazi reprisals were, as usual, terrible. Power lay at the points of the guns.

There were virtually no Italian-speakers equipped with radio and transport to go north from Brindisi to seek out prisoners and recruit helpers. So tight had been security over MONKEY, with no hint of the possibility of an Italian surrender, that recruiting had been limited. Again I blame myself.

Many resourceful individuals found their way to Brindisi, some SAS, and Popski's Private Army – and even the LRDG on its way to Istria. With his talent for improvisation and leadership, Holdsworth coordinated their efforts. Until the political fog cleared, the first task was the rescue of the prisoners. Despite the ceaseless despatch of all available transport, criticism poured in, due no doubt to the understandable belief that rescue of prisoners should have been the first consideration. One party of very senior officers was located far up the coast of the Adriatic. When transport was slow in arriving, a hint came from the north that perhaps their rescue would interfere with existing promotions. This produced an irreverent, junior comment 'That might be as well'.

They were duly rescued.

Many were lost in those weeks, among them, to my grief, John, son of Sir Stewart Symes, my chief in Khartum. He set off in some inadequate local boat and was never heard of again. But such attempts rescued many, to continue the still hard-fought struggle.

I had risked one initiative. Knowing where Amadeo d'Aosta's officers' loyalties lay, with Italy and the monarchy, I had suggested to London that, with the greatest discretion, a number of them be prepared for the earliest possible despatch from their POW camps in Africa to Italy to support the King's Government. The recent death of Aosta in Kenya – many felt of a broken heart over the disasters which had befallen his country and the war with the Allies whom he regarded as friends, as they regarded him – was a grievous blow. Had he survived, the subsequent history of Italy might have been very different. The widespread, almost universal, respect for him might well have helped him to save the monarchy and avoid much of the divisiveness still found in Italy.

The group soon arrived from Kenya and proved of great value, especially to the Allied Military Government. A particular friend was Aldo Tait, Aosta's private pilot. He became chief of operations later for Alitalia and averred that in return for what had been done for his beloved chief, he would do his best to ensure that Alitalia always used Rolls-Royce engines.

One successful venture at this time was to prove short-lived. All-OSS projects had been sought which would strengthen Donovan's hand with the White House. Realising that the Adriatic should be free for some time of enemy shipping, it was proposed that the OSS should hire, from their very substantial dollar funds, local schooners to take captured enemy weapons and ammunition and other stores to Tito's partisans. A large shipment was made to the satisfaction of all. The OSS officers concerned went back to Cairo to report and did not return, to our regret. The reason, I was only to discover many years later, was that the President had not agreed with Stalin the conditions for American support to Resistance movements in the Balkans. This was not finalised until after the Mena Conference at Cairo in December 1943. American officers were thus formally precluded from activities in the Balkans in the autumn of that year. Had this been known at the time, the OSS party could have operated in British uniform as was done on occasion – as the British sometimes wore American uniforms when more acceptable – or they could have gone in as an Allied Mission under Eisenhower. Undoubtedly great opportunities were missed during those weeks in not pressing on with these important supply operations. SOE's terms of reference authorised us to operate worldwide; we had been at work in the Balkans during the years when Russia had in effect been Germany's ally.

While Maryland was being born on the east side of Italy, other avenues were opening up on the west, in particular in Naples and Rome, for which such plans as were feasible had been made. From the USA via London had come Count Sforza, a great Italian liberal Foreign Minister before the rise of Fascism. In Algiers he discussed plans with the military. At dinner later, he had expressed useful ideas at some length. I intervened to say that these were, of course, beyond my responsibility, and that he should have discussed them with Churchill whom he had seen.

'I tried to', he replied, 'but Churchill did all the talking'. I sympathised. He also warned against proportional representation in any future constitution, for Italy or elsewhere.

'It is a good system for politicians', he said 'but bad for firm government. There must be a firm government and a credible alternative. But not a lot of small groups all wanting a share'. Many years later I found out that he was indeed wise on this point.

On my way back to Algiers I got a lift by air from Brindisi into the beach-head at Salerno. The battle had been close run. The Germans had reacted with their usual vigour and speed. To prevent a wedge being driven between the American and British forces, Alexander had put in the 201 (Guards) Brigade. The beach-head had been saved and the Germans fell back north of Naples where their supplies were assured. Saltzman was at Fifth Army Headquarters and, the danger now past, could see the funny side of Montgomery's signal 'Hang on, we are coming . . .'. But it had been a gruelling experience.

Those whom I found to be the least worried were the three 'Elderlies' – Count Sforza, Tarchiani (later Ambassador in Washington) and Cianca of the *Corriere della Sera*. They had gone in on the assault in the care of Munthe and Salvadori. If the battle had gone wrong and they had been taken prisoner, their fate under the fascists would have been unspeakable. It was a very gallant venture by the whole group.

There had been other chances for action. Salvadori had been made Mayor of Salerno on Munthe's authority. Together they had boated round the Sorrento peninsula to rescue the philosopher Benedetto Croce. In another somewhat special sortie Douglas Fairbanks picked up a message when passing Ponza, an island just north of Naples. This seemed to indicate that Mussolini was held prisoner there. When landing to investigate the next night, it was found that the Duce had been removed and the reception was not friendly; but the landing party escaped.

Our party was now moving into Naples. There they organised a number of resisters who had managed to escape from Rome and make their way by various routes to avoid the retreating Germans. They set up escape lines which were to prove invaluable in the next nine months. Leaving Emma Hamilton's villa, famous but inconvenient, to Air Chief Marshal Slessor, Munthe found a house on the hill above it with a panoramic view over the Bay of Naples. He also obtained the use of a box at the opera for Sunday afternoons.

On arrival back in Algiers, there was one Italian string to tie up. A signal had been received, and the Italians had mentioned in Brindisi, that their troops in Sardinia wished to surrender. There were still substantial German forces in the island. Every man, and woman, American and British, was already committed to Italy or Corsica. Only one remained, Sergei Obolensky. This seemed to give OSS an All-American chance such as Donovan was always seeking. Though well over fifty years of age, Obolensky agreed with his accustomed elan. He asked if he could have a British radio link as well as his own. A Massingham operator who had done his parachute training 'for fun' volunteered. The party was parachuted in. Immediate radio contacts were set up. Next day the Germans, fearing that they might be cut off from the mainland, started to withdraw. Another group of us flew in, and soon the RAF and Royal Navy were well organised there. Obolensky was decorated for his gallantry, and the Massingham radio operator received the immediate award of a Military Medal. This was, perhaps, a significant contribution to the rapid clearing of the island which, with the capture of Corsica later, could be used for attacks on the enemy in Italy and France.

Years after the war, I used to discuss these operations with the German General von Senger who commanded in Corsica and Sardinia and later at Cassino. He would wave his arm in greeting. 'It works well still', he would say. A Rhodes Scholar at Oxford in 1912, he had fallen off his horse foxhunting and broken his arm. My father, a surgeon in Oxford, had helped to mend it.

Chapter 15

Corsica: The Real Maquis

While these advances on to Italian soil were being consolidated, a victory in Corsica was setting the pattern of later joint successes between the Resistance and the liberating forces. Cesari, landed from the French submarine *Casabianca* ten months before, had used the time significantly. He had found many willing to help recruit, train and later arm and fight when the time came. Their daily work kept them mainly near the enemy-occupied centres of population. In case of need, refuge could be sought in the Maquis – the desolate, mountainous areas of the island which had been the home of outlaws for countless centuries. Thus the terms Maquis and Maquisard came to be used throughout the French Resistance.

Radio links with Massingham were quickly organised, and the supply of arms began. These came first from French stores in Algiers, and later from those weapons captured in Tunis with the usual explosives and detonators from SOE. They were transported by French and British submarines, and by a Flight of 161 Squadron from the main Special Duty base at Tempsford. Fielden himself brought them out for the monthly moon period, returning home for the usual maintenance. By September 1943, 250 tons of stores of all sorts had been delivered and were ready for action. The timetable for their use was not yet known: for a while the High Command were still undecided on the next line of advance, through Sicily to Italy or into Sardinia and Corsica. SOE had to be prepared in both areas, to support regular forces as far as possible, or to undertake Deception roles.

Progress had been made despite the earlier repression of any open support for de Gaulle. On our working level authority existed for clandestine cooperation with any who would work sincerely for liberation. There were many, too many, at that time with shortages of supply and transport. All strove well together –

only later, when officially approved, did they put up the Croix de Lorraine.

Once the decision had been taken to attack Italy and 'Brimstone' (the attack on the other islands) postponed, we had still to see what could be done within the limitation of the lack of regular forces to support any risings. In Corsica orders were issued that there must be no open action which would attract enemy reprisals until messages were sent saying that there were regular forces available to come immediately to the rescue. Such availability could not be foreseen until the outcome of the assaults on Italy was clear. It was easy to issue such instructions. In practice it proved impossible to restrain the Resistance in Corsica, or elsewhere, or to draw the line between guerrilla action and a general insurrection. All were determined to help beyond the call of duty and to contribute all in their power to liberate themselves. The braver they were, the harder to restrain. In Corsica this gallantry was rewarded. Elsewhere on occasion it was to prove disastrous as help was too far away.

By June 1943 the final, inevitable, acceptance by the Anglo-Americans of de Gaulle swept away any traces of hesitation. Colonel 'Passy' of the original Free French who had fought on in 1940 under de Gaulle was able to come to Algiers. All agreed on spheres of activity and communications into and out of France. Despite occasional tactical friction, from the summer of 1943 French/American/British joint action in and from the Club des Pins was mainly excellent, improving steadily as the action moved from clandestine to guerrilla and regular warfare.

Corsica was to be the first arena. Giraud, who had retained the command of regular troops when de Gaulle arrived, summoned us to the Palais d'été. He impressed on Dick Hewitt, our Operations Officer, and me the urgent need to make plans for full support by regular forces landing in Corsica 'when the avalanche moves' – showing, by his use of the codeword, that he knew all about the assault on Salerno. We replied that we had no control over regular forces; for these he must apply to Eisenhower. To his warning of the possible disastrous result of any premature rising, we replied that we would do all we could to prevent such an event; indeed, standing instructions to all were to avoid offering reprisal targets to the enemy, both through clandestine and guerrilla action; but nobody could judge how circumstances would restrain their enthusiastic gallantry.

Reporting this discussion to Bedell Smith, we were told that Giraud had been informed that no regular forces nor transport were available for Corsica during or directly after Avalanche; later, circumstances might change, but none knew when and how; and that he and we must do all we could to restrain the Resistance. Further, we were instructed that any action in Corsica must be entirely French, with any support we could give them. As the French themselves had at that time few resources, especially in air and sea craft and radio, the main burden of supply and communications must fall on SOE.

Inevitably in September, when the news of the Italian Armistice was received, the Maquis believed that the Italian forces in Corsica would be helpfully passive if not immediately Allied; there had been some clandestine talks with them. In the event the Italians, while of some assistance, were not as useful as all had hoped. They were tired and confused in the midst of monarchists and neo-Fascists and reprisals. The usual fast and ruthless reaction of the German forces in Corsica further discouraged co-operation. Many are the detailed accounts of the short campaign, ending with a forced withdrawal of all Germans on to the Italian mainland, pursued by the Maquisards to the end.

Some support from North Africa was possible sooner than anticipated due to the early surrender of the Italian fleet, which moved to Malta. Thus two French destroyers were freed to embark the Battaillon de Choc, a Commando-type unit. In its ranks were many determined young men who had recently escaped from France including Jacques de Beaumarchais who later became Ambassador in London. Many others who survived were to hold important post-war offices in France. I trust that they never felt demeaned by having to go to war wearing British battle dress provided, with other equipment, by Massingham in their training camp near the Club.

This joint experience and use of equipment proved invaluable for the training and operations, clandestine and open, in the coming year.

Corsica was, once secured by Allied forces, to become a valuable base for operations, air and clandestine, into Italy and

France. Bedell Smith sent for me and asked me to thank all those at Massingham, American, French and British, for what they had done for the liberation of the first part of fully metropolitan French territory.

'Eisenhower is particularly delighted that as a clandestine organisation, no credit has been claimed by you. The French can have all the credit'.

I enthusiastically concurred, adding that the credit was due to those who had done the fighting, and they, with some other air and sea crews, had all been French.

Two months or so later he sent for me again.

'I thought that we agreed that full credit would be given to the French, and the French alone, for the Corsica operation?'

I agreed.

'Then why this?' he blew up as only he could. He pointed to an American magazine, the cover emblazoned 'How OSS liberated Corsica'.

Donovan had sent out a group of Corsican-Americans who had joined most bravely in the fight. I realised that while such publicity was now embarrassing for us in Algeria, it could well help future support from the White House. So, pointing to my regimental designations, I said,

'Sir, I am British. It is you who do not have an Official Secrets Act'.

For once words, even his few, failed him.

To complete our joint association over Corsica on a more cheerful occasion, a lunch party was held to celebrate Cesari's award of the DSO. By 5.00 pm we had only reached the fish course. My last recollection was of Cesari proposing a toast to the British.

'After all you have done to help liberate our island, we now forgive you for what you did to Napoleon'.

Once the Allies had accepted de Gaulle and the Committee of National Liberation was set up in Algiers, cooperation became easier. A number of new arrivals gave increasing help.

First to come were George and Pauline Vanier; he was the Canadian Ambassador to the French Committee. They were a link between the New World and the Old, between the French and the Anglo-Saxons, and between the Commonwealth and the Rest. One result was the arrival of excellent recruits from the Royal 22nd Regt., the famous 'Van Dooze' of which General Vanier was Colonel. With their wider loyalties they were to play a unique part in coming operations.

A social occasion with Mme Vanier gave some amusement. Tito sent General Velebit to Algiers to represent him. I expected him to be a wild, bomb-happy Communist, a survivor of two years of conflict in the mountains. Mme Vanier agreed to invite him to dinner his first night in Algiers. To 'tame' him two Canadian diplomats sat down to the piano to play at our arrival. Velebit was, of course, one of the most elegant and impeccably cultured men to be found anywhere. Later he became a most effective head of the Economic Council For Europe. We would all laugh at the impact on both parties of his entry into the Vanier's villa, another error of my social judgement.

C.D. Jackson, publisher of *Life Magazine*, joined us as head of Psychological Warfare activities. His professional skill in selection and projecting information was unsurpassed. C.D. proved beyond price in joint projects, of great variety, in raising the morale of our friends in occupied areas and depressing that of the enemy. He was kept as fully informed as was necessary of clandestine capabilities and used his skill in the best use of radio, leaflets and information sent through radio receivers in the field.

Lastly Diana and Duff Cooper came to advise and cheer us. Duff had been appointed Ambassador to the French, to allow Macmillan to concentrate on the numerous political problems arising elsewhere. Duff's deep love of all things French, expressed in impeccable French, was a great asset. He took the closest interest in our work, and at the end was to pay the high compliment of taking a number of our best 'Franco-British' with him to the Embassy in Paris – among them Brooks Richards and Barley Alison. He told me that this group, having grown up with the French Resistance movements, had gained knowledge of French politics and personalities which his professional diplomatic staff could never acquire, talented though they were.

The arrival of the Duff Coopers was spectacular. Accommodation was very scarce in Algiers. Only an Arab-style house could be found at first. This the FANYs did their best to make habitable. I was invited to dinner the night of their arrival, having tried to help with wine and food. Diana and her guest pleaded fatigue and did not come into dinner. When we went into the big living room afterwards, we found two Arab ladies, immaculately cloaked in bedsheets. Diana and Joyce Grenfell gave the most hilarious unscripted performances of their lives.

Duff was to prove among the wisest of our advisers. The heart-breaking years of appeasement had finally forced him to resign from high political office and to attempt to get action taken from outside. His long experience in politics with high ministerial responsibility gave him wide authority. I was told on several occasions that our job was to kill the enemy, and to leave politics alone. Duff would support our plea that some concern with politics was essential if only to ensure that Allied lines of communication and facilities were secured in friendly hands, thus not needing troops to guard them. He could explain, more tactfully than most, the experience in Ethiopia and North Africa, and the need to avoid misunderstandings when liberation came to France. He too saw the advantage in giving due credit to the risks and achievements of the French in occupied areas – experience which neither the British nor the Americans had to endure since they never suffered the ravages of occupation.

October and November 1943 were months of unceasing activity, of operations as well as reorganisation and expansion. I had authority to fly anywhere in the Allied world on Air Force aircraft. This helped greatly since responsibility for all activities in the Western Mediterranean was still mine. These included Massingham in Algiers and the new base in Corsica under Andrew Croft, with his Scandinavian experience. An Advance Post for AFHQ, with 15 Army Group and American Fifth Army, and the Mediterranean Air Forces, had been established at Caserta in a huge building, previously partly occupied by the Italian Air Force. Naval headquarters were in Naples. From this area Munthe was already working into Rome. In Brindisi/Monopoli Holdsworth was setting up Maryland. Half his staff came from Massingham, with others from those wounded in North Africa and some sent by Gubbins from London. A duplicate organisation of all the facilities found at the Club des Pins was shortly in working order.

SOM at Bari, under a regular Major-General, was to become the main supply centre for the whole of the Balkans, and later for Italy, Poland and even France. Hamilton-Hill was pouring supplies of captured equipment into the depots. Lightweight items essential for clandestine operations, and useful for guerrillas also, were beginning to arrive. Most of these were due to American production. All Services were anxious to acquire them. On occasion I had to appeal for the decision of AFHQ on their allocation, since without a reasonable supply, clandestine work would prove ever more hazardous.

I agreed with Gubbins that the time had come for a redefinition of my duties. Massingham and Maryland were operating and expanding excellently under their existing management. All possible help had been given to SOM which was now working well with the political controls still in Cairo. My immediate task, while awaiting the early consolidation of all Allied Commands under one Chief in the Central Mediterranean, was to maintain contact with Caserta, watching developments and keeping the three operational units informed and, where required, directed.

Before final decisions could be made, I was told to go to Cairo for the Mena Conference of the President and Prime Minister, as one of Eisenhower's Allied team, to discuss support from Italy for liberation of the Balkans. Our success on MONKEY and Corsica had given us a certain status. The atmosphere at Mena was different to that at Algiers where we American and British had been working together, 'integrated' for over a year. There were strong Washington and London delegations, meeting in a virtually all-British Headquarters. Never again was such a good 'Allied' atmosphere to be found as Eisenhower had created in the previous twelve months beginning with small, selected staffs. Although later Alexander personally was as inspiring, AFHQ at Caserta became predominantly British/Middle East; while Eisenhower's appointment to the Supreme Allied Expeditionary Force (SHAEF) in early 1944 was too late to give the full 'Allied' feeling, with a largely American command superimposed on a basically British planning staff. Cooperation proved excellent, but not as close as stemmed from the smaller group which set out on 'Torch', the assault on North Africa in November 1942, and found themselves, perhaps to their surprise, a year later in Caserta.

One example forecast coming difficulties. At a meeting to discuss the next priorities for regular operations, a case was put for the Algiers group to consider the military and political advantages of an assault from the heel of Italy into Istria; the Americans had always argued against diversion of effort from the thrust through North-West Europe which they maintained was the quickest way to defeat Germany. While accepting this, it was argued that now, not foreseen six months before, there was a good springboard in Italy, and perhaps the diversion of a relatively small effort towards Central Europe from Istria could help the Russians by threatening German lines of communication, while bringing the chance of further armistices from Germany's unwilling allies in Central Europe. It could also possibly save Central Europe from Russian occupation. While the discussion waxed, an American General said suddenly, 'British imperialism seems as bad as Russian Communism'.

Although it was pointed out that the Algiers group was Anglo-American, and had put up for discussion an agreed suggestion, a decision was referred to the Heads of State. While inspired by Churchill's suggestion of 'striking at the soft underbelly of Europe', a closer examination of the north coast of the Mediterranean showed hard, rather than soft, natural features.

On my return to Algiers, Gubbins told me that he had agreed with the military authorities that I should be promoted to full Colonel, in view of the greatly increased responsibilities in Italy as well as in Algiers. I demurred, saying that my regimental designations had proved much more effective than any rank badges; that I had been made an honorary member of all American General Officers Messes; and had permission to park my motorcycle at the St George Hotel between the Eisenhower and Cunningham cars. Was that not enough? He insisted, and I duly hoisted the red cap. Perhaps the best comment came from an 18-year-old FANY at the Club who said, 'Aren't you too young to be a full Colonel? You must have got into a new racket early on'. Out of the mouths of babes . . .

CHAPTER 16

Europe Well Ablaze: Speedwell, 1944

In early January 1944 Speedwell was born. This was the code name for a small unit, of two FANY coders, a driver and some local staff. Normal Army signals were used, as they linked all SOE units. It moved to Munthe's post in Naples as he was heading for Rome through Anzio, leaving behind the Sunday box at the opera.

In military terms its function was as a Brigade Headquarters to coordinate responsibilities now split between Algiers, Naples and Brindisi; between AFHQ Main and Advanced, 15 Army Group, Mediterranean and Balkan Air Forces. During 1944 I relinquished detailed control over operations except when particular ones came my way. Loyalties were widely stretched, between military and political, Allied and national, between London, Washington, Cairo and the Mediterranean. Each of our many chiefs required primary loyalty to him. With hindsight it seems that the result might have been worse. Certainly in my relationships with so many of the protagonists in later years, few made accusations of subterfuge.

Throughout that year each unit was at fullest stretch, recruiting, training, equipping, briefing, and putting into the field; charged with carrying out, first, constant harassment of the enemy by sabotage while, second, preparing for specific tasks as liberation by regular forces approached – as it was to do over so much of Europe that year. Thanks largely to expanded American production, the availability of aircraft and equipment was only overtaken by the ever-increasing demands from the field. Priorities, military and political, became in consequence even more difficult to decide.

Naples itself was badly damaged, particularly around the railway and port installations which had been used to supply Axis forces in North Africa. Hunger among the civilian population was distressingly acute, since due to the continuing German submarine campaign few ships were available for non-military supply. One midday, hearing noises outside the back door, I went to find women and children fighting over the swill buckets. The weather was bitter. The views across the Bay of Naples to Vesuvius and the Sunday operas were small compensation.

The Mena Conference had settled on the plans for 1944. In the Mediterranean, following the securing of Naples and Foggia, the next aim was Rome and as much of Italy as possible before Allied troops, especially American and French, were due to be diverted in August to a secondary landing in the South of France (Dragoon) to support the main assault into Normany (Overlord) in June.

SOE's task was now primarily to prepare to help these assaults by cutting communications which could bring reinforcements to attack the bridgeheads; secondly, to tie up as many enemy troops as possible, from Greece to Central Europe, to prevent them from joining in the main battles; lastly, to continue the normal pressures of sabotage.

General 'Jumbo' Wilson became Supreme Commander in place of Eisenhower, but was replaced later by Alexander. I had established good relations with the latter at 15 Army Group, and he remained our main connection with the High Command, while the units liaised with the Army Commands.

When Maryland and Force 133 (SOE in Cairo) first arrived in Italy, it was thought best to keep them separate, as the former had still to emerge from the clandestine into the guerrilla stage of Special Operations. It was also important that, whatever the rights and wrongs of SOE's disputes with the military and political authorities in Cairo might be, they should not affect relations with AFHQ. Whiteley, the senior British operational officer there until he left with Eisenhower in January 1944, was insistent that the conflicts he had endured in Cairo must be avoided. AFHQ was an Allied, not just a British, Headquarters. Yet all were aware of the difficulties in Cairo. Thanks to this forewarning, relations between AFHQ and SOM under General Stawell, a friend of Alexander's, and the other operational units were constructive and friendly.

My responsibility was to keep all informed of future plans, to suggest ways SOE might contribute and then feed back to the operational units agreed projects. At the same time it was necessary to remind decision-makers that adequate supply and early notice were necessary; it was doubly difficult to prepare in occupied territory.

Political problems were often overlooked by the military. The need to consider the political feelings in liberated areas has already been described. The problem arose over diverting resources, especially air sorties, from immediate targets in the Mediterranean theatre of operations to areas outside their responsibility, especially to Poland. This seems obvious today in the modern world of War Colleges. It was not always so clear in 1944. Thus the range of my limited powers of persuasion was considerable. Much time was spent on higher policy, with the help of British and American Political Advisers. From time to time I was called in to take on some irregular action for which, like MONKEY, no existing regular unit or individual seemed qualified, or ungentlemanly enough.

Later, it was estimated that the affairs of some seventeen European countries became of greater or lesser concern to Speedwell. The year was one of intense activity, during which the efforts of the previous four years were to produce their widest effect. By the summer of 1944 most of Europe was indeed 'Ablaze'.

To attempt to describe the events of this year chronologically would create confusion. The method must be to take each country separately, although on occasion events overlapped.

Massingham: France

France must be the first, our Ally from 1939. Resistance there had been continuous in the field although our linking up with it from outside had taken time. With the prospect of liberation an early reality came the great upsurge of Resistance. The freeing of North Africa and of Corsica had coincided with the establishment of independent French Special Services in Algiers, once the Committee of National Liberation had been accepted there with de Gaulle at its Head. Réné Massigli as Foreign Minister (he had come out of France by Lysander) and Jacques Soustelle as head of the Special Service, became good allies then and thereafter. Now based on French metropolitan soil, they felt their hands and heads clearer for the forthcoming operations, clandestine and regular. There were to be disputes but they were never insoluble. They agreed with the High Command that all possible steps be taken to ensure that there would be the minimum of conflict on the lines of communication as Allied forces advanced across France to final victory in Germany. This coincided with the general wish of the French not to replace one foreign totalitarian system with another, and so keep Russian – and for other reasons Anglo-Saxon – influence to the minimum. Willie Widmer took up residence at the Club as the permanent French representative to ensure that supply into the field kept to these rules. He was to work unremittingly for Anglo-French accord until his tragic death twenty-five years later.

Massingham itself had been greatly expanded under Anstey and Brooks Richards. The OSS had also produced massive additions of equipment and personnel to supplement the training and parachute facilities. The Operational Groups (OGs) were to play a most effective part in final liberation. Their radio links through Massingham were vital. This combination of French/American/British up to and in support of Dragoon, a French/American landing, was perhaps the best Allied Special Service achievement of all.

It can only be regretted now that no records of these organisations and events survive. From 1940 it had been said 'the less the paper, the more the action'; that by the normal rules of a Secret Service, nothing would ever be written by us or about us; and that as all Intelligence was passed to SIS they would keep it safe. In Professor Foot's *SOE in France*, a footnote refers to my taking command in January 1943. That was all. No British Chiefs of Staff directive to a clandestine AFHQ unit seems to have been issued, while my terms of reference in 1943 were not left with me. By standing orders, and sensible self-protection as our base was on a deserted seashore, records were minimal and destroyed as soon as they were no longer of immediate use. After France was liberated, the Club des Pins was closed down. A FANY said to me that as she saw the last paper curl up in flames she realised that with it went the only record of two years of great interest and effort. It must be hoped that one day a senior Massingham officer will find time to record his or her memories.

For a number of FANYs and other girls bore a great part of the burden of constant attention to meticulous detail on which so many lives depended; so the loss of an aircraft or the damage to a *reseau* in the field were felt personally. This was to add to emotional stress but ensured even greater carefulness.

Constant criticism came from the field about the delays, shortages, and bad packing of radios and containers. While Algiers had many who had come from France, those still in the field did not realise the difficulties at the Club. To the original group of weekend villas had been added, with considerable American help, huts for storage and packing. They bore no resemblance to the facilities available in Britain, located in spacious stately homes. In all the circumstances results were beyond reasonable expectations – but could not always be thus regarded when things went wrong in the field. Despite this, M.R.D. Foot in *SOE in France* (page 473) states that of the air operations mounted from Algiers compared to the UK, 1,910 sorties went from Algiers out of a total of 10,485; taking 2,074 tons out of a total of 10,485; with 599 agents dropped out of a total of 1,784. (It is not clear whether this included the 250 tons of stores put into Corsica).

This shows not only the scale of French willingness to face appalling dangers if caught, but the dedication of the flying and ground staff. The latter had to organise, often at short notice due to changes in the weather, the correct containers and supplies and radios to go with each party. Most of the ground staff were girls since most of the young men, and some of the girls, had gone into the field. That memorial on the church in Wilton Crescent records some of those who met their ends in indescribable circumstances in concentration camps.

By the spring of 1944 French regular forces in North Africa were substantial. Pauline Vanier had brought me together with General Leclerc, her cousin. Fresh from his triumphs in the southern desert, he could have continued his close association with all the irregular groups, but he was required to lead his division in Overlord and to be the first into Paris. In his place came de Lattre de Tassigny, later a Marshal of France, a born leader if there ever was one. He had tried to defend the non-Occupied Zone of France when the Germans moved in in November 1942, and for his pains had been put in prison. SOE had helped in his escape. Gubbins took me to meet him in Algiers, and from then until I said goodbye in Strasbourg in 1945, he was always accessible to my requests.

Control was divided between Massingham (on behalf of AFHQ and later of the Dragoon planners) on one side, and the French military and political authorities on the other. There was considerable sympathy for the latter. Short-term military and long-term political aims could not always be the same. Anstey and Brooks Richards did wonders in reconciling them. *Ordres de Mission* and signals, checked by agreement, were sometimes reduplicated by unchecked messages. Without meticulous cross-checking, disasters to precious lives could result. For example, as noted on page 392 of *SOE in France*, the order calling out the Resistance in the Vercors did not specify exactly whether *Le Jour J* denoted the landings in Normandy or at St. Tropez ten weeks later. In consequence the rising was premature and led to one of the great disasters of the Resistance.

On 6 June Overlord, the assault on Normandy, was successfully mounted. Within a week a sudden storm threatened sea communications. A second wave of attacks by Resistance groups on enemy road and rail links was urgently called for, to slow down the enemy concentration against the bridgehead until it was more firmly established. This second wave, like the first, ranged from the Ljubljana Gap in Northern Yugoslavia throughout France and across the Low Countries and Denmark to the train ferries in Norway. Later, senior officers were to pay tribute, at least in private, to this contribution at an awkward moment.

In August came the climax of Massingham's twenty-one months of preparation. Part of the assault was mounted from Naples where de Lattre had his headquarters. The plan was to land at St Tropez and move west to capture the ports of Toulon and Marseilles and move up the Rhône valley to Lyons, to be liberated by October. The extensive demolitions prepared by the Germans in the two ports would, if touched off, restrict full use of them until the spring of 1945; only then could they be used to supply the southern front in north-east France. The French

Resistance, however, withdrew the detonators by brave clandestine actions and thereby frustrated all but minor demolitions.

Meanwhile a Lysander had gone from Corsica to Orange to bring out Colonel 'Josef' (one of the two Zeller brothers), taking Willie Widmer in. In a quick conference on the airfield, the two agreed that the French Forces of the Interior (FFI) could and would capture and patrol the Route Napoleon and thereby open the quickest line of advance to cut off the German forces in the Rhône valley.

At dinner that evening with de Lattre in Naples, I heard Col. Josef say 'As soon as I hear you have landed, I am going to blow every bridge in the south of France'.

'Please don't do that as I will have to repair them all' said the French Chief Engineer. It was Henri, the other Zeller brother. Col. Josef also reported that while he expected substantial groups to join him to help the assault, there was one 'Roger' believed to be British who had achieved, in the mountains further east, a much larger following through sheer force of his personality. This was Francis Cammaerts DSO.

In command of the assault landings was General Sandy Patch, the hero of Guadacanal. His experienced American forces were to make sure of the foothold, coordinated with air and sea bombardment. De Lattre's French forces would then provide the main part of the thrust north and west. In the event the prevention of demolitions in the ports, the move over the Route Napoleon and the weakening of the Germans in the whole south-east allowed General Devers' Army Group to reach the Belfort Gap by October – the date set to reach Lyons. In addition fifteen divisions were being supplied through the Mediterranean rather than over the Normandy beaches. Little credit has appeared for this mainly French contribution, with American help.

Gubbins summoned me to Paris at this time, to discuss the Warsaw Rising which was at its height. On the way I went to Avignon, to meet some of our fieldworkers, and assess immediate needs. There were always numberless points of concern at such a time of fast movement, forwards or backwards. Many were of the ungentlemanly warfare type unsuitable for officers and gentlemen.

In Avignon one such problem required instant attention. The

Army Command sent for the senior SOE officer; 'Take a car and interpreter and sort out what you will find about fifty miles west'.

On getting out of the staff car the officer walked round the corner of a chateau to find what appeared to be a complete German battalion drawn up. While the interpreter spoke, the British officer controlled his emotions at being alone, facing the fully armed enemy before him.

'We are Vlassov's Army' came the explanation. 'To save our lives, we joined the German Army. As soon as we heard that the Allies had landed nearby, we shot all our German officers. Before you say anything else, we want a complete assurance that under no circumstances at all will we ever be handed back to the Russians. Unless that understanding is given here, at once, we are going to shoot ourselves'.

The officer, fearing that perhaps he might be included in the slaughter, gave the assurance in the name of every General and politician he could remember. Within forty-eight hours the unit was on its way to North Africa proudly wearing the képis of the French Foreign Legion.

Soon afterwards it was reported that this occurrence had come to the attention of the Russian authorities in France and that they were threatening action against Allied prisoners-of-war unless all theirs were handed back promptly. This threat had, for good reasons, to be accepted. The same threat against Allied prisoners of war was soon to be used by the Nazis when in 1945 they warned against any attempt to rescue concentration camps. Criticism of Allied policy in handing back reluctant Russians arose on the publication of records released thirty years after the events. This criticism might be more validly levelled at the failure to change the policy once all Allied prisoners had been returned by mid-1945.

In Paris I was told to escort a senior French Security Officer who, in 1940, had remained at his post, in touch with the Americans and British until liberation. In 1940 he had destroyed all records of foreign, especially Jewish, residents who might have been of interest to the Germans. Despite having at times to appear to collaborate with the Nazis, he had been ready to stay and carry out most valuable work for France and her Allies. He knew he would risk some misunderstanding on liberation. The easiest way out was for him now to leave France. There were several others faced with this same appalling dilemma, in France and other occupied countries.

In Paris Gubbins was coordinating the part SOE could play in the link-up between the Overlord and Dragoon forces, now converging in north-east France. Huge areas of France were still occupied by German troops, and the Resistance was isolating them and trying to prevent them from getting back to Germany. This function was to play an inestimable part in freeing Allied regular troops, and in safeguarding the lines of communication.

My main discussions with Gubbins had been about what more we could do to supply our brave, original allies, the Poles in Warsaw. We both had personal links with Poland and felt powerless, despite wholehearted support from all at the High Commands. Back in Naples this was to be my priority for the next few weeks. It perhaps stopped me from giving fuller attention to other 'irregular' decisions which came to my notice.

One concerned Christine Granville, whose initiative and courage has been saluted in many a book. After unsurpassed service in Central Europe from 1939–41 she had escaped to Cairo. In 1944 she was sent to Massingham where it was decided that her courage was best restrained until nearer the time of liberation. In France she joined 'Roger', whom I have already mentioned. Francis Cammaerts, DSO, one of the fighting academics in SOE, had an unequalled record of achievement and courage. Leading a charmed life, at the very end he was caught. The story of how Christine organised his escape has been told before. Walking into the office of the Gestapo chief, she promised him amnesty for his misdeeds in the name of every one whose name she could remember, including mine. Cammaerts was released and all three made their way to our side. The first I knew of all this was when Christine came into my office in Naples and told me the story. I congratulated her most warmly on her initiative, but said that as the Gestapo chief was one of those most wanted by the Allies, I could not honour her grant of amnesty. His help would, of course, be taken into consideration at his trial. Christine then, understandably, blew up. I told her that I would try to think out another way. Later I told her that I would put the man back into France; give him forty-eight hours start, and then . . . ; that I believed this was his best chance and fairest to all . . . and that he concurred. She was not mollified. Leaving the man under guard, I went out to Caserta. Returning well after midnight, I was told that 'Higher Authority' had arrived, had made enquiries, and had ordered that the man be handed over to the French without delay. With so many other events needing most urgent attention there was nothing else I could do. Christine never forgave me, and would mention my dishonour whenever we met in later years, up to the time that she was murdered. It was only years later that I found out that the Gestapo chief had not been placed in French hands but sent to Cairo from whence, by some quirk, he had made his way home, a free man. Perhaps Christine knows now that her courageous initiative proved honourable, though not thanks to me. Perhaps 'Higher Authority' was right, in the long run. He had not been personally concerned in the horrors of clandestine action before 1944, and his judgement was the clearer for it.

In October I made my rounds of farewell visits, agreeing to meet next in Prague or Vienna or Budapest. The base at the Club des Pins was now non-operational; I was not to see it again until thirty-two years later when it had become a great holiday resort with our original villas, somewhat dated, in the midst. There was no sign of the great part, I claim, that it had played in one aspect of the worldwide struggle for freedom. My wife, who had not seen it before, stood while I recalled the activities, and the personalities who had passed through my villa and the other areas. Even the great Domaine de la Trappe, with the Bourgeaud eighteenth-century estate around it, had gone, and with it the production of food, wine and perfume which had graced it and delighted so many.

I returned to Avignon where Brooks Richards had called all our field workers to celebrate, and in many cases to meet for the first time. Our base workers were there in force also, on their way home. Some had parachuted in at the last moment against all orders. I had received a signal at Speedwell from an eighteen-year old FANY, 'Do join us' (the rest garbled).

Before leaving I issued an order that they must all be out of France as soon as reasonable. Gubbins had agreed to this, with regret, since in some cases it meant leaving French colleagues with their disagreements with the new authorities unresolved. As described, there had from 1940 always been a strong political base to Resistance. While far the greater number were patriotic and Gaullist, there was still that small but powerful group of pro-Russian Marxists, who had been clandestinely organised before 1939. Their aim to make France into a Communist state after liberation was one which we had had no intention of abetting, and we had striven through the French authorities in London and Algiers to ensure that supplies went to those who intended to set up a democratic system. All indications at base and in the field were that those who worked best for liberation were democratically inclined. This was to be proved in the later years I was to spend in international politics. In late 1944 the democrats were clearly in charge. There was still much to be done, but we must not get mixed up in the inevitable aftermath of wartime collaboration. A few particularly controversial individuals were taken away until anger simmered down; the acceptable Brooks Richards, Barley Alison and half a dozen others went to the Paris Embassy. I drove on to Lyons, to help liberate the Côte d'Or – the Burgundy country with its heaven-given gifts to mankind's enjoyment. When I entered Lyons, my red cap was mistaken for a Russian one, with mixed reactions, mostly unfavourable. A quick change and then a notice proclaimed *Les Marx Fréres 'Une Nuit à L'Opera': Où sont . . .?* When we got to the cinema the lights were turned up and 'God Save the King' played. We relaxed at last.

At my farewell to General Devers at Army Group, I found myself belatedly involved in taking a message to de Lattre, my final stop. The French had thrust ahead of the Army plan to capture Strasbourg. Army Group anxiety became intense that Allied forces might need to be diverted to beat off a possible German counter-attack which could cut off the French. By the time I arrived the crisis had eased, but there remained the need to try to persuade the French of the need for closer cooperation. I found it impossible to interpret fully the views of each side to the other. I tried but scarcely carried persuasion. 'Strasbourg' is a subject of emotion, not of logic.

Lines of Communication

Part of Massingham's responsibility was the final reception of those who escaped from Occupied Europe – from Denmark and the Low Countries and even Poland, and, of course, from France. As much of the work of organising these lines lay through neutral countries, little has been written about them beyond the experiences of some who used them with greater or lesser hardship. MI9 had been an initiative of MIR in 1940. Its ramifications and successes were to be Europe-wide. The bravery of those many who worked on the lines in occupied lands was beyond praise, with the daily chance of a double agent being passed down the line and every helper later caught, to meet a fearful death.

SOE, through F Section, had its own escape lines besides MI9; and later in areas further east SOE was to bring back many including shot-down air-crew.

Although immediate danger was lifted, hardship in Spain under pro-Axis officials was acute and prolonged. The aim of our organisations was to prevent escapers from being put in camps of which Miranda was the most notorious. If these could be avoided, final destinations in Portugal, where the reception was more friendly, or Gibraltar were soon reached. It is difficult to recall today the circumstances of 1940 when almost all the world expected Britain to accept the reality of apparent defeat. Through self-interest and sentiment many in the Iberian peninsula were overawed by fear as well as by the presence of ruthless groups of Axis agents. The devoted and often dangerous efforts of British staff in Madrid, Lisbon Gibraltar and other points slowly built up counter-organisations. There were still a number of anti-Franco groups to help. It must remain a matter for speculation whether, had the anti-Franco forces won in 1939, the left wing government would have been able and willing to withstand Russian pressure to collaborate with the Nazis. For two and a half years the dangers were acute; in particular, when Torch arrived to liberate North Africa, there was a threat of German attack on its rear, against Gibraltar as a vital air-base. SOE had plans to counter this, for which the many Spanish refugees in North Africa were willing volunteers, to be led by some SOE members who had fought on either side during the Spanish Civil War.

By 1943 this threat had evaporated. Many extra lines were soon in operation, including ones direct from France, from beaches then deserted but now crowded holiday resorts. These needed constant checking as some were in enemy hands. Once Allied victory was assured, the escapers were sent more easily through Spain and with the defeat of Italy, German influence in the peninsula was lessened.

A decade later I was to answer questions in Parliament, defending some Gibraltar sailors against imprisonment in Spain for smuggling tobacco. I waxed most indignant. Subsequently I was told that they had been SOE's best ferry service in the war.

The Base for Special Operations Mediterranean (SOM)

From September 1943 onwards, Holdsworth, Hewitt and other experienced workers from Massingham had been setting up their base in Monopoli while beginning to prepare for action in central and northern Italy. Demands were made on them for help by other special services. Never were resources so strained, but Maryland coped. Cairo sent a strong team as described. I was told by senior British officers that I would be held responsible for the initial operation of this base on the lines that had proved effective in Algiers. By early 1944 much of the political and clandestine confusion had been sorted out. SOM was to give paramilitary supply to the guerrilla forces of Balkan Resistance striving to contain the maximum number of German troops, having had success in disarming and disposing of many Italian occupation units.

I had, of course, the advantage of being an Allied officer whereas until American/Russian agreement was reached in December 1943 over the part to be taken by the USA in the Balkans, the OSS, without my knowing it, was restricted. That did not curtail better understanding with the air and naval high commands, American and British. Air Chief Marshal Sir John Slessor had been a friend from Oxford Air Squadron days. The Chief of Mediterranean Air Forces, General Ira Eaker, always gave full support. Air Marshal Elliott was Chief of Balkan Air Force. Everyone realised the value of mutual assistance in bringing back aircrews shot down on operations and in indicating targets to ensure greater accuracy, since too many civilians had been killed. Later Rebeccas, the beacons invented to guide aircraft for secret drops, were used, being placed by Resistance groups to guide bombers.

It became clear that a plastic explosive charge placed accurately by a saboteur could obviate aircraft and civilian losses. The achievement of the Norwegian Resistance in thus destroying the German heavy water plant at Rjukan was by now known to the High Command.

The Air Headquarters at Caserta were delightful to visit. The American Fifth Army had lived a Spartan life under canvas. Once when visiting Saltzman, I had put on my cap and saluted Gruenther as taught at Windsor. Touching the tent top with my flourish, the rain poured in. Thereafter I was forbidden by the General, with characteristic bonhomie, to salute at all. When the Air Forces moved in they brought huts and many amenities which led to the site being known to the other Services as The Silver Foxhole.

Operations by sea were centralised in Naples, Algiers and Brindisi. Thus SOE's operations could be controlled at these three points. Holdsworth's and Brooks Richards' naval decorations gave them fully accepted status. A rumour reached us that Admiral 'A.B.C.' Cunningham never really forgave SOE for having small ships, entitled as a last resort to fly the White Ensign, which were not fully under his command. Certainly in the Central areas, and the Adriatic with Cmdr. Morgan Giles, operations went on without hindrance.

The High Command understood that SOE had responsibilities such as Poland which were not within the Mediterranean theatre. They saw that action there was essential chiefly to harass enemy lines to the Russian front. Beyond these military objectives lay political aims; to encourage European countries to make a substantial contribution to their own liberation, with the satisfaction of thus participating in victory; and to give them the best chance to set up freely-chosen governments, of a less authoritarian nature than before 1939. It would clearly take some time, apart from any Russian imperialist intervention, to move from these pre-war forms to reasonably stable democracies. Aided by the support from outside, France, Italy, Greece and, lastly, Austria, were to achieve their freedom.

The major base was thus well organised in southern Italy as the springboard for the final phases of hostilities. The High Command had acknowledged realities of special relations. Political supervision was accepted while SOE retained operational responsibility. Supply, transport and signals were now part of the main Allied plans.

Italy and Maryland

Speedwell had taken over Munthe's post in Naples when he moved forward to Anzio. Being near Caserta with several Headquarters located there, the numerous ideas and personnel attracted to it could be sent to Maryland. An avowed republican, Count Sforza was the centre of an embryo government in opposition to Badoglio. He had to be warned that for the time being all efforts must be aimed at clearing Italy of the Germans; that there were substantial groups rallying round the King for operations in north Italy; and that similar use had been made of Darlan until the moment came for a change. It was for the High Command to decide the timing. Macmillan has described the negotiations which saved the monarchy until after the end of the war. In retrospect it is a pity that more effort was not put into encouraging democratic political parties, but all were stretched to the limit with current action. Togliatti, a Communist refugee in Russia, was brought back at Stalin's insistence. He, too, was warned that full support for the expulsion of the enemy was the only immediate task; if he was found 'playing politics', he would have to go. He at least had an idea of what that meant.

A typical recruit was Manfred Czernin, from a famous Hungarian family and with a British mother. Awarded two DFCs in Fighter Command, he was to win even higher honours in northern Italy. Max Salvadori, having delivered his 'Elderlies' safely in Naples, had proceeded to Maryland and on into North Italy.

Accompanied by one of Amadeo d'Aosta's officers from Kenya, I called on his mother at the Royal Palace at Capo di Monte in Naples. My welcome was not exactly cordial, as she believed, without any justification, that her son's death had been in part due to neglect by his captors. I shall always hope that I succeeded in conveying to her the genuine respect that all had felt for her son, and our regret that he had not survived to help at this critical time in Italy.

While the front line was stabilising just short of Cassino, it was possible to pass through the lines by night. Gerald Templer, commanding 56 Division, was helpful. I had, however, to remonstrate with Signora Lussu, Salvadori's sister. Having crossed the lines one dismal night, she walked into Naples as if she had just come from a stroll down the Via Condotti. It cheered us all to see such an impeccably dressed lady, but it was something of a give-away.

Templer had taken great interest in our work in Algiers. He might have made greater use of special operations had not an unfortunate accident, involving my Regiment, removed him. Passing a company truck on his way to the frontline, the truck hit a mine and deposited the contents on his head, breaking his neck but not severing the spinal cord. It seems agreed that the contents involved a piano, but not a bucket of ice and champagne as part of the Regimental front-line equipment. Hearing of the disaster, I called on him in hospital the next day. Seeing my regimental designations, he let out such a sustained volume of invective that I saluted, saying 'I am so glad to find there is nothing fundamentally wrong', and sent two FANYs with suitable flowers the next day. His command post on the Garigliano River, from which he could supervise the Scots Guards duck shoot, had been hospitable to special operations, and gave him practical experience which, he told me, was to prove useful subsequently in Europe and Malaya.

Another episode occurred in early 1944. I have been unable to find any who will admit responsibility for it. I only heard about it when reaching Rome, which had been declared an Open City, not to be bombed. US Air Forces had bombed the marshalling yards near the City, and as recently as 14 March the RAF had attacked them as they were being used to supply the Anzio beachhead. Meantime, Gayda, the virulent anti-Allied Fascist editor, was continuing his verbal attacks from his house down the Via Nomentana. One day, despite the veto, a single Allied aircraft dropped a bomb exactly on the house, destroying it and nothing else – a splendid act of precision bombing. To the delight of the cynical Romans, Gayda was taking an English lesson at the moment of his death.

The beachhead at Anzio was under continuous shell fire for five months. This deprived us at a critical stage of two exceptional men: Michael Gubbins, our General's son, was killed and Munthe so seriously wounded that he was out of action for the duration of the war. During their time in Anzio, I flew in to consult them. These visits brought home to me the strange contrasts of war – the noise of battle at the front, followed by a meeting at Caserta and after dinner an opera in the charming small theatre in the Palace.

Came the day when Rome was liberated. American forces, against the orders of AFHQ, turned left from Anzio to enter Rome instead of turning right to capture enemy forces retreating to the north. How long this delayed the clearing of Italy must be left to military historians to judge. Maryland already had a number of adherents in Rome, under command of Charles Mackintosh who had replaced Munthe. His experience and mine from Central Europe caused us to requisition facilities beyond normal military requirements. He had obtained a delectable location in an archeological school. The first night was spent there, but the morning revealed a Tiger tank not far away, and the news that the school belonged to a neutral country. So retreat was sounded to the Final Ditch, the Bridal Suite in the Eden Hotel. As usual we had brought our food; ordered and paid cash for our drink – and asked the band to play 'Lilli Marlene'. Overcoming their early hesitancy, they admitted that only forty-eight hours before they had been playing the same tune for the Germans.

Later a fine house belonging to a notorious neo-Fascist was taken over. From this could be organised many activities concerning Italy and countries beyond, especially those with a Roman Catholic connection. I trust I am not out of order in revealing how, as a Protestant, I was honoured with two audiences with the Pope. One was devoted primarily to the Poles, then coming under their heaviest tribulation, in which their faith never wavered. Discussions were privileged in both senses. I can only say that I gained some idea of the torment caused to His Holiness during the years of Hitler's and Mussolini's domination. For those without full knowledge of the facts and without responsibility, it is easy to criticise later. The choice often lay between two courses of action, each significantly wrong.

An immediate task was to visit the Quirinale to fetch Dick Mallaby's radio sets and other equipment. The resident staff were most accommodating. During this chaotic period we could have removed anything, even the entire Italian archives, had there been enough transport. Between Fascists and anti-Fascists, monarchists and anti-monarchists, Communists and democrats, authority was difficult for the ordinary bureaucrat to perceive.

Among the discoveries in the Quirinale was a room full of what appeared to be the contents of the British Embassy Chancery from 1930 to 1940. The story has been told before. I will only say that I trust our records are now safeguarded from external penetration of the kind which allowed locally recruited staff to be blackmailed into obtaining keys and letting outsiders enter to copy records. Some time later, at lunch at the British Embassy, a diplomat who had served there during the pre-war years pointed out the Italian servant who had betrayed his trust – he had come back as if nothing had occurred.

From the time when the Allies landed in Sicily, Leonard Woolley, the discoverer of Ur of the Chaldees, had been attached to SOE. Our orders were to help him to locate and safeguard treasures which the enemy might be trying to destroy or remove. Our workers in still occupied areas might be able to assist. First in Sicily it was reported that sixteen truckloads of fourth-century manuscripts, sent from Palermo to the monastery at Bronte, had never arrived. In Naples it was reported that the Germans had loaded much of the contents of the music museum on to trucks – and set fire to the rest. The full record of Italian losses will probably never be known, from world-famous paintings to the many centuries-old pictures, perhaps not of the highest quality, but part of their heritage, taken from churches. On the advance north the price that Italy was paying for her years of Fascism was clear to all. Italy's empire had always been a drain on her resources, which could have been better used in southern Italy. Italy was still being 'raked by war' in Churchill's phrase. Industry and communications were being destroyed, in the seemingly endless uphill-downhill advance northwards. Despite all efforts, much was irretrievably damaged, a loss to mankind and not only to the Italians.

Many of the finest pictures from all over Italy had been harboured in the Vatican. Before allowing them to be returned to their owners, an exhibition was organised in aid of the Red Cross, in Mussolini's office in the Mappa di Mundo Room in the Palazzo di Venezia – a huge room with a slippery mosaic floor designed to destabilise any visitor. For the first time I was able to look out of the window from which I had watched the Duce harangue the mob a decade earlier.

My final foray on the western side of Italy was to Florence. The Germans were making a stand there. All bridges were destroyed across the River Arno. Only the Ponte Vecchio stood unharmed. Across it the Partisans had a telephone line to Mackintosh. Under threat from the Germans to destroy the bridge unless the line was removed, Mackintosh unhappily complied.

On the east side of Italy Maryland had soon moved into full production. The operations, supply, training and signal sections were under experienced leaders. To complement the OSS parachute training unit at Massingham, Ray Wooler came out from Britain. He was an expert parachute trainer, experimenting with many new ideas and always making the first jump with them himself. Several times he was within a few feet of disaster. In the next eighteen months this unit became perhaps the largest ever to be deployed in operations of all kinds, clandestine and open.

The front line had stabilised across the middle of Italy, with only slow advances until the spring. The early flood of prisoners-of-war and refugees had fallen to a trickle. Recruiting was possible from the many anti-Fascists and anti-Communists who had made their way south, to help clear Italian soil from Neo-Fascism/Nazism. Beyond that they did not look, except to avoid the establishment of another form of totalitarian tyranny in the form of Communism. They were mostly young, hoping for a future constitutional monarchy with a democratically elected government. The King himself was, of course, tainted by long association with Mussolini. Badoglio as head of the administration was particularly unacceptable to many. But they provided a rallying point as the flow of recruits showed. After training, these soldiers were dropped into north Italy, bravely to harass enemy lines of communication and targets set by the Allied armies. These tasks they carried out as the Italian contribution to the Allied cause.

Little has been written about these two significant years of Italian national revival, from 1943 to 1945. The brave men, many of whom Maryland organised, fought under somewhat discredited banners owing to the unpopularity of the top leadership. The post-war collapse of the monarchy carried away with it much of the undoubted contribution to victory made by these patriotic non-Communists. Had Amadeo Di Savoia lived, the story of the monarchy, with its potential for unifying the still diverse parts of Italy, might have ended differently.

SOE had, of course, been linked with governments-in-exile since 1939. MONKEY had given Maryland the same standing of unofficial responsibility. This led to some difficulties with OSS. As told, I had accepted personally the need for Donovan to organise separate operations. In Massingham this still allowed excellent cooperation in the paramilitary phase, a joint endeavour under Anglo-American command. In Italian operations this association was not so productive. Officially the Eisenhower order to combine one hundred percent remained in being. In practice a virtually autonomous organisation took the field from Sicily onwards. It contained many brave and effective men, with very substantial funds. Individuals would often work in detail with SOE. Their main thrust was to comprise *coup de main* parties infiltrated behind the lines for tactical support of military advances, especially of American Fifth Army aimed at Naples and Rome.

Some anti-monarchist views were clearly reflected in OSS in Italy. A search for republicans took Count Sforza and the philosopher Croce into their orbit, despite the latter's rescue from behind enemy lines by Munthe and Salvadori during the Salerno battle. The High Command, with the experience of Darlan behind them, had issued orders that full support must be given to the King and Badoglio until the military and political positions stabilised; but implied that later there would be a change.

This change came in mid-1944, as Macmillan has recounted. Meanwhile OSS went ahead in linking up with many different groups, one officer citing to me how Massingham had built up Gaullist groups in North Africa early in 1943 before such links were officially authorised. It would have been better had the senior American political officers been kept as fully informed as were the British. A summons from Murphy, or Alexander, or Kirk, the American Ambassador in Rome, would find me as short of information on OSS activities as they were. Yet I was officially held responsible for action beyond the tactical support of the Armies. It sometimes proved almost impossible to keep a properly united front, sympathising as I did with the short-term aims of the High Command while hoping that OSS longer-term plans would help the Alliance.

Few attempts were made to build up in Italy democratic party organisations, even after the liberation of Rome where a number of future Italian leaders had been found. The Allies were divided, monarchists and anti-monarchists. Existing Communist organisations succeeded, as elsewhere, in dubbing many right-wing anti-Communists as Fascist or neo-Fascist. One Vatican official confided that, in his opinion, only 30% of voters would be influenced by Papal authority. By design or under pressure of other duties, or even through ignorance of European political parties, little was done by Allied authorities to rebuild democratic organisations. Perhaps in the event this was as well. Outside interference would have been resented; while the disparities between the north and south of Italy, united less than a century earlier, have steadily diminished under the resilience of the Italian character. It must be hoped that a Maryland officer will record its successes which, without doubt, nurtured a substantial Italian contribution to Allied victory. Mackintosh has written of the operations on the west of Italy; but the tale of the north is still untold.

Force 139: Poland and Central Europe

Directly the air base at Brindisi was secured, Henry Threlfall came out to command the SOE unit, Force 139, charged with support of the Poles and Czechs, Hungarians and Austrians. His responsibility was daunting, but carried out with selfless application and, as far as circumstances were to allow, with success.

By early 1944 the Russians were advancing steadily from the east towards Poland and Central Europe. The Allies were continuing to engage large Axis land forces in Italy. In August experienced Allied divisions were to be diverted from Italy for the thrust through France to Berlin. No attempt was to be made to send regular forces through the not-so-soft underbelly of Europe through Istria towards Central Europe. Poland and its neighbours were thus to be left open to 'liberation' by Russian armies. They could only be saved if the landings in Normandy were followed by a rapid advance to the East. Had the airborne assault at Arnhem, in which the Polish Brigade took such an heroic part, succeeded, this might have been achieved. If any substantial senior German military group, who were later to claim some credit for the July 1944 'plot', had had the real national interests at heart and cooperated to overthrow Hitler in September 1944, the history of Europe and the world would have been different. Their political pusillanimity has never been adequately explained – thus they must be condemned to bear responsibility for the betrayal of so much of German and Central European civilisation.

Britain's entry into the conflict, in September 1939, had been to sustain Poland. Gubbins had been on the Military Mission, headed by General Carton de Wiart, throughout the gallant but doomed campaign later that month. Inspired by my time in Poland in August 1939, and by my experience of the Poles' supreme Catholic faith, I had done what little I could to aid their reorganisation in Britain and the Middle East after the Battle of France. I had been concerned with the first full Polish air sorties to Occupied Poland in February 1942. There was British dedication to the liberation of a free Poland – the only country, together with the Commonwealth, which fought in World War II from beginning to the end, without sign of collaboration.

On our first arrival in the Mediterranean little was at hand to help the Poles. Only when the airfields in Tunisia, and later in Italy, were secured would it be easier to despatch planes to Poland from that area rather than from Britain.

Meanwhile the disaster of the death of General Sikorski had to be repaired. His end in an air crash at Gibraltar in July 1943 had taken with him the hopes, vain in the opinion of many, that he above all might be able to reach some political agreement with the Russians. His loss was regarded, particularly by Churchill, as the greatest tragedy. Later suggestions that this air crash was organised by some in the Allied camp are monstrous. All who recognised the interests of Poland and freedom and peace would have done their utmost to save Sikorski.

Years later I met a colleague from the Oxford Air Squadron

days who had crashed at Al Adem in Egypt for what seemed to be the same reason. To save time, mail bags were sometimes thrown into the aircraft through the holes housing the nose wheel. In his case, one bag had escaped notice and jammed the wheel and controls when retracted. Luckily for him, the crash was on land and he survived.

Had there been a plan to remove Sikorski it could clearly have been done by other methods without the loss of so many companions.

Later in the year General Sosnkowski, his successor, came to Algiers. As the local representative of the Polish action groups, I accompanied him on his visit to Eisenhower, as I had Sikorski. Judging by their bearing during these visits, I formed the opinion that neither by record, by personality nor by inspiration was the change for the better. On a visit with Sosnkowski to the Vatican a year later, I sensed that, like many others, he had grown with the top responsibility, but he lacked enough time to establish himself as fully as Sikorski.

The Poles had always been a favoured group in the Alliance. With centuries of clandestine action behind them they had educated the rest of us. They were largely self-contained, with training, codes, and direction. They needed supply – radio, delay fuses, and above all, air transport. They had authority from London to make tactical use of any personnel and equipment available in the Mediterranean. Their clandestine Home Army was said to number 300,000. Despite the murder of thousands of their officers at Katyn by the Russians, they never ceased to run great risks, sabotaging German lines of communication while waiting for the day when they could rise, to free Warsaw and as much of their beloved country as possible before the Russians, their oppressors from time immemorial, could move in to replace their other traditional foe, the Germans.

The only account, short though it is, of clandestine British/Polish cooperation is given by Jozef Garlinski in *Poland, SOE and the Allies*. The story it tells of the relatively small amount of real help given is humiliating. But it is only one facet of the appalling condition of unreadiness of the Allies in 1939.

Large Polish forces had been interned in Russia in 1939. In 1942 they were allowed to come through Iran to the Middle East, to form the Polish Corps under General Anders. Dedicated to make any sacrifice for Polish freedom, they were made the more determined by the experience of Russian as well as German deception and tyranny. They were to play a major role in the battles for Cassino, on their way, they firmly believed, to liberate Poland. Their ranks offered an inexhaustible flow of trained clandestine fighters; only shortage of air transport to their country restricted their employment.

This was the situation which Threlfall found at Brindisi. The Poles had their own personnel, holding them for final despatch in villages in the hills in conical houses called 'trulli' of prehistoric design. SOM's supply system and Wooler's parachute training were nearby. A growing number of aircraft were available as American production and OSS support built up. Air Marshal William Elliott, commanding Balkan Air Force, gave unstinted help to all Special Operations.

Pick-ups were also organised; for the long flights over enemy-occupied territory only unarmed aircraft, DC3s, were suitable. I welcomed back one such regular flight with Retinger as a passenger. He had been injured on dropping into Poland and was urgently needed for consultation. On board the aircraft was a piece of captured German equipment of the greatest interest and value. The aircraft was behind schedule, and we wondered if it had been lost. But as on other occasions it had got stuck in the mud and had spent two hours being dug out, very close to a German camp. My offer to guard the captured equipment was smartly refused. Its possessor, like a good gun dog, refused to take his hand off it until he delivered it to the Polish High Command in London. It was a vital part of the control system of V2s; and its examination in London hastened the creation of anti-V2 defences. Three years later, flying in a DC3 in Rhodesia, I noticed the pilot was wearing the 'Virtuti Militare', the Polish Victoria Cross. Named not inappropriately Donovan, he admitted that he had been one of the DC3 pilots who had flown these hazardous sorties to Poland.

Such aircrew from so many nations were to be the heroes of the attempts to supply the Warsaw Rising. Of all periods of my life, I look back on the weeks from the first of August 1943, the beginning of the Rising, to 21 September, when the last flight took place, as the most harassing. During a time of intense activity elsewhere, the Rising was my highest priority. Other operational areas had Army and Air High Commands to help. Poland was outside the Mediterranean theatre. Washington and London were far away. Daily, sometimes hourly, contact by Threlfall with Balkan Air Force and by myself with Mediterranean Air Force was essential. As so vividly described by Garlinski, pressure was brought from all over the free world to give maximum help to the Poles. But the limitations of practicality had to be accepted. At no period, I believe, in Britain as in Italy, was a greater and more intensive air effort sustained, loading, flying and maintaining aircraft, while suffering severe losses and fatigue by aircrews. The heroism of these crews – Polish, British, South African and other Commonwealth – was only matched by the valour of the Poles in Warsaw and the treachery of the Russians on its outskirts.

The Polish Home Army had waited until the Red Army had reached the east bank of the Vistula, across from Warsaw itself, before rising to free their capital city by their own efforts. The Red Army immediately halted its advance. They watched while the Germans and the Poles, the latter so ill-armed, fought it out. The highest Allied political pressure was brought to bear on Stalin, asking him to intervene in person, and at least to allow our aircraft to overfly Warsaw and refuel before their return, thus making a bigger load possible. All assistance of whatever kind was refused by the Russians, so air-drops had to continue at extreme range. If the aircraft flew too low, to drop with greater accuracy, they were more liable to be shot down. If they flew high, many of the containers fell outside the target areas. Whichever way they flew, they were shot at by both Russians as well as Germans. In the history of warfare, no episode is more cynical or disgraceful than this Russian behaviour.

During these weeks I was continuously at the Air Headquarters at Caserta, by night and by day. My admiration and gratitude remains unbounded for those who had the highest responsibility there, General Eaker and Slessor in particular. Poland was outside their immediate responsibilities in the Mediterranean theatre. Nevertheless they took full account of Polish needs. As I saw my duty, I was completely importunate. I was refused permission to fly with the sorties, to be able to report back from personal experience of what was happening. There were too many Polish volunteers, to be dropped with the supplies. Every pound weight was of value. There was no room for a non-flying return passenger. How far Slessor 'acted against his own convictions', as reported by Garlinski, I do not know. But I must plead guilty to being part of the 'pressure' recorded.

When the Rising was over and the Russians had occupied the smoking ruins of Warsaw, I was sent by Slessor to see General Smuts in Cairo, to explain to him the background which had led to the virtually entire destruction of two South African bomber squadrons. He listened carefully, and was good enough to recall our meeting in Khartum ten long years before. He said it might prove difficult, in light of the general regard for the Red Army, to describe so fully the details of these appalling and unnecessarily high losses; but agreed that the South African Air Force would share a page of Poland's immortal struggle against tyranny. He hoped that South African opinion would accept this view. Nearly four hundred aircrew, from many countries, had died between Warsaw and Italy. Yet, due to the contemporary operational difficulties and later Polish Communist suppression, this saga is unknown in Poland. On visits to Poland in post-war years I have found little knowledge of these efforts made to help their gallantry in the Rising. Even before these events I had come to appreciate the spirit of freedom and national independence among the Polish people, even if this had not had time to find expression in more democratic institutions before 1939. This must be mainly ascribed to three partitions in two centuries. There has never been any doubt in the minds of those who served with them in the war years that their indomitable national spirit, inspired and suffused by their Catholic faith, will, one day, carry them through to full independence. No Marxist nor Fascist restrictions nor alien rule can for long subdue them.

Czechoslovakia

The Czech story is different. Between the wars they had organised one of the best democratic systems in Europe. Historically they had tended to look East rather than West. The Little Entente led by France was regarded as a failure in 1938, having given no support during the Munich Crisis. Equally Russia had done nothing to help against German aggression. The breakup of their country between 1938 and 1941 had left them stunned. The removal of Heydrich, their monstrous tyrant ruler, had been followed by the most brutal suppression, ill-famed by the total destruction of Lidice with the murder of all its inhabitants. In the next three years the government-in-exile, led by Benes and Masaryk, remained based in London. As their country, unlike Poland, lay off the immediate lines of communication to the Eastern Front, they concentrated their operations on sabotage of supplies from sources like the Skoda works; and meantime kept their powder dry until the time for liberation came near and risings could be made in support, without risking another Lidice. By 1944 access was easier from the East than from Britain or from Italy. Benes realised that a compromise must be made with Russia whose army would probably reach Prague ahead of the Allies. Little could he have foreseen the results of General Patton being halted by order of the High Command before he could occupy Prague; nor of the later murder of Masaryk and the occupation of the whole country by Russia. Few sorties had been flown from Italy to support the Czechs. But their operational groups left no doubt that they too were wholly dedicated to freeing their country from alien domination.

Austria

Austria was another country which presented complex political difficulties for special operations. A number of Austrians had taken refuge in Britain after the German occupation. At first there was some confusion over the status of Austria under this uninvited Nazi domination, whether they were 'occupied', 'collaborationist' or 'neutral'. Little progress was made, therefore, in finding resistance groups. Luckily recognition of Austria's true position as 'occupied' was later accepted. This was to permit free association with the rest of Western Europe when the Treaty of 1955 brought Russian withdrawal. Although legally 'neutral' Austria's sentiments have always been strong for democratic freedom.

SOE was again inhibited by fears of premature action leading to outbreaks which could not be supported from outside. With so much to be done in areas more directly affecting the tides of warfare, Austria was a low priority. Not until 1944 was a small mission, led by Peter Wilkinson, with Charles Villiers and Edward Renton, infiltrated into southern Austria through Yugoslavia. Their task was to see what might be stirred up in that area, following reports of anti-German action encouraged by Yugoslav resistance. For six months they succeeded in tying up three thousand German troops in attempts to capture them. On withdrawing, Alfgaar Hesketh-Pritchard, one of SOE's most talented and energetic officers, was left to continue the action. He was to perish in circumstances never yet explained. It became apparent, however, that the Yugoslavs had designs on southern Austria and did not welcome outside intervention. This foray created a disproportionately large diversion of enemy resources at a critical moment – and gave to democrats further north hopes of eventual non-Communist liberation.

Hungary

Force 139 also supervised the affairs of Hungary. A number of Hungarians had sought asylum in Britain and had joined British services even before their country was overrun by Germany. Contacts were kept, but little action was possible while Hungary's status was so equivocal; having a right-wing, authoritarian, anti-Communist government, enduring an unsought occupation which was less disruptive than that of the Communist regime under Bela Kun two decades earlier. This experience had left many Hungarians in no doubt that a Marxist revolution was the greater evil. Between that aversion on one hand and the fear of an Austrian-type occupation on the other, their predicament was grave. Like most of Central Europe, and indeed elsewhere, they wished to live in peace, and to work out their own destiny in their own time and manner, even if this seemed too slow for some. In 1944 Frank Roberts carried on a clandestine negotiation with a Hungarian emissary; but it came to nought as Russian, rather than Allied forces, approached. A book published in Buda-Pest, based on documents released by Britain thirty years after the event, sold many thousands of copies in Hungary; thus showing the interest there in what might have been.

Parties were dropped in, usually near Lake Balaton, to try to contact individual groups of dissidents. One party included

Lt.-Col. Peter Boughey, a Black Watch officer with considerable Balkan experience. For security reasons he was dressed as a sergeant. The aircraft was shot down just after Boughey had jumped, and all but he were killed. When captured later, his scarlet regimental hackle was taken at first to be the emblem of the Red Army and he received rough treatment accordingly. All hope of his survival had been given up when news arrived of a sergeant in a prison camp talking like a Lt-Colonel, and we knew all was well. It took him a year to return, through Germany and Poland to Russia, where he had the usual experience of being worse treated than by the Nazis.

Force 133: The Balkans

Policy for the Balkans was laid down by SOE, Cairo, labelled Force 133. This had coalesced during the dark months of the summer of 1940, from D Section and G(R), the offshoot of MI(R) in the War Office in London. Two of my companions on the flight in May 1940 to Cairo had been George Taylor and Ian Pirie, destined for Belgrade and Athens respectively, to see what could be done to organise resistance to anticipated Nazi/Fascist aggression. To suggest at that moment in Cairo that anything could go wrong in Greece or Yugoslavia, and to propose certain pre-occupational precautions, was regarded as tantamount to defeatist lunacy. Yet within a year both countries were under the German heel.

Greece

Greece was first to be struck. The Greeks had reacted to Italian invasion with the greatest courage in the winter of 1940–41, and had held back the Fascists in the mountains of the north west of their country. In the spring of 1941 the Germans had to come to the rescue of their fellow aggressors, defeated in the Desert and thrown back in Greece. Forewarned, Wavell had halted the advance to Tripoli in Libya and had diverted forces to help the Greeks. The short campaign in Greece and the German parachute attack on Crete in the spring of 1941 were other epics of Allied bravery with inadequate resources and without time for proper preparation. However, the German diversion of forces to Greece and the Desert without doubt delayed their attack on

Russia, and so prevented the capture of Moscow before General Winter took a hand in the struggle.

Pirie later told me that as the collapse of Allied regular resistance was beginning, after many heroic counter-attacks, he besought the Prime Minister in Athens to come to Egypt to form a government-in-exile. Being met with refusal he found a Minister going to Egypt who was ready to form a government. This no doubt light-hearted over-simplification gives some indication of the chaos and confusion characteristic of attempts to take precautions before it was too late. Delays in evacuation of important nationals in good time were due to the attitude 'Why panic? nothing will happen without plenty of warning'. Despite numerous warnings from the time of Prague in 1938, when the crisis arose valuable military transport and facilities had to be diverted to rescue civilians. When the German attack began, Gubbins sent out his two most experienced SOE officers, Fleming and Wilkinson, to see what improvisation and courage could do in Greece and Crete. Both were lucky to return safely.

Had it been possible to clear Italian North Africa before the Germans came into the Desert, as Wingate had anticipated six months earlier, the course of the war in the Mediterranean could have been far different.

Later in 1941 the first Mission was sent in, to reconnoitre the indigenous Resistance which had sprung up spontaneously, and which a number of our troops left behind had joined – many to remain and lead hostilities. Supplies, always hard to obtain, went in by boat and by air. These allowed the resisters to contain substantial enemy forces, and keep alive the hopes of eventual freedom through the coming years of defeat. Unfortunately, deeply held differences of view on the political future of Greece after liberation were held among those in exile as well as among those fighting in Greece. These high emotions were to affect operations there as elsewhere in Europe.

In 1943, while Allied forces were landing at Salerno, attempts to capture Leros and other Greek islands in the Dodecanese failed when support from outside was cut off. The later Allied decision not to use further resources for such operations led to Greek resistance being used for Deception purposes, and to contain as many German forces as possible once Italy had become non-combatant. These aims had to be achieved without bringing down reprisals on Greek civilians. The Greek involvement in this success was considerable.

With the Adriatic denied to Axis shipping in late 1943, the sole remaining route for German supply was by rail from Yugoslavia to Athens. This line was cut on a number of occasions by Resistance groups led by British officers, notably by Eddie Myers against the Gorgopotamos Bridge. Later, by British alone, the Aisopos Viaduct was broken. As elsewhere in Europe there was occasionally local resistance to such major attacks for justifiable fear of extreme Axis reactions. Coordinated and continuous harassment of this railway link could possibly have forced earlier Axis withdrawal from Greece, but at an unacceptable cost to civilians nearby, and also making the forces so withdrawn available for defence nearer home.

The politically disunited Greek Resistance still gave grave concern when SOM became operational from Italy in late 1943. From its position in the heel of Italy, shorter flights and huge quantities of captured weapons made it a more effective base than Cyrenaica; while the increasing concentration and number of aircraft in Italy was to turn the semi-clandestine Greek group into guerrilla forces of substantial size.

Many accounts have been written of the Greek Resistance, among them one by Monty Woodhouse who led the first Military Mission. A brilliant Greek scholar, he was another of the fighting academics who gave gallant and decisive leadership in the field. He came out for a break just after the capture of Rome. I offered to take him there for a change, to see the Eternal City. He pondered a while, then said, 'I would much prefer to go to see Paestum (the Greek ruins near Salerno). All that modern stuff in Rome . . .'. There spoke the true philhellene. He went to Paestum.

Later a Greek guerrilla General, Zervas, came out from Epirus to see the High Command. He spoke most movingly about Monty whom he knew as 'Colonel Chris'.

'We don't know who he really is', he said. 'He tells us so much about Greece that we have never known. Although he speaks a rather strange Greek!'

Monty of course spoke, at least at the start, pure classical Greek.

Speedwell was charged with explaining how AFHQ policies were being carried out in the field. This Allied Command was absorbing a British one, with American involvement across the Adriatic still undefined. My task was made easier when, three months after reaching Italy, the American part of my responsibility was made clear.

My final involvement with Greek affairs was at Christmas 1944. On the German withdrawal from Greece an Allied force was landed at Athens to prevent a possible outbreak of civil war between monarchists and anti-monarchists. General Scobie, Chief of Staff in Khartum in 1940–41, was in command. President Roosevelt, it seemed, had ordered that no Americans or American equipment were to be used in any Restoration. Churchill and Eden were on their way to Athens. The security situation was serious. Gubbins was asked by Alexander if I was available to go to Athens to set up some organisation, free of any contact with existing SOE groups all of whom were well known in Greece; adding that our forces, even including the Prime Minister and Foreign Secretary, might be overrun by the Communists. I set forth still equipped with some American kit but without a parachute, and with two OSS officers from Italy in British uniform. We were welcomed by Scobie. He pointed out the Communist group only a few hundred yards away across Constitution Square. The Prime Minister and Eden, he said, were enjoying themselves hugely – but the security forces, still taking some politicians seriously, were worried. We dug ourselves in for a Last Stand at the Monarcho-Fascist Bar nearby. The immediate crisis was soon resolved, thanks to British troops and the Archbishop Damaskinos. The pass was held. Three years later (when the United States came to shoulder the post-War burden of sustaining the Free World) the Truman Doctrine was to include the maintenance of democracy in Greece.

Albania

Just across the sea from Brindisi lay Albania. Not inappropriately my interest had first been aroused when Aosta told me how he had tried to stop Mussolini from occupying it, the last Muslim country in Europe, on Good Friday, the day after Queen Geraldine had had a baby – thereby antagonising three important groups. It was in keeping with the Ethiopian connection that the officer in charge in Albania was Colonel Neil (Billy) Maclean. I had last seen him proceeding 'Addis Ababa-wards, camel-wise'. He was to win his long-overdue DSO in the mountains between Greece and Yugoslavia, helping to maintain the Albanian independence which endures to this day, albeit in somewhat isolationist circumstances. He and his groups were to do more than their share in containing the enemy; and in 1944 at last supply to him was the easier.

He was of outstanding use when one day a DC3, slightly off course, mistook the heel of Italy for the toe and force-landed in Albania. The cargo was especially precious, consisting of nurses. With customary gallantry, Maclean helped to arrange their safe return, after much pressure to leave at least one of them behind with him.

Yugoslavia

Yugoslavia presented many of the same problems as Greece. Taylor had made some progress in the winter of 1940–41, preparing for the anticipated Nazi aggression. After the murder of King Alexander in Marseilles in 1934, the young King Peter had been placed under the Regency of his uncle Prince Paul. In the spring of 1941 German pressure was growing to allow transit of troops to Greece. Despite victories in Ethiopia and the Desert, Allied help still seemed remote. When Prince Paul looked likely to give way, a coup, in which SOE was involved, replaced him, just in time for honourable if hopeless military resistance to be made to German invasion. The Regency went into exile; while once again in the long history of the Balkans, the patriots took to the mountains, under General Mihailovic. There the struggle was to continue, with the Italians mainly in occupation of the north-west and the Adriatic coast, and the Germans on the lines of communication to the Aegean.

In 1941 it was alleged that Croats and Slovenes were taking action against the invaders in Serbia, thus bringing down reprisals on Serbs, their age-old rivals. Once again the short-term military need for action to tie up enemy forces was in conflict with the long-term need to conserve strength until liberation was near. All groups naturally wished to try to seize political power when the moment came. Such was a comprehensible ambition among both Communists and anti-Communists. Any final judgement on how the outcome was affected, if at all, by SOE can only be made by impartial examination of such official documents as remain.

Missions were put in by SOE Cairo in later 1941 under, first, Hudson, and, later, Bailey, to keep touch with Mihailovic, the King's accredited representative. Between them resistance was kept alive for two years with minimal outside help, due, once again, to the scarcity of aircraft and supplies. By the spring of 1943 the future held at least some hopes of liberation. The Allied clearing of North Africa as a springboard for the re-entry into Europe was matched by the Russians' steady advance westwards. Although the peoples of Yugoslavia were traditionally more pro-Russian than pro-German, Mihailovic represented, as was his right and duty, the anti-Communists. From information available at the time, he had accepted help from the Italians. He was later to agree that he had done so, justifying his action as the lesser of two evils, since he saw the possibility of Italian defeat and of the Allies' arrival before that of the Russians. In any case he wished to help free Yugoslavia with as strong anti-Communist forces as possible.

Four months later the Allies were themselves cooperating with the Italians, after the Armistice of September 1943. Even more inconceivable at that time would have been the entry within a decade of a free Germany into NATO, to help defend Western freedom against Russian invasion. Thus was more than justified the assessment by Mihailovic and many others in Central and Eastern Europe that Russia was the great long-term menace, once the Nazis had been annihilated. This view of the position was strongly held by OSS as described in the published record of their early Mission 'Halyard'. The terms of American participation in the Balkans had not been finalised until the end of 1943, after President Roosevelt's discussions with Stalin at Teheran. Perhaps the President's belief in republics and his known feeling that he could influence Stalin for better if not for good, clouded his unwavering support for freedom.

Meantime, Josip Broz, alias Tito, had raised the Communist banner after the German attack on Russia. It is still uncertain whether he was in Yugoslavia or Russia during the period from 1939 until this moment of aggression, when Mihailovic was to take the lead in resistance. In early 1943 William Deakin was to win his DSO after parachuting in to discover Tito's whereabouts and report on his military strength; and once SOM was set up, to arrange for air and sea supply to his forces from nearby Italy.

Soon the High Command was to withdraw support from Mihailovic as a result of his collaboration with the Italians, thus leaving Tito as the recipient of the major supply operation which enabled him to build up his strength substantially before the liberation of Belgrade by the Russians in the autumn of 1944.

Following the decision to give the greater support to Tito, Churchill and Eden decided to upgrade the Yugoslav Mission with a Brigadier in charge. To head it in late 1943 came Fitzroy Maclean, later to become a steadfast ally of mine in domestic politics. The circumstances of his arrival were not auspicious. He had gained his freedom from the Foreign Service only by getting elected to Parliament. He had fought bravely with the SAS in the Desert. His appointment and subsequent discussions in Cairo with SOE had proved mutually distasteful. His membership of the Foreign Service and later of Parliament – the exact circumstances of which were not widely known – gave no immediate pleasure to those in Cairo and Italy, many of whom had been at war or near-war since the Ethiopian crisis of 1935, and, justly or not, blamed the Foreign Office and Parliament for the lack of prevision and provision which had led to so many disasters.

Whiteley, a senior officer from the Ethiopian campaign, said, 'I hope we have not got another Wingate'. We had not. Wingate's egotism had proved the more unacceptable to Higher Authority as he was a professional soldier himself. Maclean could provide no such irritant. Both tried, believing it their right and duty, to play the Churchill card. In neither case did it work. Others with Parliamentary contacts tried the same channel. But the military staff structure for deciding priorities was well enough established to resist undue political pressure, with local Allied political representatives to coordinate these priorities. Occasionally I had to ask to see Alexander as he had told me to do; to urge, for example, that special operational types of equipment should not all be given to one group, to the detriment of another; that useful though an item might be to the limitless requirements of paramilitary groups in the Balkans, it was vital to those still operating clandestinely in north Italy, Poland and Central Europe.

The background of Maclean's appointment and his discussions in Cairo were unknown to those who, after some years of struggle, had reached Yugoslavia and Italy by other routes. He was the only Member of Parliament to become associated with Special Operations, which often seems curious when considering their political rather than military content. To form Maclean's staff and field leaders came a number of outstanding Army and Air Force officers and men. Vivian Street, a regular officer of the highest distinction, as Chief of Staff, bore the main burden of coordinating supply and operations. Two other colleagues, Randolph Churchill and Evelyn Waugh, men of conspicuous bravery and renown, were not so constructive. But thanks to the Mission and the experienced SOM staff, with tremendous opportunities opening up in the field, cooperation was soon running efficiently.

Some had serious doubts about the accuracy of the information on which the decisions affecting Mihailovic and Tito were based. To this day these continue. Letters in the *Economist* of July, August and October 1979 from former Partisans make grave charges:

'. . . The Cairo branch (of SOE) had on its staff some Communists, fellow travellers and 'progressives' who slanted and doctored various reports to suit their political and ideological strivings. In his recent book on Mihailovic, *Patriot or Traitor*, David Martin reveals how various intelligence services succeeded in colouring reports on wartime Yugoslavia and thus misleading the Prime Minister. Churchill himself realised during the Trieste crisis of May 1945 that he had been misinformed and misled about Tito . . .'

Reports and visits from the field confirmed the anti-Allied outlook of the Partisans. All in Italy hoped that care for wounded and increasing supply of war material would modify their attitude. In addition admissions years later by dissident Partisans confirmed that they were in contact with the Germans, for exchange of prisoners and for other purposes. All of which pointed to the belief that Tito's Partisans were accepting help from wherever it was available in order to seize political power on liberation. This was the oft-repeated pattern of Communism in

Italy and Greece, as well as in France where the Gaullists came out on top.

On one occasion Street's anticipation forewarned Tito of a German attack and arranged for him to be flown to Bari. I went to the airfield at Bari when he landed. He was quickly put back on to Yugoslav soil on the island of Vis, then held by the Commandos. Every effort was made to comply with his wish to maintain that he never left Yugoslavia until the liberation of Belgrade in October 1944.

Russian forces moved on towards Germany after liberation, leaving Tito in charge. His brave and prolonged fight against absorption in the Russian Empire is a matter of history. It is a fact. It is irrelevant whether it was due to Tito's personal antipathy, or to his realisation of the nationalist pride of mountain peoples who would not accept denials of individual freedom. Only in the Voivodina was there any trace of a proletariat. All who fought and worked for Yugoslav independence in World War II can rejoice in her upward growth from wartorn socialism to a form of social democracy – all within a disparate state held together by Tito's authority until constitutional bonds could be forged.

Soon after Maclean had joined Tito in the field, the Russians sent a General to represent them at the same Headquarters. He reported somewhat unwillingly to Eisenhower, under my guidance. At dinner with the Russian Ambassador Bogomolov, I met Vyshinski whom I had last talked to a decade earlier in Moscow after the Metrovic trials. He was as cynical as ever.

'Freedom of the Press is all very well as long as it does not interfere with the business of government', was one gem.

To another, 'Democracy is like wine; it should be taken in small quantities', Macmillan replied, 'Yes, but there is no need to be a teetotaler'.

Bedell Smith told me to arrange for the General to be parachute trained. I submitted that if the 1 in 7,000 chance occurred of the parachute failing to open, I would be charged with having arranged it. He was duly airlanded.

His aircraft was loaded with boxes which, when food was needed in the field, were found to contain vodka and caviar. Later, contrary to the agreement that no Russian should enter Greece, one made his way south from Yugoslavia into Epirus, his sole sustenance being some of these boxes. Paul West, an experienced OSS officer, reported his presence, asking for instructions. Shortly afterwards he reported back that, as instructed, he had paid a return courtesy call on the Russian, departing some thirty-six hours later, with apologies for leaving so early – but the boxes were empty. The Russian withdrew.

I paid regular visits to Cairo to coordinate plans with the SOE and other Special Services there. Two events throw light on the apprehensions under which we worked.

The first was revealed after the unique coup by Paddy Leigh-Fermor and Billy Moss in capturing the German Commander-in-Chief in Crete, von Kreipe, and getting him aboard a submarine to bring to Egypt. Perhaps because of the long hours spent practising saluting at Windsor in 1939, I was sometimes flattered by being mistaken for a regular soldier, like the military head of SOE in Cairo. I was with him when the news came that von Kreipe had been landed at Alexandria.

'Absolutely splendid. We must have a drink on this', he said. Then he hesitated, turning to say, 'I am not quite sure it is the right thing, old boy. After all, von Kreipe is a regular soldier'.

The second was more distressing. After reporting to Lord Moyne, the Minister of State, I was hospitably invited to lunch at the Mohamed Ali Club. The next evening, back in Algiers, I heard that he had been murdered that morning as he got into his car to go to lunch. The assassins were a Zionist terrorist group who did not see fit to delay their activities against those still battling with the shared menace from Nazism until the war in Europe, at least, was won.

My usefulness in the Mediterranean was coming to an end. Gubbins had discussed the future with me in Paris in August. France had been cleared. Italian operations were working smoothly under Holdsworth with 15 Army Group and with an Ambassador, Sir Noel Charles, to give advice. Poland and Central Europe, then under highest pressure, were capably supported by Threlfall and Force 139. The Balkans, under General Stawell's direction at SOM and Force 133, had reached the phase of guerrilla, soon to be open, warfare. Gubbins asked whether I wished to go to the Far East or Washington. I replied that I would prefer to keep to my original interest in Europe; that there would be considerable opportunities for working into enemy-occupied areas through neutral countries and through the French Alps. He agreed, telling me to stay until Polish affairs were clearer; and to bid farewell to those who had helped SOE most.

Among others I called on Alexander, who approved of the plan. He was good enough to say that he proposed to recommend me for an honour.

'I thank you, Sir, for leave to speak.'

'Please.'

'A colleague, a young regular officer, received an honour for a brilliant coup. It proved to be, by the rules of SOE, a civilian honour. I could not believe that such would be acceptable to my Regimental Headquarters. Such risks as I have from time to time taken have been against all standing orders. Instead, please recommend for honours more of those who have run such indescribable risks in the field.' Any suggestion then that within ten years I would be a junior Foreign Office Minister under Eden in a Churchill administration with Alex as Minister of Defence would have seemed beyond the bounds of reason.

I was particularly sorry to leave my OSS colleagues. Although latterly our paths had further separated, there was an original group who kept in touch and were to do so until the end of the war and thereafter. Some local disagreements had arisen, but never so serious as to affect our basic aims under Churchill and Roosevelt, Eisenhower and Alexander, Gubbins and Donovan. They had given the top direction which led to the successes of 1943 and 1944. Apart from useful *coups de main* in Italy and the Balkans, OSS main interests had shifted to North West Europe where some of the original group were once again to be found.

It is impossible, even with hindsight, to summarise the growth and achievements, not all as planned, of Special Operations in the Western and Central Mediterranean from 1942 to 1944. More than thirty years later it is difficult to call to mind the threats and circumstances which then surrounded the still Free World. Only a restricted number knew in detail about the joint Nazi/Communist occupation of Poland. Later when the Red Army was fighting so bravely to eject their former Allies, it was thought necessary to mute the details of massacres like Katyn and the cynical betrayal of the Warsaw Rising. The full truth of the Nazi concentration camps, with the genocide of Jews and the slaughter of so many others, was yet undisclosed.

Enough was known, however, for efforts to be made by SOE to eliminate those who did not observe the Geneva Convention. To that end some had earlier sought to take action and had, on the outbreak of hostilities, been taken into 'unacknowledgeable' employment. Some outline has been given of SOE activities in the Mediterranean, from the clandestine through the paramilitary stages to liberation, by land and sea and air. No full account has been given of the facilities and equipment entrusted to a Mission Commander for very special operations. Knowledge of these was drastically restricted, not surprisingly, and scarcely within the social ambit of an 'officer and a gentleman'. But then SOE's original character, in the dark days of 1940, had been for 'ungentlemanly warfare'.

On occasion enemies, for instance Heydrich, had to be removed by means outside the Geneva Convention, as no other way lay open. After all the Germans themselves were to use captured SOE time-delay fuses in an attempt on Hitler's life. I fully respect those who believe that there can be no justification for taking the life of another, but I do not share that belief. Long before I reached Belsen, the day after its full horrors were first revealed, I was convinced that to certain types of killer there was no alternative deterrent to capital punishment. I may well be wrong. It is a personal decision which I took when joining SOE, based on my experience in Africa and Central Europe before the outbreak of war. When I brought my box of tricks, from stink bombs and itching powder to more serious toys, back to London it was not, I believe, reissued to my successor, a true officer and gentleman.

The foregoing accounts of events in the Mediterranean, especially in 1944, may give the impression of a series of disconnected incidents, each of a relevant if not decisive nature. From some of these the historian may find points of confirmation or denial of other accounts from which the truth may emerge. Its aim has also been to describe the atmosphere surrounding the expansion of often tedious organisations: for, as in most forms of modern warfare, training and preparation are usually long and slow, until final action, swift and short.

No account can be given of the hundreds of hours spent explaining, and pleading, for the first year in particular; explaining the political will underlying resistance; pleading for permission to use available facilities – ships and aircraft and airfields with which to carry out our terms of reference laid down by the All-Highests; begging for supplies of weapons and explosives and radio frequencies. There was scant proof, in the early months, of the military value of political warfare and of the realities and possibilities of sabotage and para-military action. These were 'ungentlemanly' and so described in our orders; and, therefore, to be carried out by lesser breeds but not by Anglo-Saxons. Staff Colleges did not teach clandestine action – nor did any others.

'Not cricket, old boy.'

In circles predominantly consisting of cricketers, I was fortunate in finding in the course of my early importunities several who accepted the necessity for our projects. The principles had, after all, been laid down by Churchill himself. As time went on some senior officers were to initiate proposals themselves. Donovan maintained unremitting pressure, wholeheartedly sustained by the American General Julius Holmes; while the British Air Marshals Slessor and Elliott saw the possibilities of a new application of air power. Training demonstrations shown at the Club des Pins helped at first. Successes in Corsica and with MONKEY showed different facets of Special Operations. In fairness, after a slow start, no officer of any seniority gave anything but the fullest support, often beyond the call of duty.

In November 1942 a handful of experienced SOE officers had come to Algiers from London. Later, in September 1943, they were joined in Italy by a similar party from Cairo. On this framework were set up the country sections which guided the training and supply and communication groups. Increasingly these country sections became agencies for the governments-in-exile as liberation came near. The final link-up of these with the leaders in the field, often of a somewhat different political persuasion, was embarrassing on occasion, despite all our efforts to avoid our Allies' internal differences. It was then that the result of giving radio links and arms and equipment to individuals could be more clearly seen.

The whole process had been experienced in Ethiopia in 1940–41. In Western Europe, from the small beginnings in 1940, the same pattern was emerging. All possible warnings were given to the authorities, leaving the top political decisions and their final military execution to them; in the short, military, term to avoid disarray on the lines of communication; in the longer, political, term to avoid replacing one tyranny with another.

By mid-summer 1944, a massive organisation had been established in Algiers and Italy. One estimate counted 2,700 all ranks, men and women (including 250 FANYs) from all Allied countries as well as from others like Spain, engaged in maintaining base supply, training and signal facilities, and in carrying out the detailed staff work for air and sea and land communications.

The area for action ran through Spain and France to the Low Countries, and from Poland through Central and Eastern Europe to the Balkans and Greece. How many were being helped to maintain the fight in the field will never be known. The Polish Home Army, which so little could be done to help, alone numbered 300,000. The French Forces of the Interior, the Yugoslavs and the Greeks clearly surpassed that total. The Italians also formed a large array. In addition there were the regular Air and Naval Forces without whose skill and courage little would have been possible.

Substantial advantages were flowing to SOE from the individuals and information arriving from occupied areas. As its nature changed from a British Special Service into a link with Allied paramilitary forces, confidence grew between SOE's country sections and the Allied officers. The inward traffic was shared with Intelligence, Escape, Deception and political organisations. There was no interdepartmental jealousy. SOE had no Service structure, past or future. Beyond that in the wider scene American and British, OSS and SOE, cooperated within the limitations described with mutually established trust. Especially was this found in France in the Operational Groups, and the Jedburghs, where the three-man teams further expanded the radio links which already formed a network throughout Europe.

On the personal side, I attach as an Appendix, with some

diffidence, extracts from three letters which give an idea of the sentiments of some colleagues most closely concerned in those years.

CHAPTER 17

To a Hollow Victory

Before Gubbins sent me to Paris to operate with the Supreme Headquarters (SHAEF), I spent some time at Baker Street trying to write citations for Honours and Awards for those who had served in the field, of so many nationalities. It proved an impossible task. The bravest who had contributed so much were often far from any witness. Many had joined their national forces on liberation. Others were continuing the struggle to consolidate freedom against threats from Communism. The best shrugged off any suggestion that their deeds might deserve recognition. Success and survival, in freedom, was reward enough. They were most unwilling to talk about themselves.

There were three anomalies which were never resolved. First, a member of a Regular Service if fired on in the course of his or her action would be entitled to a recommendation for a DSO or MC or DFC. If carried out, as usually instructed, in a clandestine way without thereby alerting the enemy and so without immediate detection, the individual was only entitled to an OBE or MBE. When this became known, on occasion an enemy reaction was deliberately provoked to make the more highly prized award possible. The second technicality which caused much heartache was the difficulty of getting the more coveted awards for civilians, even if in uniform, among whom, strangely enough, were the FANYs. There were so many for whom the George Cross or George Medal might have been too high, yet they deserved military rather than civilian recognition for actions and long service of sustained gallantry. Thirdly, there was some rule which seemed to preclude the King from presenting awards for bravery to foreigners, or at least to our clandestine colleagues. Cesari, whom His Majesty had met at Algiers before his great success in Corsica, was awarded the DSO, which was duly pinned on him in Algiers. I reported this to Arthur Penn, my Regimental Adjutant and a member of the Household. He told me to let him know when Cesari and any other such might come to London. He then arranged, contrary to protocol . . . It was not quite the same as receiving the original award in person, but it proved a lifelong inspiration to several.

When reporting to Regimental Headquarters I was asked if, when hostilities were over in Europe, I would consider going to Palestine as Arabic-speaking Military Assistant to the Governor, Lord Gort. I said I was most flattered and would certainly accept with great pleasure if my services were not needed in Europe operationally or clearing up the mess we had made.

Once again I had few direct instructions from Gubbins, beyond closing down as soon as convenient SOE's activities in France, after doing whatever was possible for the welfare of those who had worked so nobly with us. He was most anxious that no British should become involved in the acute political disputes which were breaking out all over France.

I reached Paris soon after the last German attack through the Ardennes had been defeated in the Battle of the Bulge. It was a fiercely cold winter. Black ice made the roads doubly dangerous. I called on Bedell Smith at SHAEF at Versailles and obtained his leave to stay in Paris rather than to travel daily to and from a large house in Chantilly. The small size of the Hotel Cecil in the Rue Laurestan thus allowed the swift reduction of the number who could remain in Paris. We found a great welcome from our French and American colleagues. The latter most generously provided our rations – a good Combined Operation of American food cooked by the French and eaten largely by the British. All in Paris were virtually starving. It was forbidden to feed any except those on our official strength. I stretched this to include a number of French who otherwise would have had to leave Paris and so be unable to cooperate in the critical work still to be done. The only foodstuff the French refused to consume was peanut butter. This proved advantageous in our first task.

A standing patrol, mainly staffed by FANYs, was kept at the Gare d'Orsay. Every scrap of food that could be spared was taken there – including the peanut butter. Thither were directed all the refugees now beginning to stream back from liberated areas and later from Germany itself. At the Reception Centre all were stripped, shaved, deloused, fed, re-clothed and given a railticket and a guide to their railway station. Many were dying. All were emaciated and distressing to behold, especially for anyone trying to recognise the features of a former colleague and friend. For among them were a number who had worked with SOE. Some of our colleagues became overwrought by the strain of this prolonged search and, understandably, broke down and had to be withdrawn.

For me a high point came late in the season. Yeo-Thomas, the 'White Rabbit', had an unsurpassed record for which he was awarded the George Cross and many French decorations. He had been a colleague at Baker Street in the early years. Caught at last, he had been taken to a concentration camp. There his life was saved through the action of a brave French doctor who had substituted him for a dead Frenchman. On the liberation of the camp, the doctor returned to Paris. There he addressed a meeting at the Pasteur Institute. When Kay Gimpel, our chief FANY, and Tony Brooks and I came in, all stood up in tribute to 'Tommy' about whom the doctor was to speak.

Weeks passed with no signs of Tommy. He was given up as dead, for the camp had been cleared and the troops had moved on, to meet the Red Army. Then, one evening, I was alone at the Cecil, the members of his section have gone to dine at the Club. Suddenly the door flew open and a figure appeared, of such a dishevelled appearance that, used though I had become to such apparitions, I began to protest at the interruption. Then, through the shock, the face . . . I think, contrary to my nature, I kissed him . . . made him bath and clean up, found clothes and drove him to the Club. Telling the waiter to provide as much champagne as required, I waited long enough to see the looks of sudden recognition dawn on his friends' faces. He recounted how, on liberation, he had joined the American troops and gone with them to meet the Russians.

My first and overt instruction was to clear up any of our activities in France and keep in touch with our French colleagues from London and Algiers. The small amount of help made possible by feeding them at the Cecil allowed some to continue their work at the political centre.

There were some embarrassments. One protest was made at

the number of French being invited to the British Embassy, regardless of their Resistance or non-Resistance records. I ventured to pass this point to the Ambassador, Duff Cooper. He replied that he fully understood these feelings; but believed that unless an individual was actually on a charge or under grave suspicion, he or she should be invited; he must do all he could to heal the breaches between the many factions among the French, who were reported to have executed by summary act after liberation more than had died during the French Revolution; while there were many thousands shut up in Fresnes Prison without trial. It was the result of pent-up emotion and the tensions of the occupation years, never endured by the Anglo-Saxons. It would hinder rather than help national reconciliation if the British took sides beyond the normal diplomatic rules. I fully accepted his judgement as did, I believe, my French colleagues. In the event, his Embassy, so splendidly supported by Lady Diana, was to be one of the success stories of post-war Franco-British relations.

The next task was to help the French authorities, from records or memory, to assess damage to industrial equipment; had it been sabotaged on Allied instructions, or worn out by working, willingly, or unwillingly, for the enemy, or just run down? The differences affected compensation. There were also cases of collaboration with the enemy in which SOE's records could help. This was a major concern which was to continue for many years. Frank Soskice's acute legal mind and compassionate outlook greatly helped in these often distressing investigations. He was particularly good at judging in cases of double crosses, or treble, or even quadruple.

It had been laid down by the High Command that no-one in uniform was to try to carry on any commercial activity until hostilities were at an end, when all could be free and equal. This order was clearly being broken by some Allies. With recollections of the post-First War industrial troubles, it seemed that the sooner industry and commerce got going the better. Further chaos and shortages would otherwise result, from which only the Communists would benefit. The general policy was, of course, correct. Any breaches of it, however, were scarcely effective before hostilities ended – and allowed a beginning to be made against deepening disaster from which within two years Europe was saved by the imagination and generosity of American Marshall Aid.

My covert instructions were to continue to work, as and when chances arose, into areas still enemy-occupied, if necessary through neutral countries in which I had had some small experience pre-war. Besides Germany and Austria, North Italy was still in enemy hands. The front from the Mediterranean to the Swiss frontier had been allotted to the French. In this area France had some ambition to acquire the Val d'Aoste, a part of the Savoie, split between France and Italy. Six years before I had heard voices in Rome claiming Nice. In the valley were substantial hydroelectric works. Plans were made to help Resistance forces in Turin and Milan through the French lines. John Stevens in Turin and Alfredo Pezzoni in Milan were the leaders needing supplies. Pezzoni was nearly caught several times as he had taken the codename Longho while the real name of the most hunted Communist was Longhi. Both Pezzoni and Stevens survived, their cool judgements taking both in later years to the highest financial positions in their countries. Despite all our most urgent appeals, French agreement to the use of routes through the Alps was not given. So other ways, longer but perhaps safer, were used, organised from Grenoble and points north east.

A consideration much in mind in the final stages of the war was the belief that the Nazis and neo-Fascists were planning and providing for a redoubt in the mountains stretching from the north of Italy to The Eagle's Nest, Hitler's house in Bavaria, near the Austrian border. Although with hindsight there proved to have been little reality in this fear, considerable effort was put into infiltrating individuals to make reconnaissances and take any action possible. This was made easier, though not easy, by the continuing presence of some fifteen million foreign workers within the ring fences of the Western, Eastern and Italian Fronts. These were now closing round the remnants of the Axis Forces.

Many of these foreign workers were finding their own ways to safety. But most were in concentration and other camps from which escape was impossible without intervention from outside. The Governments-in-exile and all Special Services were becoming increasingly insistent that efforts must be made to mount rescue operations. Reports were coming in of whole camps being eliminated by the Nazis, leaving no single survivor to bear witness against the murderers.

The only forces available were General Brereton's Airborne Army into which had been absorbed the Special Duty Squadrons formerly under independent control. Gubbins had gathered a group of SOE leaders safely returned from the field and anxious to make this final drop to rescue these camps. Robin Brook in London and I in Paris were the links between the Governments and the Airborne Army Staff at Fontainebleau. The officer in charge was Brigadier General James Stewart, sandwiching in a full tour of bomber operations and high staff responsibility between two periods of a great film career. He and his colleagues received our most pressing entreaties with great compassion. But warnings had come through neutral channels that any such airborne actions would be countered by penalising Allied prisoners of war. As Hitler had ordered in 1944, the most savage murders of Allied fighters caught behind the lines, the SAS and others, even if in uniform, had been widespread. In the early spring of 1945 there seemed no limit to the substantial executive authority which Hitler still exercised. In consequence, the decision was taken at the highest political level that no rescue sorties could be made.

Another aspect of the continuing Nazi influence I saw for myself in April. The French alerted me that a concentration camp at a place called Belsen had been overrun that morning. By driving throughout the night we arrived there within a day of its discovery. Our aim was to find some of our colleagues who might be there. We saw instead the degradation of the human spirit, the horror of which no words of mine could exaggerate; nor could I explain the attitude of the Nazi guards who, by the thousand, men and women, had administered it. The only possible redeeming feature was the incredible spirit of Resistance of so many of the survivors, especially the Jewish. The estimate that day was 15000 dead and the same number dying.

On my way back to Paris we drove through the Ruhr. I wondered then, and later that year in Berlin, whether any physical reconstruction on the same sites would ever be possible. The determination which led to the successful regeneration of these two areas in later years is difficult to reconcile with the Nazi nihilist outlook.

Such were some of the horrors which clouded any lightening of the spirit as the end of hostilities approached. They showed what an immense load of mental as well as material reconstruction awaited us. Nevertheless there were, as usual, some brighter moments. The Vic Wells Ballet Company came to Paris. As the mood of audiences was difficult to judge, we were asked to take a box and guarantee to keep it filled for each performance. By the second day we were beseiged with requests to be taken there, by American and French colleagues. In particular Robert Helpman's mime in *Facade*, leaving his hand outside the door when pursuing a girl within, will never be forgotten.

In April President Roosevelt died. To him the Free World owed an inestimable debt; indeed without him Britain might well have been overwhelmed. A Service of Thanksgiving was held at Notre Dame to which we were invited. I was accompanied by Kay Gimpel, to represent the FANY, and Tony Brooks, the leading railway saboteur. Both happened to be some eighteen inches shorter than I. We drove down the Champs Elysées just as General de Gaulle came out from the Elysée. So we alighted at Notre Dame together and walked up the aisle behind him. Some took this to have been prearranged, to show our unwavering support for him. Others smiled as they saw the contrasts in size of my companions and myself. It was a privileged moment, honouring two of the giants of those years, Roosevelt and de Gaulle.

In early May, while we were still celebrating VE Day, my telephone rang. My Personal Assistant who had orders to listen in and write down any decisions taken, said the next morning, 'You are going to stand for Parliament'.

'This is the first I have heard of such a suggestion. What do you mean?'

'Last night someone rang from London and asked you to stand instead of him as he was leaving. You said you would have a bang.'

'I can't have been that tight.'

'You must have been. You will have to get yourself out of this one . . .'

Next day, having cleared my immediate commitments, I flew to London. James Edmondson, the Member for North Oxfordshire, whom I had known since Oxford days, was not standing again. He had endured my criticisms of appeasement for many years with great forbearance.

'Now you can do something to help rebuild what you have helped destroy.'

'But I am committed to going to Palestine', I explained.

'This is a higher priority.'

After some discussion, I accepted his generous if somewhat ill-timed offer. There were only a few weeks till the Election. I could not even return to Paris to bid farewell to my colleagues. On 5 July, my thirty-sixth birthday, I found myself elected to Parliament for North Oxfordshire, after a campaign in which I found constant embarrassment from finding my face and name so widely advertised, following years of trying to avoid public notice.

CHAPTER 18

All to What Purpose?

The chopper came down quickly – or rather it is fairer to say the curtain was drawn discreetly on SOE in general and on me. Elected to Parliament, I found myself one of the fewer than two hundred backbenchers supporting Churchill, against an overwhelming Labour majority of over two hundred. Being in Opposition and no longer in uniform, all contacts with my former colleagues were cut off. The doors of Baker Street were shut on me. I was not even allowed to return to Paris to say farewell and thank those who had helped most, like the Americans General Bedell Smith and Robert Murphy.

I had endured an extraordinary ten years, from 1935 to 1945; on occasions moving in the highest international military and political circles, and next conniving in some deep chicanery; taking part in discussions between senior Allied decision-makers and heads of Governments, and then treble-checking the minutiae of clandestine operations on which lives depended; one day facilitating the transport of a high-ranking morale-boosting lady and later examining under stereoscopic scrutiny photographs taken from 15,000 feet above a proposed Lysander pick-up ground, to decide whether a track across it was more than a few inches deep and so liable to break an axle.

None of this would have been possible had I not enjoyed the full confidence and support of Gubbins. My position in the Mediterranean was, in microcosm, as anomalous as his in London. One great difference was that in the course of a distinguished professional military career, the welfare of individuals and democratic institutions in many parts of the world came to rest on him as on few others. I was but his nominee, temporary and expendable, to be replaced at any time when our masters tired of our importunities and mistakes. As I have described, only the accident of my personal association with Whiteley and

Saltzman had saved us in Algiers in 1942. I was thus lucky in being a link in a chain, from Gubbins to numberless groups and individuals throughout many parts of the world, free and occupied.

Gubbins held a unique personal position, respected in private by so many Allied political and military leaders as secondary only to Churchill and Eden in helpful understanding of their difficulties. This did not endear him to some of his military colleagues, nor did politicians and diplomats always welcome his, and thus my lesser, interventions in political decisions and diplomatic exchanges. This was understandable. Our terms of reference from Churchill and our Ministers, Dalton and Selborne, were shown to, but not filed with, Supreme Commanders and political chiefs, least of all to Allied ones. To have done so might have implied our acceptance of total subordination to theatre commanders and thus have accepted their right of veto, when often part at least of our responsibilities lay outside the theatre. To balance these loyalties was a constant preoccupation, as was the need to consult without passing operational decisions to others. Thanks to Gubbins' unwavering support I claim, with some diffidence, that I was able to gain and retain the confidence of some of the key decision-makers in the Western and Central Mediterranean in the two years 1943 and 1944; and thereby hold my position against certain intrigues in London and locally among some who thought, rightly perhaps, that they would do the job better. They may well have failed to realise the conditions of personal trust and of achievement which were so essential if help was to be given, the full use of which could sometimes not be explained.

Immediately the war was over, Gubbins was 'retired'. His normal military career had been curtailed by his being outside Regular Army employment after commanding the Independent Companies in Norway in 1940. No diplomatic nor civilian employment in government seems to have been offered to him, to make use of his great experience and energy. He might have helped create some international non-party political link, transmuting the earlier British predominance of 1940–45 into an association better balanced. Fear of his independence of mind might have influenced those who could recommend him. So his potential use to his country came to an end, beyond some constructive commercial work. Among the many Allied leaders I had been privileged to observe, I came to regard him in his way, for imagination, courage and energy, as being in the highest class. Few saw his work since so much was covert. I had the good fortune to be one of the few, during many of those six years in which, from a scratch start, he built up, under the most difficult conditions, a worldwide organisation although he and others had been precluded from making any pre-occupation preparations while there was yet time.

The impressive and moving service at St Martin-in-the-Fields in 1976, giving thanks for his life, was attended by over a thousand men and women from many nations, free and still occupied, saluting the leadership which they had been so proud to follow and through which many had survived.

SOE was disbanded as soon as the War against Japan was won. Both SOE and OSS had been composed of amateurs, although by 1945 they each had an impressive record. There was no core of a profession as in other special services. Politicians, diplomats and military believed, with some justification, that their own proper functions had been usurped by the OSS and SOE while some minor shortcomings had been exaggerated. Two British financiers had muddied the waters of the Mediterranean somewhat; one had been found making personal financial deals while another had been reported as using genuine, not occupation, dollars – leading to a report to the Foreign Office that 'SOE is setting up its post-war organisation'. This was unfair and untrue. All whom I knew were activists, and as such only too anxious to return to their former employment.

The same was true of the OSS. President Truman, to whom we were to owe so much, thanked Donovan for his services to his country, but made it clear that he was not interested in Donovan's ideas for a post-war organisation. Three vital years were thus wasted, with the experienced OSS personnel returning to their former employment. Later, in 1948, the first American peacetime special service was formed on very much the lines proposed by Donovan in 1945.

At the time I had little knowledge of all this. In July 1945 I had a new trade to learn. I had also to earn a living, beyond the £600 a year which the grateful electorate lavished on their Members of Parliament – my gratuity from six years in uniform had just paid my Election expenses. Matrimony took pride of place, with politics, constituency and domestic, second, and pre-1945 interests last.

I called on Ernest Bevin, telling him of my special employment and suggesting that there was considerable overseas support for Britain above party politics. He later set up, with Christopher Mayhew and Ernest Davies, joint activities which were perhaps of some national benefit. I was to find that those who had served in the Coalition Government in war, in the greatest crisis in our history, were never fully to revert to partisan party politics. This spirit of cooperation was to last for the next decade.

I had also been elected Secretary of the Conservative Imperial Affairs Committee. Oliver Stanley was Chairman, with Gerald Sayers the sole support from the Research Department, a colleague of great experience and sagacity. We covered the affairs of a quarter of the world, including India, Palestine, the 'Dominions' and the still dependent territories of the Colonial Empire.

With these preoccupations and the persistent negative official attitude towards SOE and all its associations, there was little an Opposition Member could do. But one afternoon early in 1946, I was summoned to Churchill's room with half a dozen others.

'If we are to win the future', he said, 'we must set aside the past'. He went on to say that he had summoned us as ones who had held positions of some responsibility affecting the politics of Europe. He was undertaking a move to unite Europe by institutions not yet defined. He lacked the full facilities to organise as he had done after 10 May 1940. Above all, he continued, Germany must be included in the unity. Past Nazi actions must be 'set aside' if her great qualities were to be contained in the cause of freedom.

'If some of you do not feel you can agree to this, after all you have seen, I shall quite understand'.

As far as I can recall, no-one demurred.

One outcome were the informal gatherings at Konigswinter near Bonn, organised by Frau (later the first foreign Dame, DCMG) Lilo Milchsach. The first two Germans whom she told me to welcome in 1950 turned out to be Dr von Brentano and Karl Carstens, both to become the best of allies when I was in the

Churchill Administration. The result of such friendships made possible through Konigswinter can never be exaggerated.

From Eisenhower's instruction in September 1943 to 'be the leading pro-Italian' came my closer association with the republican Count Sforza and his son, with Pizzoni and with Aosta's friends.

I count these two initiatives to build relations with ex-enemy countries as a direct result of my service in SOE. My more direct involvement in Europe in later years is another story. In brief, an opportunity was lost to use the Resistance workers to build an international group dedicated to defend Europe against further tyranny, by uniting primarily to avoid future European civil wars. 'Finding a few to begin' was much like the search in the early years of SOE in Britain and in Europe. These new colleagues from ex-enemy countries together with the Resistance could have formed an immediate network. Delay was due mainly to the needs of domestic politics – in a bankrupt, bombed Britain as well as in the liberated countries where disputes arose between the Resistance and the returned exiles. In Britain Churchill lacked adequate finance and facilities for the European Movement. The negative attitude towards SOE, if not to the Resistance, precluded more overt use being made of the goodwill towards Britain. Little was done to institutionalise Churchill's ideas beyond the creation of the Council of Europe and the European Movement. In 1951 he himself took up yet again the reins of government. However the Bonn Conventions, converting the three Western Zones of Germany into the Federal Republic, and Western European Union in 1954 were important steps towards uniting Europe. The ill-judged failure to join the Economic Community in 1955 and help to 'write the rules' cost Britain dear, for a later application made in 1961 was blocked by de Gaulle who had returned to power in 1958.

How such misjudgements and failures to utilise existing goodwill and experience worked to the national detriment, made clearer after a third of a century, is part of that other story.*

In the summer of 1945 all these events lay shrouded in the mists of the future. At that moment there was no time or inclin-

* See *Political Eunuch* by Douglas Dodds-Parker

ation to look back. Too much to be done lay ahead. Only now, more than three decades later, with the advantage of hindsight, do I try to assess. It is not for me to judge. I am too much of a partisan. What has been written herein may be of assistance to historians, added to access to documents as they exist and become available. These latter can correct and amplify the personal recollections of the few who have laboured to record them. Thereby perhaps more balanced judgements may be formed on the value, military, economic and political, of Resistance.

Churchill's belated accession to the office of Prime Minister on 10 May 1940 had coincided with the opening day of the Battle for Western Europe. Without a conscious word of command, the few special operators had begun to take action. From that day until Victory Day I never heard a single word of recrimination among my colleagues, who had been the strongest opponents of appeasement; and even more, the most active advocates of making preparations for action, overt and covert, directly after the occupation of the Rhineland in early 1934, contrary to the Treaty of Versailles. They believed that Churchill should have been made Minister of Defence, at latest after 'Munich' in 1938; and that the use of his talents, experience and energy could well have avoided the 'Unnecessary War' as I was to hear him describe it in later years. Under his leadership from May 1940, there was always so much to do, to ensure the confident determination of all to win the war, the more speedily and predictably once the Red Army and later the Americans were involved. In 1939 I had predicted it would take six years. I was two weeks out.

Five years later victory in Europe had allowed a General Election. Labour succeeded a ten-year-old National Government, mainly Tory, elected with an overwhelming majority, and a mandate for some rearmament. The Fulham bye-election in 1936, swinging a big Tory majority to Labour fighting against rearmament, had partly unnerved the Government. By 1945 public opinion had swung far against that Government. Any Tory fighting the 1945 Election will recall the charges – failure to stop the Dictators; appeasement was worth a try if supported by adequate rearmament; unemployment still high, and not used to speed defence; Churchill kept out of office by 'the Tories'; he had brought into public life many who had helped win the war; if 'the

Tories' won, would they throw Churchill and these others out again?

The same sentiments were found among the Resistance. They came from every political party. Their individual patriotism had overridden normal political practice. In 1945 it was too early to assess the changes which would result from the disasters of the previous decade. The material destruction of industrial capacity and communications had been enormous. Maybe forty million had died premature deaths, often under the most degrading circumstances. Eastern and Central Europe, emerging from moderately benevolent autocracies, were being thrust back under alien tyranny.

In 1939 the Empire had responded magnificently to the call to defend freedom; not only the self-governing Dominions but the all-volunteer armies from the still dependent territories. There was growing realisation of the value of the Free Society, and of the institutions necessary to protect, and the administration to support, it. The even greater number of the educated aspired, naturally enough, to govern themselves, within some continuing association with Britain. Who, looking at the state of Europe in 1945, could seriously claim that their indigenous leaders could make worse decisions than the European politicians of the inter-war years?

The same subconscious, unspoken resolve underlay the aims of those from so many countries with whom we had worked through those long five years. They believed that British institutions had somehow withstood the temptations of authoritarian rule, Fascist, Nazi or Marxist, as a way to ease economic and social problems. They wished to continue to work with Britain in the future, to build together institutions through which to guard personal freedom domestically while supporting each other internationally against external aggression. In this respect they paid tribute to the manner in which the Empire had rallied for mutual defence in 1939.

Any such long-term considerations were in embryo in 1945. Food and shelter were the main concern, of an immediacy difficult now to recall. All in the true Resistance were determined to avoid another, Marxist, tyranny – although its true nature, used as a cloak for Russian imperialism, had been concealed by the bravery of the Red Army. In Yugoslavia alone was there to be found an indigenous Marxist regime strong enough to survive without the Red Army behind it. Thanks to Tito Russian domination was kept at bay. The price of Resistance there, as throughout Europe, had been beyond imagination, to the nation as well as to individuals. Names like Lidice, the Warsaw Ghetto, the Warsaw Rising, Katyn, Vercors, Oradour had entered the vocabulary of international horror.

The moral damage was perhaps even greater and longer enduring than was realised at the time. All had been encouraged to oppose their normally constituted authority – governments and factory managers and parents – unless these were working against the invaders or collaborators. They were taught how to do so, overtly or covertly.

Not until 1966 was the official ban against 'access to documents' raised to allow Professor Michael Foot to write *SOE in France*. Through no fault of his, some embarrassment was caused. Another fifteen years were then to elapse until, after representations from Earl Mountbatten of Burma just before his murder, access to documents was given to Charles Cruikshank to write about Special Operations in the South East Asia Command. Mountbatten had always been regarded as the Supreme Commander who best understood and encouraged special operations. This was partly due to his professional skill as a signals officer, which showed him how the practical reality of good signals led to enormous psychological confidence in communications in their widest sense. All, however remote, felt in contact.

High authority has never decided whether SOE was a full special service whose records would thereby never become available for public scrutiny; or whether it should fall, perhaps with the usual eliminations, under the thirty-year rule. MIR had been recruited on the understanding that nothing done or written by us should ever be made public by us or about us. Names have often been made public, not always adversely, in various books. The inevitable conclusion must be that if accounts are to be written, let them be as accurate as any records and surviving memories make possible. To this end the time ban on official documents being available has been reduced from fifty to thirty years. This has been helpful. Beginning with Cruikshank's book, access has been given to documents with reasonable safeguards, and provided no charge falls on public funds. Even this is hard to explain to overseas colleagues who find it still difficult to understand why the British do not want to make public the part they played, as shown in Foot's *SOE in France*, in the achievements of those years. They wish to have available histories, as complete and official as possible, to be compiled with all blemishes and failures as well as successes – to show the essential links which SOE provided between the Resistance and the outside forces of liberation.

This account seeks to salute those who perished for their ideals. It avoids casting blame on the few, if sometimes crucial, opponents who were to be swept aside by events. Above all, it tries to give some belated credit to those who survived, who, setting behind them the years of violence, have made substantial contributions to education and the arts, to commerce and industry, to create health and happiness, whose panache and verve and elan suffused their actions throughout those ten fraught years from 1935 to 1945 and thereafter. Men and women from so many nations and creeds, charged with the usual human failings, but filled with such hopes as seldom inspired so many before – hopes of a world in which all might stand straight, without fear, without rancour. For their ideals they had been ready to endure and die, if needs must. Even more positively they have striven to ensure that such sacrifices shall never again be needed – and to strive for this ideal.

Appendix

Extracts from three letters to the author, in order of date.

1. From Gerry Holdsworth, Brindisi, Italy,
   dated 31 January 1944:

'It is now a far cry from those late autumn days in 1942 when a small body of men drifted in and out of a top floor back room (in Baker Street) gathering together their kit and ideas and chucking them in a heap on the floor.

It was not very much later before the men, the kit and the ideas had reached the Mediterranean and were busy snow-balling their way from Matifou to the Club. They were all like dust particles in the sunshine bumping up against each other without any sense of rhythm or direction. It was about this time that you took command and gave us sense of direction. From then till now my life, and that of the majority of officers who have served under you, has been crammed full of interest and I do think that you are entitled to be most gratified with what has been achieved . . .'

2. From Dick Hewitt, Special Force No. 1, Italy,
   dated 9 October 1944:

'I would not like you to leave the Mediterranean without a word of thanks and congratulations from me. During the six and a half months that I worked as one of your staff officers in Algiers, and since then working for Gerry, first with your supervision and later with your interest and assistance, it has always been clear to me that the success and goodwill that SOE has won in the Mediterranean has been very largely due to you. No one at Massingham or Maryland has ever doubted that and I would like you to know we feel that way . . .'

3. From Colin Gubbins, in England,
   dated 1 June 1975:

'Massingham under you certainly turned out a winner for SOE – the cradle for all kinds of splendid subversive operations; a forcing house, too, for bringing forward a bevy of very able chaps who rose to high responsibilities far in advance of their years, and a focal point as exploited by you for making and maintaining contact with allies and others of political influence that has served our country well . . . To British people not connected with SOE it always seems strange that there should still very actively exist these wartime associations. What they forget is that for nearly all the occupied countries their only 'war' was resistance . . . and Resistance can never forget how Britain brought them back into the war and restored their pride – an essential element if Europe were to recover . . .'

Colin Gubbins' last instructions in 1975 to me were to do my best to help keep the Special Forces Club going, as a memorial to past and future international accord and achievement. I took this on with his admirers as a tribute to his leadership. The success that the Committee and helpers had in carrying out his wishes was due, as in earlier years, to the major contribution by those 'in the field' who responded so generously. Once again the technique was never one of 'under command' – rather of hunting a thrusting if somewhat unruly pack of hounds. The presentation of Enzo Plazotta's statuette 'Spirit of Freedom' marked the end of my term of office. This token, with the three letters quoted above will be cherished more, I trust not over-sentimentally, than any three letters before or after my name.

Index

Individuals are referred to by names under which they are usually known; the omission of prefixes denotes no lack of respect.

Ace of Spades, 86
Acland, Peter, 56, 63
Air operations, 89
Airborne Forces, 88
Airey, General Terence 60, 129
Akavia, Avraham, 62, 65
Akrat, Mekkawi Suliman, 13
Alamein, 79, 111
Albania, 23, 191–92
Alexander, General, 129, 134, 144, 149, 158, 198
Algeria, 111
Algiers, 109–17, 112, 201
Alison, Barley, 156, 170
Allen, W.E.D. (Bill), 57, 66
Allied Force Headquarters (AFHQ), 77
Aloisi, Baron, 9
Amadeo Duca D'Aosta, 23, 147
Amerigo Vespucci, 144
Anfa Conference, 121
Anglo–Egyptian Sudan. See Sudan
Anstey, John, 127, 165
Anstruther, Colonel, 116
ANTHROPOID, 96
Appleyard, 'Apple', 88
Atiyah, Edward, 20
Auschnitt, Litzi, 26
Austin, Wing Cdr John, 84, 93, 94
Australia, 47
Austria, 186–87
Avalanche, 153, 154
Avignon, 166, 169

Badoglio, Marshal, 12, 110, 136, 139, 140, 144, 146
Bagnold, Ralph, 51
Bailey, John, 30
Balkans, 133, 142, 143, 144, 147, 149, 172, 188
Ball-bearings, 99
Barry, Colonel, R.H., 37, 77, 79
Battaillon de Choc, 154
Battle of Britain, 17, 44, 98
Bedell Smith, General, 117, 120, 125, 137, 138, 141, 143, 154, 155, 196, 204, 211
Belgium, 85
Belsen, 199, 208
Benes, President, 26, 96
Bernhard, Prince, 101
Bethouart, General, 115
Bevan, Oliver, 32
Bevin, Ernest, 214
Binney, George, 33
Blida, 119
Bloom, Sol, 10
Blue Nile Province, 12
Bogomolov, Ambassador, 196
Bolshoi Ballet, 8
Bonn Conventions, 215
Bonnier de la Chapelle, Lt. Rene, 115, 116
Boughey, Lt–Col Peter, 188
Boustead, Hugh, 56, 67
Boyd, 'Stumps', 29
Bren gun, 67
Brereton, General, 208
Briggs, Brigadier, 56
Bright, Joan, 40
Brimstone, 153
Brindisi, 144, 146, 147, 183
British Empire, 217
Brocklehurst Mission, 59
Brook, Robin, 37, 208
Brooks, Richards, 80, 101, 116, 127, 156, 165, 170, 173
Brooks, Tony, 86, 209
Brown, Alan, 57, 64
Browning, General 'Boy', 88, 134
Broz, Josip. See Tito
Bruce, David, 103
Bruning, Dr, 5

Cadman, John, 7
Cairo, 51
Cambridge, 35
Cammaerts, Francis, 166, 168
Carrington, Peter, 29
Carstens, Karl, 214
Carton de Wiart, General, 40, 42
Casabianca, 119, 122, 152
Caserta, 157, 158, 173
Castellano, General, 136, 137
Central Europe, 180–85
Chamberlain, N, 16
Chapman–Andrews, Andrew, 58, 65
Charles, Sir Noel, 197
Chatterton, Sergeant, 30
Chaudhauri, Muchu, 60
Cheeseman, 'Uncle Robert', 57
Churchill, Randolph, 195
Churchill, Winston, 3, 10, 17, 18, 36, 38, 42, 44, 46, 54, 59, 61, 74, 94, 114, 122, 149, 195, 200, 211, 212, 214, 215, 216, 217
Cianca, 150
Clarke, Brigadier Dudley, 73, 123
Clark, General Mark, 104
Clark, R.T., 38
Clifford, Alexander, 64
Club des Pins, 112, 118, 153, 157, 163–64, 169, 200
Codenames, 93
Codes, 87
Codewords, 94
Collins, Ian, 134
Collis, Flt. Lt, 61
Colonna d'Istria (Cesari), 114, 152, 155, 203, 204
Communists, 36, 78, 81, 86, 94, 127, 146, 170, 178, 191, 193, 203, 206
Concentration camps, 207, 208
Coningham, Air Marshal, 'Maori', 129
Connaught, HRH The Duke of, 32
Conrad, Josef, 98
Conservative Imperial Affairs Committee, 214
Copper Horse, 30
Corbett, Major, 119, 133
Corsica, 110, 111, 114, 122, 129, 152–59, 154, 200
'Corsica, Tunis, Nice' demands, 21
Corvedale, Oliver, 66
Cote d'Or, 170
Council of Europe, 215
Coward, Noel, 33
Cowburn, Captain Ben, 83
Crawford, Joan, 87
Crockatt, Norman, 44
Croft, Andrew, 37, 42, 157
Croix de Lorraine, 153
Cromer, Rowley, 29
Cruikshank, Charles, 218
Cumming, Duncan, 7, 20, 57
Cunningham, General, 65, 69
Czech Legion, 25
Czechoslovakia, 18, 85, 96, 185–86
Czernin, Manfred, 174

D Section, 35, 44, 78
Dalton, Dr, 54, 76, 212
Danish Resistance, 99
Darlan, Admiral, 109, 112–13, 115
D'Astier de la Vigerie, 126
Davies, Ernest, 214
Davies, Tommy, 37, 40, 42, 43
de Beaumarchais, Jacques, 154
de Brantes, Marquis, 27
de Gaulle, General, 46, 82, 83, 114, 122, 126, 152, 153, 209, 215
de Guelis, Jacques, 82, 114, 127
de Kersauson, Captain, 50
de Larminat, Colonel, 50, 52
de Lattre, de Tassigny, Marshal, 113, 164–65, 171
de Rougement, Dicky, 29
Deakin, William, 194
Denmark, 99
Devers, General, 170
Dieppe Raid, 109
Dimbleby, Richard, 64, 66
Dinder River, 64, 65
Dodson, Derek, 79
Dolfuss, Dr.. 9
Domaine de la Trappe, 169
Donovan, General 'Big Bill', 103, 104, 117, 118, 121, 124, 125, 155, 200, 213
Dragoon, 161, 163
Duff Cooper, 38, 156, 206
Duff Cooper, Lady Diana, 156, 157, 206
Dufour, John Nesbitt, 90

Eaker, General Ira, 172, 184
Eddy, Colonel William, 117, 128
Eden, Anthony, 9, 38, 58, 59
Edmondson, James, 209
Egypt, 48
Eighth Army, 110, 124, 139
Eisenhower, General, 117, 120, 125, 129, 134, 136, 138, 140, 141, 147, 155, 158, 179
ELAS, 72
Elliott, Air Marshal William, 172, 183, 200
Eritrea, 20
Ethiopia, 9, 12–15, 20, 23–26, 36, 43, 48, 50, 55–73, 201
Europe, 214
European Economic Community, 215
European Movement, 215

F Section, 118, 171
Facade, 209
Fairbanks, Jr., Douglas, 130
False rumours, 86
FANY, 84, 89, 94, 96, 99, 119, 120, 130, 156, 160, 164, 169, 203, 204, 209
Farley, S/Ldr, 90, 91, 95
Fawkes, Capt 'Barney', 119

Fielden, Wing-Commander 'Mouse', 100, 119, 130, 152
Fifth Army, 179
Fingerprinting, 87
Fitzwilliam, Peter (Milton), 33
Fleming, Peter, 19, 24, 37, 40, 42, 74, 189
Florence, 178
Foggia, 142, 143, 146
Foot, Professor Michael, 82, 91, 163, 164, 218, 219
Force–133, 188
Force–139, 187–88
Ford, Christopher, 29
Foulds, Golly, 96
France, 41, 82, 83, 95, 111, 127, 153, 157, 162–70, 204
Free French (RF) section, 83
Free French Forces, 84
Frenay, Henri, 126
French Forces of the Interior (FFI), 166
French Resistance, 99, 152, 156
Fulham bye-election, 216

Gallabat, 64–65
Garland, Judy, 87
Garlinski, Jozef, 98, 182, 184
Garrod, Air Marshal Guy, 27
Gauleiters, 35
Gayda, 175
Geneva Convention, 85, 199
George V, King, 14
George VI, King, 130–31
Germany, 48, 84, 85, 96, 214, 215
Gibraltar, 111, 172,
Gideon Force, 66, 68, 70, 71, 72
Giles, Cmdr Morgan, 173
Gillan, Angus, 18
Gimpel, Kay, 209
Giraud, General, 116
Giraud, General 'Papa', 114, 153, 154
Giscard D'Estaing, Valery, 28
Gort, Lord, 204
Grand, Col Laurence, 35, 40
Granville, Christine, 168–69
Greece, 127, 132, 188–91
Greek Resistance, 190
Green, George, 49
Green frontiers, 25, 43, 85
Gregg, Ralph, 40
Grenadiers, 27
Grenfell, David, 16
Grenfell, Joyce, 157
Gruenther, General Al, 104, 173
Gubbins Major-General Colin, 35, 37, 42, 74, 76, 81, 85, 95, 102, 103, 105, 117, 121, 133, 157, 158, 159, 165, 166, 168, 181, 189, 197, 208, 211, 212, 221
Gubbins, Michael, 175
Guerrilla warfare, 36, 86, 88

Hailu, Ras, 72
Halyard, 193
Hambro, Sir Charles, 76
Hamilton, John, 25
Hamilton-Hill, Donald, 129, 158
Hanning, Arthur, 28
Harcourt, Lord, 147
Harington, Charles, 79
Harriman, Averell, 103
Harris, Air Marshal, 79
Helford River, 80, 101
Helpman, Robert, 209
Henderson, Ian, 147
Hesketh-Pritchard, Alfgaar, 187
Hewitt, Richard, 153, Appendix
Heydrich, 96, 97, 199
Hichens, Commander Robert, 101
Himmler, 77

Hindus, Maurice, 16
Hitler, 5, 8, 9, 10, 23, 26, 208
Hockey, G Capt, 96
Holdsworth, Comdr G. A., 37, 80, 101, 144, 146, 157, 173, 220
Holland, Col Joe, 35, 40
Holmes, General Julius, 200
Homing pigeons, 90
Honours and Awards, 203
Hopkinson, General, 144
Hopkinson, Henry, 9, 41
Hotchkiss factory, 85
Hungary, 187–88
Hunt, John, 90
Hutchison, Colonel James, 83, 84
Hutton, Clayton, 87

Imperial Airways, 8
Insaisisable sabotage, 36
Intelligence, 36
Intelligence Officers, 36
Istria, 159
Italian Armistice, 136–41, 154
Italian–Ethiopian War, 1935–8, 12–15
Italy, 43, 110, 127, 133, 142, 147, 153, 159, 174–80, 201 *see also* Ethiopia
Itching powder, 86

Jackson, Ann, 40
Jackson, C.D., 156
Jaksch, Wenzel, 16, 17
Jebb, Gladwyn, 41, 76
Jedburghs, 73, 145, 201
Jefferies, Colonel Millis, 86
Jibuti, 52
'Joes' 76, 80
Josephine B, 82

Kassa, Amaha, 12
Keary, Capt, 96
Kemp, Peter, 98
Kennedy, A.L., 19
Kennedy, John, 40
Keswick, David, 111, 114, 115
Khartum, 20–22, 52, 55
Knickerbocker, 16
Konigswinter, 214–215

Laming, Dick, 101
Laval, Pierre, 9
Lawrence, Arthur, 46
Lawrence, James, 103
Le Blanc, Captain, 64
League of Nations, 9
Leclerc, General, 164
Leigh-Fermor, Patrick, 197
L'Herminier, Captain, 119
Lidice, 97
Lincoln, General 'Abe', 103
Lines of communication, 170–72
Livermore, Russell, 128
London, 74–105
Long, Vera, 40
Long Range Desert Group (LRDG), 51, 60, 124, 147
Low Countries, 41, 85
Lussu, Signora, 175
'Lyon', General, 130
Lysander aircraft, 80, 90, 100

MacDonald, Ramsay, 23
MacIntyre, Mary, 138
Macintosh, Charles, 143, 176
Maclean, Colonel Neil (Billy), 57, 192
Maclean, Brigadier Fitzroy, 194, 195, 196
Macmillan, Harold, 122, 196
Macphail, 46
Macpherson, G.P.S., 147

Mafia, 125
Maidstone, HMS, 119
Makins, Roger, 9, 121
Mallaby, Dick, 133, 138, 139, 145
Malta, 132, 154
Maquis, 114, 152–59
March-Phillips, Gus, 88
Margesson, David, 17
Marks, Leo, 87
Marshall, Geoffrey, 80
Marshall Aid, 207
Martin, David, 195
Marxism, 103, 170, 217, 218
Mary, H.M. Queen, 31
Maryland, 4, 142–51, 158, 174–80
Masaryk, Jan, 26, 77, 85, 96
Mason, Michael, 51, 123
Massey, Vincent, 19
Massigli, Réné, 162
Massingham, 4, 111, 116, 118, 152, 154, 155, 158, 162–70, 178, 221
Mast, General, 115
Maurice, Jack, 70
Mayhew, Christopher, 214
Mena Conference, 149, 158, 161
Mesfin, 15, 66
Messervy, Brigadier, 56
MI6, 123
MI9, 44, 91, 171
Middle East, 45, 47
Mihailovic, General, 192, 193, 194, 195
Milchsach, Lilo, 214
Minesweeping, 80
MIR, 24, 27, 35, 39, 42, 43, 44, 51, 78, 171, 218
MONKEY, 120, 136–41, 179, 200
Montgomery, General, 134
Montsambert, General, 111
MOONSHINE/OPINION, 93
Moore, General Rodney, 29
Moorehead, Alan, 64
Morrison, Herbert, 38
Morshead, Sir Owen, 32
Moss, Billy, 197
Moulin, Jean 'Rex', 99
Mountbatten of Burma, Earl, 218
MOUSSE, 94
Moyne, Lord, 197
Munthe, Malcolm, 37, 42, 143, 150, 157, 160, 175
Murphy, Robert, 112–13, 211
Murphy, 'Sticky', 90, 100
Mussolini, 9, 23, 48, 51, 110, 135, 136, 147
Myers, Brigadier Eddie, 190

Naples, 142
NATO, 193
Navigation aids, 89
Nelson, Sir Frank, 76
New Zealand, 47
Newton, John, 81
Nicholls, Arthur, 79
NKVD, 95
Norgeby House, 74
Norstad, General, 112
Northumberland, Duke of, 32, 33
Norway, 39, 42, 95
Norwegian Resistance, 173

Obolensky, Sergei, 150–51
Office of Strategic Services (OSS), 103, 163, 172, 179, 180, 201, 213
Operation Torch, 101
Operation Centres, 72, 73, 163
Operational Planning Division, 104
Oradour, 97
Oran, 112
Overlord, 110, 161, 164, 165
OVRA, 111, 142

Packard, Reynolds & Phoebe, 16
Palestine, 50

Palmer, Freddy, 64
Parachuting, 88, 119, 178, 196
Parliament, 209–11
Partei Tag, 10
'Passy', Colonel (Comte André de Wavrin), 83
Patch, General Sandy, 166
Patton, General George, 134
Pauphilet, M., 112–13
Pearl Habour, 103, 109
Penn, Arthur, 34, 203
Penney, Jose, 20, 57
Perkins, 45
Pétain, Marshal, 47
Pezzoni, Alfredo, 142, 207, 215
Philby, Kim, 25, 27
Philby, St John, 25
PIAT, 67
Pilcher, Col John, 28
Pilkington, Richard, 10
Pirie, Ian, 46, 188
Platt, General, 56, 61, 65, 69
Plazotta, Enzo, 221
Poland, 25, 82, 84, 85, 96, 97, 102, 162, 168, 180–85
Polish Home Army, 201
Pope, His Holiness the, 176
Popski's Private Army, 124, 147
Portal, Air Marshal, 79
Portugal, 136
Postmaster, 88
Potter, Warwick, 103
Prague, 1938, 16–19
Prendergast, Guy, 51
Prescott, Col John, 34
Psychological Warfare, 156
Poulton, F/Lt, 95

Queen Elizabeth, HMS, 17
Queen Mary, HMS, 10
Quirinale, 176–77

Radio beacon, 98
Radio links, 87
Raikes, David, 17
Rea, Lord, 90, 100
Rebecca/Eureka, 98, 172
Red Army, 184, 185, 198, 218
Renton, Edward, 187
Resistance, 3, 78, 81, 104, 216, 217, 218, 219
Retinger, Josef, 98, 183
Ringrose, Basil, 57
Rivet, Colonel, 41, 114
Rjukan, 173
Roberts, Douglas, 37, 39, 40, 49
Roberts, Frank, 10, 187–88
Robertson, Major, 28
Robinson, Sergt., 29
Romanov, Boris, 95
Rome, 175, 176, 190
Roosevelt, Kermit, 42
Roosevelt, President, 42, 43, 51, 56, 114, 191, 209
Rowan, Leslie, 101
Rucker, Major, 119
Russia, 7, 25, 26, 84, 85, 94, 96, 102, 110, 132, 159, 167, 182, 184, 196–97, 217

S–phone, 90
Sabatier, Capitaine, 115, 116
Sabotage, 85
Salerno, 110, 139, 140, 153, 189
Saltzman, General, 103, 104, 121, 149
Salvadori, Max, 143, 150, 174
Sandford, Brigadier, 55
Sardinia, 129, 130
Sawbridgeworth, 91
Sayers, Gerald, 214
Scandinavia, 38, 85
Scobie, Lt General, 71, 191
Scythia, 119
Second (Social Democrat) International, 86
Secret Intelligence Service (SIS), 24, 35, 77
Selbourne, Lord, 76, 117, 212
Sforza, Count, 149, 150, 174, 179, 215
Shertok, Moshe (Moshe Sharett), 53
Shetland Bus Service, 85, 102
'Sibs', 86
Sicily, 110, 129, 134, 135, 139, 143, 177
Sidi Barrani, 9, 47
Sikorski, General, 181
Simon, André, 83
Simpson, Colonel Adrian, 39
Slessor, Air Chief Marshal, 150, 172, 184, 200
Slim, Brigadier, 56
Sloane, Colonel, 141
Small Scale Raiding Force, 88
Smith, Lt. General Arthur, 48
Smuts, General, 8, 58, 185
Soskice, Frank, 206
Sosnkowski, General, 182
Soustelle, Jacques, 126, 163
South African Air Force, 185
Spaak, M., 94
Spain, 25, 131–32, 136, 171, 172
Spears, General, 46
Special Air Service (SAS), 124, 147, 208
Special Forces Club, 221
Special Operational Planning and Action, 37
Special Operations, 36, 37, 40, 44, 48, 55, 198, 200, 218
Special Operations Executive (SOE), 3–4, 72, 73, 74–105, 85, 162, 179, 186, 192, 193, 199, 201, 211, 213, 214, 215, 218, 219
Special Operations Mediterranean (SOM), 158, 172–74
Speedwell, 4, 160–202
Spoleto, Duke of, 147
Springs, the, 113
St. George's Chapel, 32
Stafford, Dr, 54, 75
Stalin, 94
Stalingrad, 79
Stanley, Oliver, 214
Stawell, General, 161, 197
Steer, George, 66
Sten gun, 67, 97
Stevens, John, 207
Stewart, Brigadier General James, 208
Stink bombs, 86
Stirling, Col William, 124
Stirling, David, 124
Storch, 16
Strasbourg, 170
Street, Colonel Vivian, 195, 196
Strong, General, 137
Sudan, 20–22; see also Khartum
Sudan Political Service, 7
Suez Canal, 50
Sullivan, Staff Sergt, 112
Supply Organisation, 104
Supreme Headquarters Allied Expeditionary Force (SHAEF), 158, 203
Survival training, 88
Sweet-Escott, Bickham, 37
Swinton, Lord, 17
Switzerland, 134
Sykes, Christopher, 59
Symes, John, 148
Symes, Sir Stewart, 8, 148

Tait, Aldo, 148
Tamplin, Guy, 49
Tarchiani, 150
Taylor, General Max, 144
Taylor, George, 37, 46, 188
Templer, General, 35, 174–75
Thompson, Geoffrey, 43
Threlfall, Henry, 180, 183, 184
Tito, Marshal, 193–94, 218
Togliatti, 174
Torch, 158, 171
Tracy, Spencer, 87
Truman, President, 213
Tunis, 123
Tunisia, 111, 123, 127, 128, 129, 139

Ultra, 77
Um Idla, 65
Umbria, SS, 50
United States, 103, 109, 125

V2, 183
'Van Dooze', 156
Van Maurik, 'Van', 90
Vanier, General George, 155, 156
Vanier, Mme Pauline, 155, 156, 164
Vatican, 177
Velebit, General, 156
Vercors, 97
Verity, G Capt Hugh, 91, 100, 126
Vic Wells Ballet Company, 209
Villeneuve, Colonel, 41, 114
Villiers, Charles, 187
Vlassov's Army, 167
von Brentano, Dr, 214
von Kreipe, 197
von Reichenau, General, 38
von Rheinbaben, 19, 71
Von Rosen, Carl, 12
von Senger, General, 151
Vyshinski, 7, 196

Wadsworth, Mr. 7
War Office, 35–50
Warsaw Rising, 166, 183–84, 199
Wauchope, Leslie, 40
Waugh, Evelyn, 195
Wavell, General, 39, 47, 49, 51, 58, 109
Weizmann, Chaim, 25
Wellington, Duke of, 32
West, Paul, 197
Western Europe, 201
WHISKY, 95
Whitaker, John, 16
White House, 10
Whiteley, Major-General 'Jock', 116, 117, 121, 161, 194
Wickes, Picquet, 79
Widmer, Willie, 163
Wilkinson, Col Peter, 37, 39, 40, 41, 44, 45, 74, 187, 189
Wills, Colonel, 86
Wilson, General 'Jumbo', 47, 161
Wilson, Jack, 102
Windsor, 27–34
Wingate, Orde, 59–72, 194
Wise Bay, Major Alec, 49
Wise, Fred, 4
Women's Royal Air Force (WAAF), 84
Woodhouse, Col Monty, 190
Wooler, Ray, 88, 119, 178
Woolley, Leonard, 177
Wrightson, John, 25

Yalta Agreement, 84
Yeo–Thomas, 'Tommy', 84, 205
Yugoslavia, 127, 132, 192–97, 218

Zeller, Col Henri, 166
Zeller, Col Josef, 166
Zervas, General, 190
ZNO, 91, 92